PRAISE FOR
MAMA SAYS, DON'T

"To quote the author, Ergor Rubreck, is the 'wisest, most talented, most intuitive, most skilled and experienced, and most knowledgeable caver in the world today.' While such claims may or may not be true, they ignore the most salient fact: *Mama Says, Don't Cave* will make you laugh so hard that the dog or perhaps your spouse will go hide under the table. Its pithy lines evoke unexpected chuckles in crawlways. As you negotiate that awkward belay or recalled passageway it may loosen such a torrent of giggles that members of your party launch an immediate rescue. This is the best cave humor to emerge in decades, written by the alter-ego of a legendary caver, Don't miss it."

> —Michael Taylor, author of
> *Cave Passages* and *Hidden Nature*

"At last, the tales of globe-trotting super caver Ergor Rubreck, previously published only in caving newsletters, have been gathered in one volume. Aptly, Ego is contained in his first name, and as the many humorous stories reveal. His ego has no bounds where it comes to his many subterranean adventures, revealing alternate facts which will stretch your credibility as well as your funny bone."

> —Dave Bunnell, former editor *NSS News*

"When it comes to cavers, I've met many good ones, a few great ones, but only one Greatest of All Time. The evidence of greatness can be found in the pages of this book, or you might just ask him, as Ergor always has time to expound on his favorite subject . . . himself."

> —Bob Lodge, Expedition Leader,
> Cave Research Foundation

"Ergor Rubreck has taken us on a masterful tour of his adventures understanding and exploring caves in his book *Mama Says, Don't Cave*. He launches the reader into the world of Ergor's unbelievable experiences dissecting the realities of sport and scientific caving. This enlightening work on the dark underworld serves to reward the reader by raising the joys of exploration to a new level. There is little further to add to his comprehensive collection of stories experienced by Ergor Rubreck. This unique volume deserves to be stuffed in the back of every caver's cave pack or vehicle."

—Stanley D. Sides, MD, past president,
Cave Research Foundation

Mama Says,

DON'T CAVE

Ergor's Unbelievable Cave Stories

ERGOR RUBRECK

Illustrated by Clariona Sewursbhry

Published 2024
Printed in the United States of America
Print: 979-8-9903297-0-6
E-book: 979-8-9903297-1-3
Library of Congress Control Number: 2024912435

Cover and interior design by Tabitha Lahr
Front cover illustration © Ergor Rubreck

CONTENTS

FOREWORD BY DANNY A. BRASS

Cave-related activities encompass a wide array of disciplines. Exploration and discovery to a host of speleological sciences. Cavers use specialized skills and expertise in select fields of scholarship to make many contributions to culture and society. From relatively humble beginnings, the value of a growing list of significant contributions by cavers and speleologists is being recognized. Cave-related research endeavors are being funded and drawn into mainstream research initiatives.

In the rarefied atmosphere of expedition caving or related research endeavors, it often falls upon cavers to be self-reliant in the rigors of underground travel and competent in a range of technical skills. This is especially true when a team is operating far from the possibility of surface support or rescue.

Regardless of whether an underground operation is government funded or a private enterprise, gathering capable team members and a talented and resourceful leader is an absolute imperative. And so, the question arises again and again: when specialized skills, in-depth know-how, and a wealth of experience are required for difficult or dangerous cave-related enterprises—who ya gonna call?

In high-stakes caving there is really only one answer to this question—the wisest, most talented, most intuitive, most skilled and experienced, and most knowledgeable caver in the world today: Ergor Rubreck. And if you don't believe me, just ask him.

Ergor is a highly skilled and accomplished cave explorer. His expertise is rooted in decades of experience honed within cave systems around the globe. Ergor Rubreck also is a gifted teacher with a rare insight into virtually every facet of the cave-related sciences. With nary a thought to the wisdom of conventional scientific principles, he is able to illuminate the most difficult concepts in speleology in such a way that even the average individual with little grasp of the technicalities inherent in scientific research, will be able to understand. He often turns science on its head or twists orthodox doctrine inside out as he articulates his own singular vision of cave science.

Exploration and research, of course, are often highly competitive endeavors; jealousy and suspicion abound. It is little wonder, indeed, that speleologists of lesser note often find fault with Ergor's unique theories and penetrating insights. They may label him a screwball, prone to championing wacky, unproven, or non-falsifiable ideas. If you can get Ergor Rubreck to produce important and meaningful data to support your own research interests, you may consider yourself fortunate indeed.

Ergor is also a clever and creative inventor. His penchant is for designing novel instrumentation or engineering existing technology in ways that have never before been dreamed of—or likely ever will be again. His ongoing efforts to probe the darkest and most arcane secrets of the world beneath our feet have sometimes been known to work.

In praising his inventive genius, I am reminded of the now-extinct Ridiculodon, one of Mother Nature's own intriguing experiments in evolution. This giant flying reptile of the late Triassic Period is now known only from the fossil record. Unable to take flight directly from the ground, this imposing creature is believed to have launched itself from the summit of towering cliffs and could attain speeds in excess of one hundred miles per hour. . . once.

He is a true renaissance caver. Ergor's reputation for excellence and meticulous research is exceeded only by the depth of his eccentricities. Never one to miss an opportunity to publicize his (mostly) near-accomplishments, tales of Ergor's underground (mis) adventures afford readers important lessons in an assortment of subjects They range from caving safety, underground exploration, and scientific research to protocols dealing with corporate practices and international intrigue.

In this spellbinding anthology of Ergor's most exciting and daring adventures, Roger Brucker—whose name, by some inexplicable coincidence, just happens to be an anagram of Ergor's own name—introduces readers to a man at the very top (or should I say bottom?) of his game in the world of speleology. These stories chronicle many of Ergor's thrilling underground exploits. They call attention to his dramatic impact on the field of speleology in this exciting blend of fact, fiction, satire, and humor, Roger and Ergor both highlight the depth and breadth of modern cave activity as it is played out within the sweeping panorama of the subterranean world.

No cave-related research task is out of bounds for Ergor or beyond his professed expertise, and no obstacle to exploration is a hurdle that, for the right price, he will not try to overcome. You need only read his business card to know that this is true. And if this witty and entertaining text is not in itself sufficient to conjure up an image of the world's most fantastic caver submerged (and, hopefully, not drowning) in his own element, many of Ergor's tall tales are beautifully illustrated by famed cartoonist Clariona Sewursbhry Her name bears a striking resemblance to one of the founding members of the NSS Fine Arts Salon.

Having been an active member of the caving community for more than seventy years, Roger Brucker (NSS 1999 and honorary life fellow of the National Speleological Society) is very familiar with the nature of cavers, caves, and caving. His many publications—he has authored or coauthored four nonfiction books and one historical novel on cave-related subjects—have been perennial favorites for several generations of cavers. I believe Roger inspired Ergor!

As such, he is in a unique position to appreciate the full spectrum of caving-related activities and, by extension, the significance of Ergor's boundless contributions to exploration and the cave sciences. The wit and humor that he brings to this most recent publication is sure to bring a knowing smile to most everyone in the adventure community.

—DANNY A. BRASS, Author of *Rabies in Bats*, and
  Editor "Connecticut Underground"

INTRODUCTION

When I decided to become a cave explorer, my mama said, "DON'T CAVE." Her meaning was clear—don't you go caving! Or could she have meant I should not quit (cave in), give up, or surrender? Or was she pointing to the name of a cave—DON'T CAVE. (Once I named a pit DON'T'S PIT, cautioning cavers not to throw rocks in or spit-test the pit depth.)

Mom was so worried that she never read my books or stories. On the following pages, I have collected about seventy-three of my very finest stories. They are best read aloud.

A lawyer cautioned I should issue a warning: This is a book of fiction. No characters, living or dead, are real persons, and any antics real persons may have undertaken that Ergor has done are completely coincidental. My motto is "True If Interesting." But that would not exactly be true. More rigorously, I have a probability theory of truth. Take the sentence, "I took Santa Claus into Mammoth Cave." Obviously, that is fiction . . . or is it? Mammoth Cave is a real place. I have taken people into Mammoth Cave. Is Santa Claus real? Two-thirds of my example sentence is nonfiction. You be the judge. Truth or fiction? Is truth stranger than fiction? Read the Afterword for the real scoop.

Who am I, Ergor Rubreck? I am the self-styled most wonderful caver. I have many certificates suitable for framing, countless plaques, and a few ribbons attesting to my wonderfulness. In the beginning, I was about seventy and a half inches tall, but now I measure sixty-nine inches. I have gained so much wisdom that I have shrunk with many years of marvelous cave experience. Formerly I wore blond dreadlocks, but now I have a gray crew cut and wear glasses over my blue eyes to project seriousness.

After reading some of these breathtaking, exciting stories, you may want to try caving, I suggest you contact the National Speleological Society, 6001 Pulaski Pk NW, Huntsville, AL 35810, website: https://caves.org/. They will guide you into safe caving.

Cave Conservation

Caves are fragile in many ways. Their features take thousands to millions of years to form. Many cave-dwelling animals such as blind fish are rare and always live in precarious ecological balance. Cave features can be destroyed by people who enter caves ignorant of cave fragility, preservation, and conservation. Irreparable damage has been done by people who take speleothems such as stalactites and stalagmites or leave their names and graffiti on walls. Never disturb bats, especially in winter when hibernation food stores are scarce. Bats are dying from fatal white-nose syndrome, which can be spread from cave to cave by humans.

Ergor's Rules of Caving

1. Never cave alone
2. Tell someone where you are going
3. Take three independent sources of light
4. Dress warmly enough.
5. Insure yourself heavily and list Ergor Rubreck as your beneficiary

—Ergor Rubreck

Mama Says,

DON'T CAVE

MAMA SAYS, DON'T CAVE

When I was very young, my Mama said, "Don't cave. Cave exploring is dangerous. You can fall down pits. Rocks can fall on you. Bats can tangle in your hair. You could be trapped and drowned in rising water during a flood. You'll die from suffocation in bad air. Impale yourself on a stalactite and bleed out. You're my only son."

Her warning just made me want to cave more than ever! I pretended she had instead warned me not to give up, not to surrender, don't cave. After I took up active caving, she vowed never to read any of my trip reports, cave stories, or books. "It would make me worry about you more than I do already. I wouldn't be able to sleep." I thought she would relent, read my stories if I avoided flamboyant, vivid writing that would alarm her and terrify anybody.

Should I have respected my mama by abiding by her wishes? Would it have been smart to be intimidated by her ultimatum? Stay out of caves forever?

The answer is my curiosity won out. I made secret passages in our old house as a result of mystery stories read to me by my mom from *Child Life* magazine. At age six I pleaded, and she took me on a vacation to Mammoth Cave. In those days they offered the All-Day Trip, with lunch in the Snowball Dining Room. "Your little legs can't handle all day," she said.

"No!" I said, " All-Day Trip!"

I saved my allowance and bought a flashlight to shine in dark places. There were no electric lights in Mammoth Cave then. We carried kerosene lanterns, and the guide threw kerosene-soaked torches into pits and on high ledges. "Whoosh!" The acrid odor of flaming kerosene torch arced high onto a small ledge.

My aunt took me into three chilly caves on Put-in-Bay in Lake Erie one summer. It was a further incentive to continue caving in defiance of Mama. But don't you see that she aided and abetted my obsession? My aunt's encouragement and mom's discouragement made me a cave explorer! It's their fault!

It's all their fault!

You can either go through life regretting you didn't do the goofy stuff you wanted to do, or you can go ahead and seek adventure and take risks. Fortunately, my mom never held it against me for scaring her to pieces. I think her parents probably treated her the same way growing up. "Give kids unconditional love and plenty of opportunities to fail cheaply" became a central truth in my life.

Now, many decades later, my mom is long gone, but I know she was a good mama despite her foibles. Over the years, her love endured a thousand worries. She was a social worker. I learned later that social workers are trained to conceal their emotions to prevent their clients from forming undesirable attachments.

What have I learned from decades of caving? Several important things:

1. When you are faced with a baffling, complex puzzle, such as a big cave, make a map of the passages. You will see the cave a lot more slowly than the cave-exploring hotshots who scoop a cave by running through its passages. They are reduced to describing the big cave with sweeping arm gestures and superlatives. Tex Swifty used to race through tiny crawlways to wear out me and other new cavers. It was his idea of a joke. But it pissed me off.

Meanwhile, I learned to plot the cave on paper and see it unfold into an understandable network. Add the topographic lines and see the relation of the cave to the surface. Sometimes people will pay money for a cave map; most will complain, "It looks like spaghetti!"

2. Share the fun and companionship of fellow cave explorers. Solo caving is not evil, although it is peaceful and awe-inspiring, if dangerous. But as a practical matter, if an emergency occurs, resourceful cavers will rescue the victim (most of the time). A friend once bragged about his expensive new Brunton compass. We were miles up an underground river with mud everywhere. I heard a "plop," as he dropped the compass into the muddy water. He moaned. We all felt the river bottom with our feet. I struck the submerged compass with my foot. We continued swishing this way and that for a long time.

I said, "Alan, your compass is totally lost. If I find it, can I have it?" In resignation, he said yes.

"Ta-dah," I clucked. "Guess what!" I plunged my hand underwater and pulled the compass from the depth, water pouring off. He registered astonishment, then disgust. I let the disaster soak in—a cruel joke. He stowed the waterlogged Brunton. I had learned from Tex.

Teach new cavers how to survey, crawl, climb, and descend. With just the right sneer, you can teach newbies that they know all you taught them, but not all you know.

3. Follow the water to discover more cave. Most caves are made by underground water trickling or roaring through passages that drain away the water. Passages tend to become larger downstream. Sometimes you can follow the air blowing. If you follow ceiling canyons, you can occasionally find hidden places where the water came or went. Don't explain that it's anything but magic when you discover passages. If somebody tells you, "That's been looked at," do not believe them.

"Does it end?" is *the* discovery question.

4. Connecting caves gives you a sense of accomplishment. This is because nearly every cave is a fraction of the original cave. Caves break down, entrances collapse or open, and passages flood or drift shut with fill. Understanding and enjoyment reaches high excitement levels when you find a connection between caves once thought to be separate. The proper response: "I knew it all along."

5. Cave photography lets you create with light, since caves are naturally dark. Beyond the satisfying visual image, you can find small creatures that enjoy interactive lives within the limited environment. How they prey and are preyed upon spins a life-web of understanding. Discovery is what caving is about.

It took several years before I learned just the right way to say, "Aw shucks." And how to suggest that my companions nominate me for big rewards without seeming to be a blow-hard.

Finally, I believe every person receives the gifts of curiosity, free will, and opportunities at birth. Cave exploring is a better way than most because the elements and challenges are simpler than most problems and offer a chance to understand what is important. Mama believed that to be true, even if her sense of danger often overwhelmed her curiosity, and her professional expertise hid her feelings.

MY VISIT TO MAMMOTH CAVE

I decided to visit Mammoth Cave National Park and to check out what has been called "the longest cave." I drove south on I-65 to Cave City, Kentucky. The entrance to the park is only a few miles from there. At the new visitor center, I saw a new museum where the wonders of Mammoth Cave were described in minute detail. A computer map of the whole cave was revolving on a plasma screen—spaghetti observed from every vantage point. Looking at the cave sideways, I saw a single long yellow line, described by the narrator as over 420 miles of horizontal cave occurring in only 300 vertical feet of rock.

Exhibits told about early and contemporary explorers. Secrets of every cave-making process were laid bare. I spent two hours in the museum and missed my tour altogether. Maybe since I learned so much secret stuff and mysterious minutia, I would not have to go into the cave after all. Too much knowledge and experience can spoil a cave trip. However, I realized my own selfishness: The question is what I could contribute to others' experience, not whether I could learn any more.

Our guide said we would have to leave behind all backpacks, crutches. firearms, and fireworks. There would be no smoking. There would be no restroom stop. We heard more from the guide at the top of the entrance stairs: "A hunter named Houchins was the first Caucasian to enter the cave in 1795. He was chasing a bear, or vice versa." In reality, Native Americans entered the cave thousands of years before Houchins to gather gypsum and laxative salts. Perhaps they performed rituals such as tailgate parties, hide-and-seek, and bar mitzvahs. During the War of 1812, African American slaves were brought into Mammoth to mine saltpeter. After the war, saltpeter dropped to about twenty cents a pound, so the cave shifted to a tourist attraction.

While going down the stairs into the cave, I encountered a spray of water falling off the drip line of the cave roof. All cavers know the cave does not begin until a point directly under the drip line. I saw my chance to make the climax discovery by making a permanent extension of the drip line outward approximately three feet. That would increase the actual length of the cave some three feet beyond any subsequent claim.

The rest of the tour was instructive and wonderful. Sort of. We stopped in River Hall. The guide sat us down and told us a long story of Stephen Bishop, the seventeen-year-old African American slave who was brought to the cave in 1838. He guided trips and explored far beyond the eight miles of surveyed routes in the cave. Stephen made a good map of twenty miles of Mammoth Cave and was given full credit for drafting it. I nearly wept at the injustice of it.

I spoke up by observing that, in view of Stephen's accomplishments, we need to petition Congress to change the name of Mammoth Cave to Bishop Cave. After all, we have the Washington Monument, Lincoln Memorial, and Jefferson Memorial. The name of Boulder Dam was changed to Hoover Dam. I gave seven good reasons why the cave name should be changed. Then, I shouted that all who agreed with me should line up on the far side of River Hall. Three members of the tour joined me.

I shouted that we would not leave Bishop Cave until everyone agreed with me to demand the name change.

Of course, the guides (there are two for each party) protested, claiming I was behaving in an objectionable manner, and that I would have to exit the cave in the company of the trailer guide "who has the full authority to arrest you."

I made several spirited, loud comments about free speech, liberty, Gestapo, and KGB. I think my suggestions were taken the wrong way, because 95 percent of the tour booed and made unpleasant noises and gestures while the 5 percent next to me cheered me on.

Some of my 5 percent elected to march out of the cave with me in solidarity. We were met just beyond the drip line and the pitter-patter of its waterfall by four rangers with sidearms. The head honcho, a Major Ranger, explained that I was under arrest for inciting a riot and disorderly conduct. Evidently, my casual remarks about changing the name of the cave were not well received. I pleaded for the release of my three tourist supporters since they had been caught up in the excitement of the moment and were strangers to me. I was read my rights and placed in a green Range Rover for the trip to Bowling Green, Kentucky, where the US magistrate held office.

I was told I could plead guilty, not guilty, or nolo contendere. I asked if I could approach the magistrate. I said I was an innocent tourist, very sorry for any commotion I had caused, and that I would not do it again. He told me to plea *nolo*, and I did. The rangers who returned me to the park said I must never set foot on a tour again that year unless I wanted to do ten days in the electric chair.

That afternoon I bought everything I needed at the hardware store in Cave City. After dark, I packed the stuff down to the Historic Entrance. I put several cakes of dry ice in a couple of buckets of water to make a dense mist roiling around the cave in a thick cloud. I carefully moved out on the arch of rock over the cave entrance to the place where several springs of water joined for the plunge from the natural drip line. I jammed a three-foot (one-meter) section of roof gutter into the mud of the springs and heaped mud and stones into dikes that directed the water to the metal gutter. To support the outer end of the gutter, I attached one end of a stainless-steel wire to the gutter and wired the other end to a tree about six feet upslope from the cave entrance arch. In one brilliant engineering feat, I had diverted the water demarcating the actual drip line to a point some three feet farther out. This effectively made the cave some three feet longer than whatever people might claim the cave length to be. I withdrew silently just as the last of the dry ice had stopped cloud-forming.

In my hotel room, I prepared a news release to be sprung any time somebody claimed that Mammoth Cave was five hundred miles long.

EXPLORING THE CAVES OF VENICE

The phone call was an obvious prank.

Who could be calling me from Venus? After all, Venus is forty million kilometers (twenty-five million miles) from Earth. I listened anyway. The voice on the line was Doctor Antonio Spumoni, President of the Società Veneziana di Speleologica in Venice, Italy. He informed me I had won an all-expense-paid tour of the caves of Venice. Now, I am keenly aware of the Nigerian Lottery scam, so naturally, I was skeptical, to say the least.

Dr. Spumoni said I was the unanimous choice of their board since I was the most famous and foremost speleologist and cave explorer of all time. I asked for some verification to make sure this was not a scam. He quoted my Social Security number digit for digit, and then he quoted his Italian Social Security number. I concluded this was not a scam because he sounded so sincere. He said he would wire the money into my bank account if I gave my bank's routing number and my account number.

On the airplane to Venice, I had second thoughts. Aren't the caves of Venice flooded? I was not a PADI-certified cave diver, nor even a cavern diver, although I had breathed through a scuba outfit in a resort swimming pool. How difficult can it be to explore underwater caves, even with my limited experience?

Dr. Spumoni's firm handshake and warm greeting at the arrival gate assured me that I had made the right choice in accepting his invitation. We rode a vaporetto—a kind of boat—to the

Villa Parcheesi, a historic structure leaning dangerously into the Grand Canal. This was the society's headquarters and accommodations for distinguished visiting speleologists. My bedroom walls were lined with six portraits of men, each with a black line around the matted picture. I was able to decipher that they were distinguished speleologists who had perished in a cave in Venice.

After a delicious lunch of pasta, fruit, and wine, Dr. Spumoni said they had brought me over for a specific secret purpose, not just to tour the caves. They wanted to connect a newly found cave to the largest cave beneath Venice; thus, I was their choice for the expert who could help. "Did you not connect Mammoth Cave with Carlsbad Caverns?" asked Dr. Spumoni.

"Yes!" I said enthusiastically. "I did not connect those two caves and many others as well." I think he did not understand my meaning but told me to pack for an expedition this very afternoon. Naturally, I did not bring diving gear, but just my regular caving kit. We climbed aboard a gondola and the gondolier made for the Villa Bologna in a seedy part of the city. He made fast to a pole sticking out of the water thirty meters (about ninety-nine feet) from the dilapidated villa. There he removed the cover from a manhole that barely topped the surface of the water and bade me to enter. I climbed down a cable ladder and heard Dr. Spumoni dismiss the gondolier; then the ladder shook as he descended into my light. We were in a room about the size of my bedroom, with water beads and drips on the walls. There was an odd smell, like pizza mixed with excrement. A cave entrance complete with stalactites led out from the room.

"How is it possible that this cave is not water-filled?" I wondered. We were several meters underwater, and surely the walls must leak.

Dr. Spumoni explained: "Many centuries ago, this was karst terrane with numerous caves and polje. The entire area was captured by a Tuscan warlord. His chief engineer was an ancestor of Leonardo da Vinci. The warlord and Leonardo's predecessor decided to develop a marine subdivision so they plotted streets to create canals and began to pump seawater in, but they could not pump fast enough to fill the streets. The sinkholes drained away the water. The engineer wisely saw that the trouble was the caves draining away the water, but to plug up the caves was unthinkable because they might later become a tourist attraction. The engineer, being an inventor in the line of the famous Leonardo, developed a reverse siphon based upon arcane physics and alchemy. Operating automatically by the gravitational attraction of the moon and tidal forces, the siphon kept the caves relatively dry, and the subsequent air pressure kept the sea out. "We know the caves are connected because, so far, the reverse siphon has been found to work in every cave discovered to date. We cannot find the connections. That is why we have brought you, Ergor."

I was humbled by Dr. Spumoni's confidence in me as we pressed our way into the cavern. It was a cave of beauty—dripping and adorned with speleothems. There were nice stalactites, drapery, stalagmites, and columns, too! "I'll leave you here," said Dr. Spumoni. "I doubt if you will want others to learn your secret methods for finding cave connections."

"Oh no, you don't! Caving alone is not safe. And I failed to notice the sequence of twists and turns to find the entrance," I protested. Many times in West Virginia, Kentucky, and Missouri, we left novice cavers alone to explore as a joke. Twenty-three of them never came back, so we discontinued that kind of tomfoolery long ago.

"Very well, I will stay behind you," replied Tony, as he asked to be called. I know that to connect caves you must follow the water. But in this cave, there was no water, thanks to the effective DaVinci reverse siphon. I thought hard. What would be the opposite equivalent of water? Aha! Air—I would follow the air that was now gently blowing on my left cheek.

My aeolian friend led me down ancient corridors, up slopes, down drops, and through squeezes. Where multiple leads branched, I paused motionless until I could discern the faint waft of a cooling breeze on my face. We came at last to a mud belly crawl so tiny I had to remove my helmet to squeeze in. Tony elected to stay behind to "fix his lamp," he said, but I knew fatigue in any language. I told him that if I was not back in eight hours to leave without me and name it Rubreck Cave. He was spent, but I was just warming up. "If I'm not back in twenty-four hours, call the International Cave Rescue Federation," I said to the sagging Dr. S.

Air whistled through the squeeze as I squirmed ahead, wriggling worm-fashion through the ooze. We do stuff like this all the time in Kentucky, but Euro cavers may not like to get down in the grubbies. The Brits spend all their time in the grubbies, so they do not know what good cave looks like unless they go to Borneo, Sumatra, or China. After 1,200 meters (3,600 feet) of crawl, I sensed the ceiling rise a bit. And there was the familiar odor again—the faint whiff of pizza and excrement!

I crawled on my hands and knees. I stood. I saw a bouquet of red, white, and green flagging tied to a bolt sunk in the wall. A sign said: FARTHEST PENETRATION in seven languages. GRUPO DE SPELEOLOGICA DE VENEZIA. Beyond it, I saw a tourist trail. I had connected, and surely would have to wash the lingering odor out of my coveralls at the earliest opportunity. I gathered my muddy kit and trudged along the trail for several kilometers until I came to a lighted entrance. A ticket taker asked for my ticket, but I told him I had lost it. He said I had been given two tickets, one to get in and one to get out. I thrust my muddy bundle toward his nose, and he swung the gate wide to let me pass out of the cave.

The cave was on a small island, so I walked to the dock and hailed a gondola. "Take me to the secret cave," I ordered.

"Bellissimo," he said shoving us off into the canal. After twenty minutes we arrived at the pole, and there was Dr. Spumoni waiting atop the manhole cover.

"Congratulations!" he said. "You have connected the caves. I knew if anybody could do it, you would!" He gave me a kiss on both cheeks but backed off when he smelled my clothes. Back at the Villa Parcheesi, I was awarded the Italian Medal of Magnificence, a certificate suitable for framing, and a bottle of wine. Thank heaven they did not add my picture to the row of framed, distinguished cave heroes in my bedroom.

AMBER ROOM MYSTERY

An enduring mystery is, what happened to the Amber Room? Peter the Great constructed the Catherine Palace near St. Petersburg, Russia, around the mid-eighteenth century. He had been given the gift of six tons of amber in 1716 to construct the ornate palace. A spectacular feature of that edifice was the Amber Room, a 590-square-foot chamber adorned with 24-karat gold leaf and many kilograms of precious amber. The Amber Room was created by craftsmen working for four years inlaying amber and gold in the walls. The glittering space was called the Eighth Wonder of the World.

Amber is a solidified, fossilized resin produced millions of years ago when sap oozed from coniferous trees. In its viscous liquid state, it trapped small insects such as bees and ants, lizards, feathers, and leaves. The bugs remained encased as the yellow, orange, and brown amber cured and hardened. Jewelry is crafted from amber and is highly desirable because it is light in weight compared to semiprecious stones and is warm to the touch.

Alas, the Amber Room disappeared in World War II. It was reported that the Russians disassembled it and stored it in a basement in 1941 to protect it from the invading Nazis. One account claimed the Amber Room was destroyed in 1944 a casualty of war; another rumor claimed the Nazis shipped the dismantled Amber Room to an underground limestone mine as part of their systematic looting of European art treasures. For practical purposes, the priceless Amber Room no longer exists.

After the war, a drive to duplicate the Amber Room began in 1979 and was finally finished in 2003. Was the new Amber Room as fine as the original? A controversial issue.

Meanwhile, in a rural hospital eight km from St. Petersburg, an aged Russian speleologist lay gasping for breath on his deathbed. A former Cossack, Hugo Buzzov, uttered the words, "Amber Room . . . sister Anastasia. . . ." His last words made no sense, but when I read the account of his demise in a Russian speleological journal, I connected two and two.

Jim White, the cowboy who discovered Carlsbad Caverns in 1903, had a grandniece, Anastasia Buzzov. Around 1946, she had lived in Carlsbad, New Mexico. She had received a large shipment of heavy boxes, and she disappeared shortly thereafter.

I journeyed to New Mexico to see if I could pick up the trail. The scorching sun blasted a 115-degree blowtorch the day I arrived. I located Caliente Cartage, a local trucking company, and asked the ancient owner, Pedro Caliente, if he remembered Ms. Buzzov.

"You bet your sweet ass . . . she stiffed me out of four hundred thirty-five dollars back in forty-fix or forty-seven. Had us pick up a bunch of heavy crates at Railway Express and haul 'em out to Carlsbad Caverns National Park," Pedro Caliente was still angry and could remember the bitter details. "We unloaded at the far end of the parking lot around dusk. They was a gang of roustabouts there, but I didn't stick around."

In the Paloma Bar in Carlsbad, I found a few patrons nursing beers. "Anybody here know anything about a bunch of heavy boxes delivered to Carlsbad Caverns in the late forties?" I really did not expect anyone to remember an event so many years ago.

A customer in a ten-gallon hat turned from his stool, "My pap did. He passed in eighty-eight. But he used to tell of the day he and his three brothers made a thousand bucks apiece." He said they never worked so hard in their lives. They had a key to the cave gate, and they hauled the boxes down to Carlsbad Cavern's

Big Room. They spent all night gluing the contents of the crates to the stalactites, stalagmites, and flowstone columns.

Pap said, "It was real purty stuff, gold pieces, thousands of golden yellow and orange plastic pieces." But when they got done and switched on the lights, they couldn't see any of it because it was the same color as all the formations.

The Amber Room mystery was solved! The evidence was in plain sight. I'd just drive out to the Caverns and verify it for myself. I followed the winding road to Carlsbad Caverns National Park. As I drove, I reconstructed the sequence in my mind. Hugo, the Cossack, had located the looted dismantled Amber Room in a Russian cave. For safekeeping, he shipped the boxes to his sister in the USA and told her to hide the contents in plain sight. He sent her enough money to cover expenses, plus pay her way out of town. Hugo may never have figured out the end game—but I was well on the way to recovering the priceless world-renown Amber Room.

I bought a cave ticket. Our tour descended the zigzag cave trail and a little later we arrived in the Big Room. I was nearly blinded by the vastness of the largest underground room, 8.2 acres (3.3 hectares) of orange and cream, tan and ocher-colored formations (speleothems) of every size and shape, rank after rank. Where was the Amber Room?

It was hidden in plain sight. Same color. There was absolutely nothing to give away the location of the dismantled parts of the Amber Room. They blended in! I moved sideways off the trail to take a closer look.

"Sir, return to the trail! Departure from the trail is punishable by a ten-thousand-dollar fine," said the cave guide. She pointed to her badge. I stammered that I was just doing speleological research . . . in the name of science. "I won't warn you again!" she said. "Ranger'll be here in two minutes flat."

I thought I saw a bug on the edge of a column. But in my haste to get back on the trail, I couldn't be sure.

TOURING A SECRET CAVE
UNDER WOLF CREEK DAM

As all enlisted personnel of the Ohio Navy know, Wolf Creek Dam, which holds back Lake Cumberland in Kentucky, is leaking. The lake level is abnormally low and is threatening to strand some of the larger houseboats crosswise in the narrow arms of the lake. The US Army Corps of Engineers (USACOE) has paid $340 million to an Italian contractor to pump grout into the cave passages beneath the dam. Antonio Manacotti, Engineer in Charge of Pastafazoo Engineering, Ltd. said, "I am one hundred percent absolutely and positively certain that after we finish placing the grout curtain inside and under the earthen portion of the dam, there will be no more leaks." He said they had pumped three billion yards of cement into the cave below and were bringing in larger grout pumps the following week to be able to pump around the clock.

To investigate this project for myself, I wrote to the contractor and the USACOE for permission to visit the site. As the world's foremost cave explorer and authority on speleological ephemera, I presented my credentials. Needless to say, I was shocked when I was denied permission due to Homeland Security provisions that exclude individuals with foreign-sounding names. "We must enforce the Precautionary Principle and the Law of Unintended Consequences," said Major General Luigi Linguini.

I next wrote to a renegade caver from Summerset, Kentucky, to see if he could get me into the cave beneath Wolf Creek Dam. He had heard of my reputation for extreme honesty, bravery, and tact, so he invited me to join him for a "cave trip to an unknown place." We met at midnight at a marina south of the city and boarded his cigarette boat for a blackout run down the lake. A speedometer on the boat indicated 210 knots, which he said was why he was entering the Mayor's Lake Cumberland Regatta & Race this summer.

Never have I traveled so fast on a boat, nor thrown up from one end of the lake to the other. We arrived around 12:20 a.m. on the moonless night at a pier not far from the dam. I followed my host through the woods to a place where a door was set into a rock cliff face. He used his key, and we turned on our Sten lamps, entering a diagonal tunnel with stairsteps leading downward in it, much like the Carmichael Entrance to Mammoth Cave. Moisture dripped from the ceiling. The stairway bottomed in a trunk passage extending in the direction of the dam. I had brought my compass to verify the direction.

We walked 1,250 paces to where there was a thirty-six-inch-diameter pipe extending out of the ceiling and emptying into a vast tank. Semi-liquid grout poured from the pipe into the tank, where a front loader bladed the gray stuff the length of the tank. Another front loader shoveled the goop into a dump truck. My host and I walked the length of the tank just in time to see the loaded dump truck drive off farther into the cave. I expressed my astonishment to my caver host, and he said the best was yet to come.

We hitched a ride on the next dump truck, which drove about a mile through the cave passage to a brilliantly lighted rotunda-like cave room filled with conveyors and pouring stations. Workers were pouring the grout into molds. "We make concrete lawn ornaments, here." My host pointed out cast birdbaths, lawn deer, giant planting pots, frogs, parking barriers, nude ladies with jars on their shoulders, footmen in jockey uniforms, garden benches, sitting dogs, doorstops, and fountains. I thought the religious statues were interesting.

"Aren't you afraid you'll saturate the market for concrete lawn ornaments?"

His eyes twinkled as he said, "This is healthier than making moonshine. And if business slacks off, we can shift to making musical tombstones." He showed me several boxes of letters and numbers that could be inserted into tombstone molds, along with an assortment of ornamental horses, guns, hot rods, guitars, and bass boats—depicting the name, dates, and favorite hobbies of the deceased.

I asked my host if he wasn't worried about the lake above collapsing into the cave and sweeping the lawn ornament business into downtown Nashville. "Nah, I ain't skeered," he said. "Over in the next side passage, we got a water bottling line set up in case we need it." He fished out a label from his cave pack, CUMBERLAND WATER 100% H2O. "Reckon we can handle any part of the stimulus package that comes our way."

As we shook hands at the dock after our exciting cave trip beneath the Wolf Creek Dam, my host reminded me that tact dictated I not reveal his name. "It's the Code of the Cavers."

AUSTRALIAN DRUMSTICK

My speleological knowledge is legendary, although I am the first to confess to gaps in understanding. For instance, I do not know much about paleontology—the study and classification of ancient animals and plants. Many years ago, Brother Nicholas Sullivan, PhD, gained a stellar reputation for his paleontological study of a filled sinkhole in Maryland. A road cut revealed a cave that was mostly filled with red sediment and hundreds of thousands of bones! Sullivan spent months excavating and identifying the bones—bats, mice, shrews, moles, raccoons, ferrets, chipmunks, rats, guinea fowl, chickens, sparrows, and a snake. I never really envied his scientific prowess, but I was a little jealous of the fuss made by others over his Pleistocene graveyard hunt for itty-bitty bones.

One day, I asked Sullivan why he didn't seek larger bones, ones you could wrap your hand around or heft with two hands. "You could go for the big bones," he explained, "but peccary, jaguar, bison, deer, and antelope are as big as you find around here. You'd have to go to Australia to find really big bones in a cave."

I wrote to the international secretary of the Australian Speleological Society (unfortunate initials), and he replied within a fortnight. The Sydney Chapter of the ASS was mounting a speleological expedition to the caves of the Nullarbor Plateau two months from now. The expedition roster had a vacancy for a paleontologist with cave experience. I immediately applied for the position, believing that two months would allow sufficient time for me to cram all there was to know about cave paleontology specific to Australia.

My local library had little in the way of reference material: "Frog Hair Classification in New Zealand," and "Enamel Formation in Paleolithic Hens Teeth of New South Wales." The university library collection was far richer. I devoted five hours a day to "bone up" on paleontology in Australia. Fortunately, after one month, a letter arrived saying the Sydney Chapter had exhausted all efforts to recruit a cave paleontologist from Europe, North and South America, the Middle East, and Asia. I was thus invited to participate provided I paid my way. I was delighted and wired my acceptance.

Fearing there still might be gaps in my newly acquired knowledge, I called Brother Sullivan. "What should I do if I am asked about something beyond my knowledge?" Sullivan should know if anyone did.

"Change the subject," was his advice. "You know all that is worth knowing plus everything else about caves. Tell them of your cenote dives in Yucatan, trephine patterns in waterlogged skulls, tibia, and fibula fibs. You know, dazzle them."

Before packing, I shopped for appropriate tools—brushes and whisk brooms, dental scalers and explorers, tiny trowels and spatulas, and a reading glass. I bought a twenty-five-pound container of plaster of paris. Homeland security wanted to confiscate my plaster of paris, but I convinced them it was not cocaine by sniffing it and sneezing uncontrollably for ten minutes. Altogether I hefted two duffle bags of kit onto the scales at the Qantas Airline ticket counter check-in. The flight was the longest of my life, and I was happy to land in Australia days later. The Sydney Chapter expedition leader in his Range Rover made me feel at home. He kept calling me "mate." He did pronounce it "mite," however, and my newfound paleontology knowledge warned me he could be calling me a bug. I gave him the benefit of the doubt as we shared a stuffed kangaroo pocket over several brews at a pub.

Our plane flew west from Sydney with the entire expedition crew on board. I tried to enliven the trip by singing a few verses of "Bless 'Em All," but nobody joined in. It was hot as blazes—over one hundred degrees—when we landed. We journeyed to the cave at once. "I see this cave was developed in the Nullarbor limestone of Late Eocene, Oligocene, and Middle Miocene age," I volunteered, seeking to demonstrate I intended to hold up my end of the science.

Due to the high ambient temperature of the cave, we all wore Speedos and sweated like peccaries. Inside the first room was a small pool, and in it were round marble-like spheres. "Cave pearls, eh mite?" said John Eyre, leader of the expedition.

"Any caver would guess that" I said, "but in reality, we have an example of Lepidoptera testes—in other words, moth balls. *Laothoe populi* testes to be more specific." This silenced any critics that may have been in the party. "The so-called hawk moth preys upon wombat scat and is attracted to light from cave glowworms."

"How do you know that?" asked the leader. "How do you know it's wombat scat?"

"Simple! By taste alone, you can tell. Here, try some." I thrust at him a half of a Tootsie Roll." He refused it with a disgusted scowl. Clearly, my superior knowledge was buying me expertise by attribution. I popped the Tootsie Roll into my mouth and made sucking, pleasurable noises swallowing it.

The survey from the entrance had extended nearly a thousand meters into the cave when a shout came from the point setter. "Get Ergor up here. We found a big bone!"

There in the passage was a fossilized bone, the biggest drumstick I had ever seen. It was about two meters long with characteristic joint bulges on both ends. I had never seen anything like it except at Thanksgiving when I carved a turkey. Only that was microscopic compared to this gigantic bone at our feet. "Well," said John, "can you ID it? We did not pay you big bucks to fly you over here for this moment. The entire success of the expedition depends on your incontrovertible identification of what must be a speleological record." (Actually, I did pay my way.)

I studied the bone with my magnifying glass and carefully brushed aside the red ocher sediment. Truth be told, I had no idea what the bloody bone was! I remembered Brother Sullivan's advice: change the subject. "Notice that there are no other bones in situ. Nor do we have any feathers. It reminds me of a Pliocene guácharo oil bird fossil I discovered in Argentina in 1989. The femur of that bird measured thirty-three centimeters, which for several years held the Argentine record for largest avian femur." They seemed to believe what I said. "On the other hand, this femur is far larger—six feet or so—and is from an ostrich-like bird native to the Australian Outback. But it is *not* an ostrich femur!"

The crew gasped, "It's not?"

"*No!* It is the femur of an emir—a long-extinct giant bird that lived in Australia in the Pliocene Epoch. It will set the femur length record for the subcontinent, if not the entire world." The cavers clearly wanted to know more and pressed me for details. I thought fast. "Climate change is responsible for the demise of the emir; that and a combination of a volcanic eruption that dwarfed Krakatoa and a meteorite that impacted Mesopotamia. The noise deafened all the emirs, and they could no longer hear the warning noise of approaching predators. A few, like this one, fled into the caves of the Nullarbor where there used to be glowworms to sustain life. But when the glowworms gave out due to the heating effect of the sun, the emir became extinct. And this single remnant of a giant emir is evidence of all I have told you. Now, encase the femur with plaster of paris for protection."

The cave ended in a breakdown around the next corner, and the expedition packed up its Speedos and left the Nullarbor. As I was about to board my plane back to the States, John Eyre said as I walked out onto the tarmac, "Ergor, I think you should have known that word is *not* emir. An emir is an Arabian potentate. You misidentified what is actually the femur of an emu. While it does set the Australian record for femur length, I am very disappointed, and I think you are not the paleontology expert you claimed to be."

"Emir, emu, femur, femir . . . anyone could make a mistake like that. And I never claimed to be a paleontologist, despite my vast experience in caves worldwide and now, Australia." I don't think he bought my explanation, and I may have to wait until the scientific paper is published to find out.

ERGOR INTRODUCES EVIDENCE TO THE AUSSIES AND OFFERS A BITE

STARTLING DISCOVERY IN THE SOVEREIGN STYGIAN SEVENTH

The seventh continent, according to geographers, is Antarctica. Until last year, only Antarctica had no known caves. Since global warming is real, I have been following the retreating ice sheets in both the Arctic and Antarctic. My perusal of Google Earth photos of Antarctica revealed to me a heretofore unobserved black spot in a location previously covered by ice. Could this be the first cave on the last continent? If so, it would qualify for the time being as the longest, biggest, and best cave in Antarctica—in other words a Stygian Sovereign! I immediately booked a first-class seat on Patagonian Airways Flight 7 to McMurdo Sound.

I had already explored the Sovereign Stygian Six. Those are the longest, biggest, and best caves on each continent. Mammoth Cave in North America is the best-known example. So, it is not surprising that I wanted to be the first cave explorer to conquer the Sovereign Stygian Seventh. Normally, I would not think of caving alone. Yet, I was well aware of the controversy in the conquest of Everest—was it Sherpa Tenzing or Sir Edmund Hilary who first reached the sovereign summit? I reasoned that if I alone explored the Sovereign Stygian Seventh, it would avoid embarrassing controversy.

Fortunately for me, there is no baggage limit on Patagonia Airways flights, as my kit included 527 pounds (1,146.4 kg) of equipment. My Sno-Doo scooter was most of that cargo, but layers of clothing, a tent, and complete cave gear composed the rest of it. For food, I packed concentrated high-tech super-energy Snickers (yummy when frozen).

Immediately upon landing, I set off for the GPS coordinates I had calculated from the aerial photo. I motored over snow to the edge of the retreating ice pack and set up camp. Driving stakes into the limestone bedrock was out of the question, so I used my lithium battery-powered hammer drill to install bolts. After two bolts I decided to use rocks to hold down the tent. I nearly faced death when I bit into a Snickers bar. It was hard as steel from the cold, and as the first bite melted in thirty minutes, it also pulled out a filling in my molar.

In the morning, I entered the yawning cave—the Sovereign Stygian Seventh. Residual ice and snow drifts nearly blocked the entrance, but I used my ice axe and crampons to hack and chop my way through the entrance barrier. No footprints! I was first!

A disgusting smell assailed my nostrils. The cave air was slightly warmer than outside, and I was out of the wind. My surroundings were devoid of speleothems. There were no stalactites or stalagmites either. The trunk passage descended at -4.5° as displayed on my Leica Disto-Z for about 2,567.8 m. Suddenly, I stopped! Ahead, I heard a rustling, a continuous sound of motion, and small footfalls. Around the bend, I saw them—a large flock of eyeless cave-adapted penguins. Where penguins have eyes, these birds had none, nor even vestigial pigmentation. They had entirely white feathers, bills, and feet and seemed to sense my intrusion. Those on the outside of the flock waddled around as if in a daze. Those near the center revolved in place, like some eerie Christmas display in a department store window. The stench was nearly overpowering, and I sought the source of the nauseating odor. The floor of the cave beneath their feet was dazzling white, no doubt due to centuries of droppings.

Here was the most sensational natural discovery of all time, eclipsing the discovery of Lucy, the first humanoid. It did not shock me that these all-white birds were silent, as that is characteristic of these penguins. But what did they eat? Vegetation was out of the question in this deep, underground cavern.

I pressed onward and came to a circular pool of water. Before my very eyes, two penguins popped to the surface, shook off the water, and wobbled their way toward the rest of the flock. Suddenly a large specimen surfaced with a fish in its mouth. I recognized it as a giant *Amblyopsis spelaea,* a cave blindfish that I estimated to be a quarter meter in length! It, too, had no eyes and was nearly translucent. Now the source of their sustenance was apparent—no wonder the subterranean birds seemed sleek and well-fed.

In an experimental frame of mind. I pulled out a Snickers and handed it to a large outlier. He sensed I was proximate and bobbed his head quizzically, then snatched the candy bar from my mittened hand. He swallowed it whole. Maybe I should have removed the wrapper. I was sure that was his conclusion as he defecated on my snow boot, a steaming white pile. As if by some silent signal, all the cave penguins began to move in agitation, spreading their wings, gyrating, and clearly disturbed. Was I dreaming? They silently arranged themselves in straight lines rank on rank. The largest of the birds stepped out in front and turned. I would say he eyed me menacingly, except he had no eyes. Then he planted his right foot toward me, then his left. Now the mass was moving as one menacing body toward me, inexorable, as automatons in a *Star Wars* robot battle formation!

Panic seized me! They were not slowing or stopping! I jettisoned my Snickers. Their ranks flowed over breakdown on the floor like a slow-motion bore tide in the Bay of Fundy. If I could not escape, they would envelop me, maybe smother me. They forced me to retreat toward the pool. Step by step. I should have made my will before this trip, and my thoughtless Snickers bar proffer must have inflamed their leader's passions.

Good thing I had brought along my rebreather scuba pack. I hastily swung it around and clamped down on the mouthpiece. I hit the Emergency On valve and all LED indicators glowed green. Good to go! I tipped backward into the pool and sank in the chilly water. My $1,800 lithium Scurry-On lamp cut through the stygian deep water, and I could see rank after rank of penguins diving in hot pursuit. Breathe slow, Ergor! Kick hard! The penguins were coming closer!

My helmet bumped into something soft, yet hard. I recognized the striations of a whale and grasped a fin as it approached. Fortunately, the whale seemed to be heading rapidly for open water rather than deep diving to four hundred fathoms. He breached. I let go. I fell back into the water and struck out for the nearby beach where the cave mouth loomed to my right and my Sno-Do was parked at my left. Within an hour, I reached the McMurdo Sound airport just in time to board outbound Patagonia Airways Flight 9. Alas, they had no first-class seats, so I had to settle for tourist class.

I was lucky to escape alive. Needless to say, I had lost all my kit, cave gear, camping gear, Disto-Z, and Go-Pro camera. There was no time to load the Sno-Go on the plane. But I'd had the satisfaction of conquering the Sovereign Stygian Seventh and reporting on a strange new species of cave penguins—who hate Snickers.

Addendum. Tom Brucker, a semi-famous caver, read about the blind cave penguins in Antarctica. He emailed me as follows: Dear Ergor, you idiot! Everybody knows that penguins prefer Zero bars to all other fruit. Next time you encounter penguins be sure you have a supply of Zero bars at the ready, and devoid of wrappers. —Tom Brucker

Tom Brucker resides in Nashville and will probably tell me next what kind of music penguins like. Isn't it a shame that when cavers think they are expert on one thing, they think they are expert on all things?
—E. R.

NOOT NOOT !
NOOT NOOT !
NOOT NOOT !
NOOT NOOT !
NOOT NOOT
NOOT NOOT
NOOT NOOT
Noot Noot!
Noot?
Clariona Gewursthry

HOW I SAVED CIVILIZATION

ecently, I have seen science fiction movies where grotesque monsters who are angry about something decide to try to conquer our civilized world. They don't send a polite message or even a demand—no, they invade with fireworks from space or emerge from a steamy swamp somewhere, generally due to the thoughtless mistake of a deranged scientist.

A lesson for cavers is this: If you are exploring in a cave and come across cave pearls as big as weather balloons, for Pete's sake do not puncture them! If you hear scary music in a cave, do not call the governor of your state to send in the National Guard. And do not leave your party to check out a side lead unless you want the rest of your party to come after you, and later find you a pile of raw bleeding hamburger. That can only lead to endless misfortune.

All really good scientists are skeptics. Despite the evidence from realistic movies, I remain skeptical that enemy aliens from other planets would come to us violently as depicted in the movies in which they rise up out of the ocean looking like Model T Fords laden with household junk right out of *The Grapes of Wrath*. Only a million times larger! The creatures have abnormally large heads and carry fancy ray guns. Their movements may resemble the shifting gyrations of giant inflated attention-getters in used car lots in Los Angeles. My skepticism tells me that hostile aliens would not come upon us so obviously like this.

Why? In these science fiction movies, civilization always wins because, while the early humans get liquidated, heroic government forces or true patriots eventually prevail and send the creatures back to hell in bits. Or wherever they came from. In other words, if you are a space alien and want to conquer Earth, do not come on like invincible gigantic mechanical monsters with unstoppable firepower. That will always end badly for you.

How do I know? Once, we discovered a cave in southern Ohio. The mud was thick and gooey, like cottage cheese, in the small passage leading to the Big Room. We were astonished to find the room packed with orange highway barrels, some of which had yellow flashing lights. Who could have stacked them in this remote cave? Why were they here? The survey consisted of five stations—extensive for Ohio caves. After we left the cave, the entrance collapsed, much like in the movies where the good guys run out of the mine before the whole mountain lets go. We did not think much about Orange Barrel Cave after the map was finally plotted.

But in the past few days, I have realized a startling truth: alien invaders of Earth will not come as warlike monsters. No, they will disguise themselves as orange barrels! They will build their forces into an invincible army before they launch their surprise attack and wipe out civilization. I have since seen orange barrels lined up in formation along many roads. Their commanders flash yellow lights.

Orange barrels are everywhere! Earth is doomed, if my suspicions are true. They are waiting until all mankind is asleep, then *whamm*!

Yet, what if I am wrong? Maybe the evil aliens are zucchini! In summer, zucchini multiply and are everywhere. If you have grown zucchini, you know that you can't get rid of them. We used to sneak into supermarket parking lots and load six or eight zucchini into each unlocked car. Maybe the attack of the killer zucchini is just around the corner. The *Attack of the Killer Tomatoes* may not be just the creative brainstorm of a science fiction movie.

Or stop signs. Those red octagonal stop signs could be the growing army of an advanced planet's military buildup. Stealth incarnate! They're controlling our movements for sinister purposes—making us stop. They laugh—we are so easily controlled! We anticipate the frightening arrival of giant monsters accompanied by ominous movie music, but—woe is us—they are already here! Doom is around the corner.

Armed with this flash of insight, I wrote a letter to the president of the United States. In the movies, presidents always ignore warnings like mine. Science is disrespected at the highest levels. Boy, was I surprised when a letter arrived in my mailbox from the White House! The president thanked me for the warning and said he had forwarded it to his Secretary of Homeland Security. He also asked me to send a campaign contribution, so I know the letter was authentic.

I urge all cavers to be alert for orange barrels in caves. You can't very well attack them outdoors with long guns and baseball bats without running afoul of ignorant local authorities. But in caves, you can bring down the roof! Focus on the barrels with flashing yellow lights—the platoon commanders. Put their leaders out of action, and the troops will die of confusion. Cave conservation nuts will immediately protest or even organize demonstrations, but our civilization is at risk! No time to lose.

Just for the record, I have not seen any caves filled with zucchini. Nor any filled with stop signs. However, their ubiquitous presence in plain sight, rank on rank—along nearly all highways—convinces me that *they* are among us.

Could it be that the orange barrels in caves are their reserve armies? When the forces of Earth eventually conquer the obvious invaders, and we are lulled into complacency by joyous movie music, the orange barrels will emerge from their hideout caves and *strike*!

Wake up, world! Otherworldly aliens are inside the gates. Their reserves are marshaled in ranks deep underground, waiting for the digital message from their home planet to annihilate civilization as we know it. Cavers have warned Earthlings! Ergor Rubreck has done his duty, so now it is up to cavers to carry the message to all who value humanity. Time is short. Resolve can yet save the day and all we hold dear.

PROOF OF FLAT EARTH IN A CAVE

For most of my life, I have believed that the earth was an oblate spheroid, sometimes called a geoid. To call the earth an ideal Earth-shaped sphere is like calling a caver caver-shaped. In a similar vein, I had heard of flat-earthers—individuals claiming the earth was flat despite more than ten ways to check its shape for yourself. The modern Flat Earth Society exists, I learned to my amazement when I saw a four-color membership certificate, suitable for framing, hanging on the wall of a friend's office.

"Charlie," I said, "You look like a dork with that certificate hanging on your wall."

"Hold on, Ergor, your insult is unbecoming of a caver of your intellect. Haven't you heard of the Four Corners Monument?" Four Corners is the junction of the states of Utah, Colorado, Arizona, and New Mexico. Of course, I had heard of it, but I realized I had insensitively insulted my friend.

Seeking to recover, I said, "I apologize, but don't you think it would be better to buy a frame for your membership certificate?" He nodded approvingly at my request for forgiveness.

"You should investigate before you shoot off your mouth," Charlie said. So, I investigated by calling the Four Corner Monument manager at his office in Utah.

Edward Standing Tall answered the phone. "I am Ergor Rubreck, famous and wonderful cave explorer, and I'm calling to inquire about. . . ."

"Oh!" he interrupted. "You're calling about the cave! Timely indeed. Some members of our steering committee found what we think is a cave entrance about three hundred feet southwest of the monument, but we haven't entered the cave. We discussed our next move and decided to contact a prominent cave explorer. I was about to call you. When can you come?"

I consulted my busy calendar. "How about next Monday?" I asked.

"Fine, I'll pick you up at the Salt Lake City airport if you tell me your flight number. So you can recognize me, I'm seven feet tall without my headdress."

Indeed, Edward stood out. I would have recognized him immediately, even without his feathered headdress. "So, are you a Native American," I asked.

"I am. I'm a leader in the Teec Nos Pos chapter of the Navajo Nation, and this year's manager of the Four Corners Monument. Welcome! We'll drive to the cave entrance at once."

We drove up a dusty road to the Monument where the parking lot was flanked with souvenir stands. We unloaded and hiked off in a southwest direction about the distance of a football field. I suited up, checked my many light sources, and climbed into the entrance. My Disto-Z indicated a heading of 45° with -4° down and a distance of 310.4 feet. The scalloped canyon walls were eight feet apart, and the passage was 78 inches high—Edward would have bent his feathers.

The cave ended in a roughly circular chamber about 175 feet in diameter by ten feet high. I reckoned we must be directly under the Four Corners Monument. When the dust cleared, I decided to check the walls. I came to an eight-inch-wide vertical joint, peculiar in that the bedrock wall on one side was limestone and the other side was sandstone! I continued walking around the circular wall and found another eight-inch-wide vertical joint, sandstone on the near wall and shale on the continuing wall. All the joints showed slickenside, shiny surfaces. The rock on either side of the joints had moved relative to one another, so because I know so much geology, I realized that these features weren't joints at all! They were faults!

Except in high-angle, thrust-fault mountainous areas, I had never seen dissimilar wall rocks horizontally adjacent to each other. Most road cuts show sandwich-like layers of bedrock, one on top of the other. At the next eight-inch vertical joint, the shale adjoined an igneous diorite. Now I reached the first joint I had seen 360° back—the limestone again. I took a few rock samples from each of the four rock zones, hoping some paleomagnetic or fossil evidence would clear up this astounding mystery.

My sketch showed the four quadrants—limestone, sandstone, shale, diorite—each separated by an eight-inch vertical joint or fault that met at the center of the room's ceiling. I said goodbye to Edward Standing Tall and promised to send him a map and report after further investigation.

Back at my lab, I turned on my sensitive micro-magnetometer (Model R-16) and electron microscope. I prepared several slabs of the four different rocks. I recorded the earliest geomagnetic indicators of reversal in each rock, discovering a far earlier magnetic chron (interval) not described in the literature (I'm calling it the Rubreck Precambrian chron, eleven billion years old), subject to further study. The paleomagnetic dipoles pointed to the ancient North Pole but in several directions, which seemed widely divergent. All lines should have pointed consistently in one direction.

The only way I could account for the diverse paleomagnetic directions was if the original earth had been flat, consisting of four end-joined segments, each resembling a flattened fourth of a basketball. My working hypothesis is that indeed *the earth was flat in the beginning*, but instead of a flat rectangle, it had a quatrefoil plan or outline with the "basketball segments" joined at one end. Centrifugal and centripetal forces, together with the Coriolis and Coanda effects had gently forced the four segments up, out, and in to form an oblate spheroid! The top four corners met in the cave!

If you examine a library globe, you will see it is made from similar segments—called gores—printed flat and pasted on a spheroid. Their junction was evident in the rocks at Four Corners!

A few scientists may be skeptical of my conclusion. Dinosaurs did not exist in the Precambrian era, which makes these bones so rare. But like plate tectonics, the far-fetched-sounding theory that became accepted geologic history, my flat-earth finding will gladden the hearts of flat-earthers everywhere. Mark my words: Ergor said it first!

I cut a melon to show how this works.

HUNTING THE BLIND ALABASTER

A few years back while on a cave expedition to Australia, I identified the femur of an emir, a giant bird resembling an ostrich. My identification proved controversial, especially by zoologists who mainly know about surface animals and not so much about underground birds. Because my usual hourly rate was less than qualified experts, I was asked to lead a caving expedition to find the probably extinct (maybe not) blind alabaster.

If you have not heard of the blind alabaster, consider these truthful facts: it cannot see straight because it cannot see at all. Nobody has seen a blind alabaster in twenty years. Skeptics deny that alabasters in any form exist and insist they are mythical, like the unicorn. (If there are blind unicorns, I am willing to hunt for them.) An alabaster can see equally well from both ends. What, exactly, is a blind alabaster?

It is an extremophile, a rare cave-dwelling animal that lives in caves 24/7/365. If you can imagine a small white animal, physically a cross between an armadillo and an miniature hodag 0.2mm from head to tail, with pigment for eyes (vestigial eyes?), then you can imagine a blind alabaster. They roll up into tiny white balls when asleep or frightened. They are found in an Outer Seychelle Island cave at sea level. With climate change, the cave is endangered by rising water and embittered by shifting sand.

The expedition to investigate them and take pictures for the *National Geographic* was funded by the Timex Division of the Rolex Chronometer Foundation, headquartered in Bora-Bora.

For many years, they sponsored the Frobisher to Tierra del Fuego Stilt Race until the Panama Canal was dug open in 1914. Their sponsorship switched to expeditions a few years later. My expedition had a 256,000,000 outski (4,950:1.0 US) budget ($51,717), covering the airfare tourist class and a couple of Zebra lights. The budget covered one investigator—me.

The Seychelle Islands (115 of them) are in the Indian Ocean. Aldabra Atoll consists of four coral islands, noted for its large population of giant tortoises. Lesser Aldabra is small, so I rented a Zodiac and packed a cooler of sandwiches and Bootstrap Stout. I found the small island on the first try, beached the Zodiac, and saw the cave at the base of a spiral "smoke column" of departing bats. A ten-foot-wide tortoise guarded the cave entrance. Bat poop covered his shell. He blinked slowly, as if in a torpor. I timed my cave entry between blinks.

Most coral caves I have seen are bathed in creamy orange flowstone stalactites, stalagmites, and columns. This cave was no exception. I examined a pool to see if I could catch sight of the illusive blind alabaster. Back when I inventoried the Kentucky Cave shrimp in Mammoth Cave, I stretched out on a foam rubber mattress prepared with food and drink to spend hours staring into the water. Then, the critters were so transparent they could only be seen when their tiny shadow moved. At 0.2mm, the blind alabaster might be even harder to detect.

It was my hope to capture a male and female breeding pair so the alabaster could be raised in captivity back in the laboratory or in a colony to study predation. In a forty-eight-hour-long vigil, I saw only one suspected blind alabaster, sex undetermined. He (or she) was too quick and escaped my tea strainer net. I thought of using a lure, but the literature is silent on what alabasters eat—their diet is a mystery. Back in Kentucky, the preferred bait for cave beetles and cave crickets is horse poop. Could tortoise poop lure the alabaster? Or bat poop? I went to the mouth of the cave to secure a handful of each. The tortoise shit won the day, or rather the next day.

I spread the poop on a small rock and placed it in the pool. The next day, the rock with the tortoise lure was covered with a blanket of white blind alabasters. I could see the individuals without magnification. Now the question was how to get the animals back home alive for further study? How could I control the environment to keep them happy and alive? Would I have to take along the giant ten-foot tortoise to supply alabaster attractant?

Extra weight of rocks could be costly. So instead, I cut the tortoise poop into round coupons, similar to quarters. I placed a dozen of these in various cave pools.

The next morning, I retrieved the twelve poop coupons, and each was covered by blind alabasters! My quest was a success. I arranged the coupons neatly in a plastic box, covering the colonies with natural pool water. Mission accomplished. Time to go home.

I met an unexpected problem from Homeland Security at New York City airport as I checked in to my home flight. An inspector examined my carry-on luggage and found the plastic box containing the blind alabasters on the tortoise poop coupons. "Hey, what's with the box of candy? Those look like nonpareils to me. We'd better check," he said to the other inspectors.

"No," I said, "Nonpareils are dark chocolate disks covered with small white candy balls. Nonpareil means 'no equal.' These alabasters are from the Seychelles, not nonpareil candy."

Federal inspectors began yelling to each other, "This passenger is acting suspicious! We'd better test this stuff. There's plenty for all of us to check it out." Three more inspectors converged from up and down the screening lines. They opened the box, passed out the round coupons, and devoured the blind alabasters!

They reacted as if they had been poisoned. One retched. Another ran for the restroom. I tried to explain what the inspectors had eaten, but the sound of vomiting drowned me out. Panic ensued among the waiting passengers.

My science trip was ruined. My sponsors never forgave me.

CAVE RESCUES

Everybody knows caves are dangerous and that cave rescues make gripping headlines. I have rescued victims from caves a few times. Sometimes the fault is the cavers themselves, as when children enter caves with only a flashlight. Other times, the cave owner may be at fault. Or nobody is at fault.

Two years ago, I visited WunderFull Cave in Missouri. They advertised two tours: #1 was $10 and #2 was $60. Neither tour was described, so I chose the #1 tour to see what wonders the cave had in store for me. As is my custom, I entered the cave in my full caving regalia: red coveralls, helmet and light, boots, kneepads, and carry bag. I find it helps establish my caving creds with the guide, who may (or may not) recognize me as Ergor Rubreck, famous explorer.

Only this time there was no guide for #1 tour. The turnstile into the dark cave clicked on a dim light—the management's gesture toward natural cave lighting—and I read the sign explaining that #1 was a self-guided tour. ENJOY! admonished the sign. I marched into the murky darkness past some pointy formations to the next sign and light switch. ECHO HALL was about forty-two feet in diameter and lit with a single LED. In the feeble light I could not detect an echo but gave management the benefit of the doubt.

Several hundred feet farther, I stumbled onto another sign, LAKE ROOM. The lake appeared about two inches deep with a sailboat of indeterminate size silhouetted with an LED on the far shore. I followed an intricate twisting passage deeper into the cave, feeling drip water soaking my coveralls. The path led me up and down past numerous dark side leads, barely distinguishable in the thick gloom.

After about an hour, I saw a glint of light far ahead and entered a small room containing four visitors huddled together. They explained they had taken #1 Tour and had been trapped there because none of the lights would switch on in reverse, leaving them at the mercy of a pitch-black, confusing cave. A vending machine in one corner of the room contained the lighted message: INSERT CREDIT CARD FOR TOUR #2 TICKET BACK OUT OF WUNDERFULL CAVE. Nobody had brought a credit card, and the four visitors had waited three and a half hours for a rescue. I used my headlamp to lead the four out of the cave to safety, not only saving their lives but saving us between $60 and $300.

On another occasion, I was summoned to Paregoric Cave in Patagonia to aid in the rescue of a table tennis team trapped by high water in the cave. The Patagonian Speleological Institute of Cave History Operations (PSICHO) knew they needed an expert's skill set to extricate the two stranded victims. Since no expert was available, they contacted me. Not being certified in cave diving, I needed another technique to rescue them successfully.

Fortunately, I had changed my US money to 243,000 pesos at the port of entry. So, I was able to buy out the entire stock of paper towels and yellow sponges at the three grocery stores near the cave. Members of PSICHO and I stuffed paper towels and sponges into the flooded cave mouth, sopped up sufficient water to create a one-meter opening, and brought out the table tennis team hungry but thankful to be alive. I was pleased to learn later that the Patagonian table tennis team had won the brass medal in that sport at the 2016 Olympic Games.

Rescues from vertical shafts in caves can require nerves of nylon. An unnamed, deep TAG (**T**ennessee, **A**labama, **G**eorgia) cave was the scene of another of my rescue involvements. I got the call when I was in the shower. Pat Longtress had rappelled into a 132-foot vertical shaft near Norris Lake on a 120-foot Blue Water rope. She used an eight-bar rack, and her long blond hair had become woven among the bars about eighty feet down. She could neither slide down to the overhand knot in the end of the rope nor change over to her ascenders due to her scalp being pulled tangential to the rope, generally immobilizing her.

A waterfall poured into the pit, luckily missing the fixed descending rope altogether, so immediate hypothermia was not the main risk. Pat dangled and thrashed in the eight-foot-diameter shaft for an hour before the others in her party called me.

I rappelled down to her on my own 156-foot rope. I suggested that she stop flailing her extremities and rest. "Help me, Ergor, I'm in a terrible fix!" she screamed over the thundering waterfall.

"If you ain't broke, don't fix it!" I yelled to cheer her up a bit and encourage her spirits. "We can't hoist you up to the top because there is no room at the top to tie off a hoisting line." I gave her three cups of chocolate pudding and a plastic spoon to get her blood flowing. Then I continued down to the bottom of the shaft. All the water was draining through a six-inch hole in the bottom. I pondered the situation for a few minutes, then climbed past Pat to the top of the shaft. "Don't go anywhere while I go to town," I advised.

At a nearby marina chandlery, I purchased a sewer test plug and a personal flotation device, size medium. And a six-pack of chocolate pudding.

Back at the vertical shaft, I slipped several cups of pudding to Pat and continued to the bottom. The test plug fit snugly into the drain orifice, and I used my Leatherman monkey wrench to tighten the expansion nut atop the plug. Snug plug, glug-glug, the water began to pool in the shaft floor. I mounted my ropewalker ascender set and hiked back up my rope to Pat.

She said she had dropped the spoon as I was slipping the life preserver vest around her shoulders.

It took only seven hours and forty-three minutes for Pat to float to the top where we cut her golden hair to free her from the brake bar rack. She was so grateful she gave me her brake bar rack and rope.

Pat Longtress—now short tress—tells of her rescue by Ergor at every opportunity.

Me, I'm still picking long yellow hairs out of my new eight-bar rack.

FIND AT OAK ISLAND

Oak Island, site of the Money Pit in Nova Scotia, supposedly holds a buried treasure trove of fabulous and mysterious valuables. Some treasure has been found. What remains? Gold doubloons? Marie Antoinette's crown jewels? King Arthur's magic sword? The Ark of the Covenant? The Holy Grail? Groucho Marx's mustache? Accounts said a prophetic note reads, "Seven must die!" to find the treasure; however, six are already dead, which cuts down the odds. Me, I couldn't care less for treasure; exploring interesting caves is everything! On the other hand, non-cavers always ask me, "Find anything valuable in them caves?"

I contacted a Canadian caver, Hoser MacSuds, who had explored caves in the slipperiest parts of West Virginia, Castle-guard, and Kings Pub in Montreal. We made a pact to explore Oak Island caves together, sealed by a pint of Bunker C. "We'll do it right, mate, since the provincial government bolloxed the split-treasure law aborning," he proclaimed.

We met in the seaport city of Halifax, Nova Scotia, and rented a lorry for our excursion to Oak Island. Oak Island is privately owned. Photos reveal that much of it is strewn with junk cars, rusting machinery, hoists, petards, windlasses, jack screws, cable, chains, and whips. These abandoned artifacts spoil most views on the island. Expeditions mounted by mountebanks, freebooters, contractors, businessmen, and ne'er-do-wells have exhausted their patrons' patience and fortunes digging, drilling, pumping, and otherwise seeking the treasure buried there.

Why would any self-respecting pirate bury treasure there, when there are at least eight other islands larger and more readily accessible in Mahone Bay? Only a wealth of *stories* has been generated, plus a beat-up ancient coin, some coconut fibers, rotten wood, and a lost stone tablet containing an undeciphered coded inscription (which I deciphered, by the way; translation later).

Hoser wanted to crowdfund our go at the money pit, but I told him we needed a reconnaissance first before we went after the heavy coin. We left the big city, stopping at a general store in the small town of Mahon Bay. The proprietor looked over forty, so I told him we were cave explorers looking for the Oak Island treasure. "How many treasure hunters have you seen?" I asked.

"You're the twentieth and twenty-first," he said. Then he added, "This week." He offered to sell us an Oak Island treasure map for two loonies. I objected to being called crazy, but Hoser wisely restrained my arm as I drew back to smite him.

Hoser told him, "No thanks, lad. We downloaded the exclusive Oak Island treasure map from Google. Fresh off the internet." The shopkeeper allowed as how we were spelunkers, we might want a map of nearby Acorn Island. He said it was an island karst complete with flank margin caves, sinkholes, rillenstein, and karren. (I failed to ask for Karren's phone number.) We paid twenty bob for "the only copy" of the *Acorn Island Treasure Map; An Annotated Guide to Money Pits and Gold Hoards.* © 2012 by Clothes Press. We departed after loading up with bangers and mash for lunch.

There is no causeway or bridge to Acorn Island. But we found a fisherperson who owned a landing ship tank (LST) from World War II and would ferry our lorry to Acorn Island for $50 C. Through the mist, we could see waves breaking on Oak Island a few miles away. Our 4WD climbed on an unpaved road around the island to a flank margin cave near a beach containing several shipwrecks, and several crosses. A cryptic sign said AVAST THERE and on the reverse side said AARGH. I guessed these were pirate signs, so if there *was* pirate treasure, we were on the right track. Hoser and I donned our boiler suits, helmets, headlamps, and ditty bags of emergency rations and plunged into the cave. In 234 meters, we came to an abrupt wall—the end of the cave. Propped against the wall was an exact copy of the undecipherable inscription-coded rock that supposedly referred to the Oak Island Money Pit.

Suddenly Hoser cried out, "Water! Run for your life. Tide's coming in!" The sea was now lapping my ankles and Hoser was heading pell-mell toward the exit. I lingered for a few minutes and unholstered my camera. Confirming everything we had heard and read, the inscription was gibberish. But as the water rose, it soon reached the halfway point on the rock, covering the lower half of the symbols. The upper half of the coded inscription was reflected in the inrushing water. I fired a burst of twenty shots, then high-tailed out of the cave chin-deep in water. Suddenly, I had it!

I screamed for Hoser to build a fire at once on the beach . . . our signal for summoning the fisherperson's WWII LST. Back at our room in the Ritz Hotel in Mahone Bay, I printed out my photos of the undecipherable coded inscription rock. One frame struck me like a thunderbolt.

A CORN IS LAND M I T OK IS LAND

I puzzled at the half-inscription, half-reflection in my photo. Several hours later, we headed northeast up the coast. Just before the small town of Western Shore, we turned right onto the narrow causeway to Oak Island. The owner's agent hailed us to stop and pay $100 C (Aha! The Oak Island treasure—a toll for access!). Hoser and I pooled our cash and paid, not waiting for a receipt. Dusk was at hand, light fading fast. We drove the lorry to where the junk was scattered abundantly. "Hoser, what do you see?"

"Just junk," said Hoser, surveying the abandoned machinery.

"Over there, next to the ancient boiler . . . see, it's a rusted Ford Model T! That's the clue everybody has missed since 1923." It was finally dark, and Hoser gave up looking. We agreed to rise at first light and examine the old car hulk. We pitched our tent, brewed coffee, ate the last of the bangers and mash, and turned in.

The first light this far east was at 5:32 a.m. Hoser was already up. We sprinted to the rusting Model T Ford. Under a rotting floorboard, we found a rusting metal toolbox. We prized it open. It contained a hoard of coins, twenty in all. They were goonies, a rare Canadian coin, only forty of which were struck in 1920. They bore an image of an upside down bi-wing airplane—obviously, a misstrike. Hoser was a numismatist—a coin collector and money expert. He said these were worth a fortune, perhaps $200 C!

"How did you know where to look?" asked Hoser. I told him the undecipherable coded inscription—when reflected in the advancing tide—told the story. I had held that photo up to my mirror, which I always carry in my caving emergency kit, and saw . . . nonsense! However, the letters in reverse spelled A CORN IS LAND M I T OK IS LAND. If you put all the letters together, and divide them differently, it spells *ACORN ISLAND MY T OAK ISLAND*. I remembered seeing an abandoned Ford Model T among the junk scattered around on Oak Island.

On our way back along the causeway, we were stopped by a crown official. "The Provincial Parliament has just enacted a law that one-half of any treasure find is claimed by the Province," he explained. We showed him the hoard of twenty goonies, and he counted out ten, giving us an official receipt. Our causeway fee of $100 C and our $100 goony-confiscation meant we had almost broken even, despite our find on Oak Island.

FAST FANDANGO

I was invited to Spain to assist in the exploration of a newly discovered, strange cave on the outskirts of Madrid. The only known entrance was a one-meter hole in the corner of a rail yard of the Ferrocarril de Cordoba y Valencia. The Spanish Speleological Society invited me after a rapid phone call. Sr. Gorge S. Mendez, Director General said, "Sr. Rubreck, have you not explored the famous Snowy River Cueva in Arizona?"

I replied, "Yes, I have not explored Snowy River." He was referring to the famous thirty-mile-long cave with only one entrance where a river of gypsum seems to have no end. Survey trips in that cave are the most arduous on Earth because camping is not allowed, and trips must be of thirty hours duration.

"We need you to advise us on long-duration trips," Mendez said. "We send you a ticket to come to Spain, courtesy of the Museo de las Estudias de Amblentales. You leave mañana." He hung up before I could learn the details, but since I have participated in long cave trips, I assumed my worldwide fame had come to the attention of Spanish cavers. The electronic ticket voucher arrived an hour later, so I packed my lightweight cave gear and passport.

Sr. Mendez met me at the Madrid International Airport with a warm handshake and a cheery "Hola!" The drive to the rail yard took forty-five minutes. A steel tripod was rigged over the hole in the ground, and my host beckoned me to clip onto a carabineer on the hoisting cable. (Some European cavers use electric winches for descents and ascents.)

On the bottom, my stun light revealed a white strip of gypsum trailing into the distance in a passageway ten meters wide by fifteen meters high. It curved gently to the left. Sr. Mendez alighted at my side. "We explore, no?" Before setting off, I drew my boot across the white path. Instead of it feeling crunchy, like gypsum, it felt soft like talcum powder—strange. The mark was to tell me when we had returned to the entrance spot; the trench would remind me to look up for the cable.

As we trudged ahead, I explained to Sr. Mendez that we always survey as we explore. It saves us from party leaders who return with hand-waving stories of immense passages and unspeakable grandeur but have no idea where this magnificent discovery is located. "No, we don't do that. We enjoy good stories," Mendez said.

Fortunately, I had brought along my pedometer and checked it from time to time. We had walked seven miles (11.2 km), and my boots were white along with my pants up to my knees. Sr. Mendez was similarly covered with white stuff. Suddenly I saw it dead ahead in the beam of my light—the trench I had scraped with my boot at the bottom of the drop.

We had marched in a complete circle. Mendez apparently did not see the mark and kept walking. I asked him how far it was to the end of the cave. He replied, "We have not come to the end. We turned around at twenty-five kilometers and backtracked." I knew then that Mendez and his companions had gone around twice and turned around, not recognizing anything. They were lucky finally to see the hole in the ceiling.

"Alto!" I called, "Stop. We have passed our entry point." Sr. Mendez shook his head vigorously from side to side, a universal *no*. I pointed to the ceiling where a cable dangled just out of reach. He raised both arms in astonishment.

Suddenly, I saw light coming around the tunnel curve ahead of us. The light grew larger in size, and I heard a whooshing sound, as if made by a locomotive churning fast toward us. A cloud of white powder framed the churning mass. If we did not move, the train-like vehicle would run us over. Mendez was tinkering with his harness, paying no attention to the speeding train.

I made a flying tackle to shove Mendez to the right side of the tunnel just as the train thundered by, covering us in a cloud of white powder. It missed us by inches (millimeters).

We lay in the dust panting and coughing to clear our lungs. My impression was the locomotive had a swastika emblem below its headlight, but I could have been wrong. The engine was followed by one baggage car, but the train had passed around the bend by the time I sought to verify the vehicle.

We ascended by hoist, emerging in darkness lighted only by the orange glow of a sodium vapor light. What had I learned? I'd learned that the uniform tunnel formed a giant circle some 11.2 km in circumference. I scooped up a vial of the white powder to analyze later. I had checked the white trail to see if there were steel rails covered beneath. No rails, just smooth hard floor. How indeed had a train come, if it was a train? Mendez had no idea what had happened. He tried to swear me to secrecy saying, "You must swear never to tell of this, or we will be the laughingstock of speleologists everywhere."

I replied, "Yes, I will never swear to tell of this adventure." That seemed to satisfy him.

Sr. Mendez deposited me at the departure lounge. Waiting for my flight home, I opened my computer to search for answers to this stupendous mystery. I Googled *Nazi circle*. On page 6 was a puzzling note: *Nostradamus*. I clicked on the so-called prophet's writings to find the following:

*Hister allied with two leaders will incur wrath of people
to the north, discern magic, and hoard.*

Gibberish! Yet, one or two things caught my eye: Hister and discern. Hmm. Proponents of Nostradamus had observed that Hister is really Hitler—Adolf Hitler, the Führer of Germany. The word *discern* contains the word CERN. CERN is the home of the twenty-seven-mile-long circular Hadron Collider. It hurls particles around a circular tunnel to collide with irresistible force to split atoms and possibly discover new elements. How does Hitler fit in? I clicked on *Hitler atom*. Wow! A Wikipedia article on Hitler's secret atomic program said his scientists had an idea that atoms could be split if accelerated faster than the speed of light and then collide with atoms.

Particles would be cast off, perhaps a new deadly weapon. A history of the run-up to World War II said that Hitler made a pact with Benito Mussolini of Italy and Generalissimo Franco of Spain to experiment with a collider. A secret research facility was actually constructed underground somewhere in Spain in 1935. Could that secret program have been a failure, and Hitler turned to heavy water as a different approach? Norwegian Commando raids early in 1942 sabotaged this Nazi plan, ending by sending a ferry boat and its cargo of heavy water to the bottom of Lake Tinn in 1945.

My analysis of the white powder indicated it was harmless spent neutrino dust, originally gray but turned white when oxidized. Pieces of the puzzle were fitting together. Enemies to the north? Of course, that would be the Basque separatists in the north of Spain. Franco, the Spanish dictator, had loaded the enormous electric power cost of the collider onto the electric bills of this group of people living in the north of Spain. This and other forms of economic injustice and cruelty had made the Basques mortal enemies of the Spanish government.

Still unanswered was the train in the "cave." I searched on *Nazi trains*. Bingo! In the last days of the regime, Hitler had loaded a train with gold to finance his "retirement," but the train was never found. All blown-up tunnels were opened, abandoned train sheds were explored—no gold train. Maybe the mystery was solved by Mendez and me in that circular cave. Yet, trains must run on rails, and there were no rails beneath the white neutrino powder.

Trains can use magnetic repulsion to levitate the train above any surface. No rails necessary. Nazi scientists had discovered the Maglev principle first. After all, the first electric train was developed in Germany by Werner von Siemens in 1879 and is still running today, so the inventive capacity had been available near the end of the war.

Gold. Gold? Why had Sr. Gorge S. Mendez demanded secrecy, especially with his remark that Spanish cavers enjoyed good stories? Once again, I Googled, this time on Gorge S. Mendez. His biography came back with a plausible answer. His full name is Gorge Sishtruber Mendez. No relation to anything . . . but wait . . . Hister = Hitler. Could Schicklgruber (Hitler's original family name) be equivalent to Sishtruber? Schicklegruber = Shistruber?

What else could it be?

EGYPTIAN CAVE MISSING

Seven years ago, I was contracted by the government of Egypt to survey the cave systems of the Western Desert District southwest of Giza. For millennia, Egypt has been a treasure trove of archaeology, including ancient architecture. As a competent numerologist, I already knew the Egyptians had determined the value of pi (in 1650 BCE before the discovery of that value by Ptolemy in 150 AD. Supposedly, it was derived from the dimensions of the pyramids. However, I was the one who solved the mystery: the Egyptians laid out the pyramid dimensions using a measuring wheel, so the value of pi comes accidentally and naturally out of the wheel circumference, not the pyramid itself!

Before the ink was dry on my contract, I had invited the famous Egyptologist, Dr. Hardeharhar, to accompany my expedition. We traveled from Cairo by Land Rover caravan southwest to the Djara cave area, an arid karst region containing several caves. I immediately calibrated my Disto-X survey instrument. Dr. Hardeharhar read the hieroglyphic inscription over the entrance of the first cave and translated it as "Mummy Cave."

The cave revealed a simple linear dendritic pattern roughly paralleling the shallow dip of the Eocene limestone with one tributary passage entering on the right (south) side, and one diversion passage departing northward from a canyon in the floor. Nubbins of broken stalactites covered the ceiling. Altogether, Mummy Cave measured 314.16m from beginning to end. Had this been the origin of pi? We failed to find any mummies, despite the inscription. Dr. Hardeharhar said the mummies probably had been looted in the Third Dynasty, but I had not seen that TV program, so I cannot vouch for his conclusion.

The startling find for me was the discovery of an open-pit limestone quarry one kilometer away where I reasoned the next cave should be located. The excavation measured 1131m by 314.16m by 14.16m deep. Dr. H. thought the quarry could have been mined for pyramid-building stone many years ago.

About one kilometer still farther southwest, beyond the quarry, yawned the entrance to another cave. It had no inscription, but a rectangular patch 1.3m by 1.416m had been chiseled out of the limestone to a depth of 3.1cm. Dr. H speculated that looters had stolen the nameplate of the cave and it probably rested in the basement of the Louvre in Paris. I know that in Paris there are Louvres on many major street corners.

Our second cave was 314.16m long with no side passages and a few dusty stalagmite bases, but no stalagmites, further evidence of looting. It was uniformly 3.5m to 5.5m high. Broken stalactite nubbins jutted from the ceiling. There were no mummies, but there were niches where mummies could have been placed.

Since I had many demands on my expertise and time, I could no longer linger in the Djara region, so we folded the expedition without having much to show for it except for the two modest cave maps.

Spring ahead to 2017. Scientists of the ScanPyramids Project (SPP) say they have found am internal hidden chamber in Egypt's Great Pyramid of Giza, otherwise known as the Pyramid of Cheops. A thirty-meter-deep hollow inside the pyramid is located above the pyramid's Grand Gallery. The computed void is about eight hundred cubic meters. No entry passage has been discovered. The puzzle is whether the void contains antiquities.

The scientists of the SPP made the discovery using muon tomography measurements—subatomic particles that penetrate solid rock much like X-rays, only more energetic such that they penetrate deeper. Voids amplify the cosmic-ray muon density. Evidence of a void was described by Dr. Kunihiro Morishima, and wave forms were captured three different ways: on nuclear emulsion films; on scintillator hodoscopes, and on micro-pattern gaseous detectors, giving strong evidence of the void. Yet there are skeptics who poo-poo the reported discovery. Dr. Hardeharhar said, "I have known about it for many years." Other Egyptologists dismissed the claims as "rubbish."

I called Dr. Morishima of SPP to verify the report, and he confirmed that the fine dimensions of the hidden void were unknown. They could not be determined until physical access could be found. I asked him to describe the muon traces he recorded. He said they resemble a sawtooth mountain range—fairly uniform in size.

Aha! Those sharp points are stalactites inside the missing cave of Djara! Hemon, the architect of the Great Pyramid, must have ordered his stone masons to mine out the second Djara cave and transport the cave—surrounding rock and all—to the pyramid! The volume of rock missing from the quarry could easily contain an eight-hundred-cubic-meter cave! The cave was installed vertically so its hidden profile was oriented to mirror the Grand Gallery. My scenario could predict why no entrance to the second cave would ever be found. If discovered one day, I was sure the sharp stalactites revealed in the muon waveform would confirm my prediction that the missing Djara cave resides *inside* the Grand Pyramid of Giza. By brilliance, acumen, and sagacity as the world's most wonderful cave scientist, my conclusion was 99 percent digitally confirmed by this astounding feat of logical inference.

I rushed back excitedly to Cairo to explain my conclusion to Dr. Hardeharhar. He fingered his glasses and finally said, "I have known about it for many years. What else could it be?" He said he would check out my hypothesis and conclusion in Wikipedia. But he was confident it was "old news."

PANAMA CANAL BYPASS

I had a good thing going for a while. I used to collect about $20 a day every day as a royalty on a discovery I made in 1995. The only reason I can reveal this secret now is that my discovery has been made obsolete since 2016. It's a fascinating story—some would say unbelievable—but you can audit my income taxes for 2015 and 2017 and see that my reported income dropped from $7,200 in 2015 to zero in 2017. There's nothing crooked or shady (heaven forbid!)

In 2002, I became interested in the Isthmus of Panama. Geologically, it is a mixed fruit salad in a world-class dinner of Earth history. The North American Plate and South American Plate collided with the Pacific Plate and Atlantic Plate and two other oceanic plates 150 million years ago. This was a slow meeting as junctions go, and 2.8 million years ago Central America was completed. What had been relatively flat plains and seas became shallow seas from surrounding uplift and erosion. Subsequent volcanism produced islands, numerous fractures and joints, eventual connections, and finally a land bridge between North and South America. Floral and faunal interchange began with birds and bats leading the way in both directions.

Late Cretaceous and Early Tertiary sedimentary deposits produced sandstones, shales, and limestones. And, yes, several caves. The most notable is Bayano River Cave seventy miles east of Panama City (for $150 you can take an excursion from Panama

City to the cave). It's a flowing river cave complete with boat rides plus a zillion exotic birds fluttering around every entrance and window to the sky. Where you find one cave, you may find two or more.

The lens of Miocene limestone rose to the southeast of Bayano to a mesa. No caves were known in the mesa, so I began to look carefully. A sinkhole near the Pacific Ocean blew abundant air, evidenced by birds that swooped in on level flight and immediately ascended vertically as if rocket propelled when they flew over the sinkhole.

I hacked my way through the lush jungle by a circuitous route and reached the blowhole. It was easy to enlarge. The loosened dirt was ejected skyward leaving no telltale fresh earth behind. I rappelled 220 feet to a pool of water. I changed over to ascending gear, grabbed my Zodiac and motor, and reentered the cave. The passage was 151.5 feet wide by 180.5 feet high, with wall-to-wall water. The depth was 41.5 feet. I could hardly believe the immense size of the passage, more like the great subterranean chambers in Sumatra and China.

I motored off to the southwest for many miles. At the battery half-life, I reversed direction and near the end of the battery, found my line descending from the entrance. Where I turned around at the far end, sunlight filtered through the terminal pool, apparently the Atlantic Ocean! Can you imagine my excitement—I had found a deep-water underground route more than 150 feet wide and 180 feet tall extending from the Pacific Ocean to the Atlantic. Alas, there were no stalactites or stalagmites, no flowstone decorations whatsoever. It would never make it as a tourist attraction!

Something aroused my curiosity. I visited the Panama Canal Authority Library in Panama City. There I learned that the canal could handle ships up to 106 feet wide by 950 feet long, with a draft of 39.5 feet. The term "PanaMax" designated ships that could fit through the canal; All US Navy ships were built to fit the canal, the battleship *Wisconsin* just squeezing through with three inches on each side. Older, smaller commercial ships used the canal, yet none bigger.

But there were larger ships. Those were container ships, ore and oil carriers limited to either ocean unless they sailed around Cape Horn. I decided the Panama Canal Authority should be apprised of my discovery, seeking transparency and full account-ability in my explorations.

The Commissioner-in-Chief Pedro Gondola listened skeptically to my cave trip report, taking copious notes. At the end he said, "Señor Rubreck, if this cave is as you describe, we can open both ends and allow passage of larger ships—those that now do not now fit the locks. What do you require if you show us this remarkable discovery?"

I thought I'd be sitting pretty for the rest of my life if I gave Sr. Gondola a reasonable royalty figure. "How about paying me a royalty of one US dollar for every ship that passes through my new cave?"

"Agreed!" he said, sliding a blank sheet of paper toward me with a pen. "Just sign," he said. "We will fill in the details." That was trust indeed!

Little did I know that even then, plans were being drawn up for a third set of locks for the canal! Those new locks would handle "post-PanaMax ships," those gigantic vessels up to 1,200 feet long by 160 feet wide and 50-foot-deep draft. That project started in 2007 and was completed in 2016. The new locks made my cave a has-been. My revenue dropped to zero!

The other day I spoke to the captain of the *Maersk Biggie Gigundo*, a container ship that can carry 15,000 twenty-foot containers. I hoped for sympathy for my loss. He said, "Bah, your cursed cave passage was anathema to me and my crew. We had to burn all our lights all the way through our six-hour transit time. No stalactites. No flowstone. No light. No good." He said the new locks make passage through the Panama Canal a delightful breeze.

For a brief time, smarting from my loss, I thought of renting an old diesel submarine and collecting $1 for every ship that I failed to torpedo. Getting paid for *not* doing something is better than real work. But then I considered the ethics of demanding a ransom, and the terrible loss of containers the first time I carried out my threat. Reluctantly, I decided honesty is the best policy—a principle that has always governed my life as a highly principled, moral, competent, and wonderful caver of internationally justified fame.

CAVEMOBILE AUTO-WASH

For several years, I have been impressed by NSS Grotto cave cleanup efforts. The Nashville Grotto removed 3,141 tons of trash from Wretched Cave last year. There were 467 old auto tires, 513 appliances, 52 bedsprings, and more than 2,115 tons of miscellaneous garbage and litter. They scrubbed the walls of many layers of graffiti thus enlarging the cave by fourteen cubic meters. The Louisville Grotto and Bowling Green Grotto cleaned up 723 sinkholes, including a like-new Aztek automobile, and deposited the trash in the Radford, Kentucky, landfill (closing that facility for good).

I finally responded to an opportunity I had been waiting for. A broker in West Virginia called me about making an offer on ten used garbage trucks. This fleet was on its last legs. The minimum bid was $25 for the lot. No previous bids had met the minimum. Could I turn these trucks into campers for cavers? I said no. Some cavers are dirtier after caving than any camper could accommodate. But, I did enter my bid for $25, certified check accepted.

Upon inspection, I found many of the old garbage trucks still operable. I surveyed the storage yard and discovered a mobile auto-wash unit in the far corner. For another $25, I bought that too. Back in my Ohio headquarters, I modified the auto-wash vehicle by adding a 20,000-pound winch to the front bumper. Now for a shakedown tryout. My clean-cave caravan was fueled and ready.

Uglylitter Cave in Adams County, Ohio, had been a local party cave and trash magnet for a score of years. Limestone had been quarried near the entrance. I waded through vermin, flotsam, jetsam, and graffiti to the back wall of the cave. There I hoisted my lithium-powered hammer drill with a three-quarter-inch bit and bored a five-inch-deep hole. I installed a lead anchor and a half-inch galvanized steel eyebolt. I unspooled 307 feet of half-inch braided steel cable from the bumper winch and hooked it onto the newly embedded eyebolt. Outside, I set the winch to low speed and pulled Uglylitter Cave inside out, like pulling off a rubber glove! It made a loud sucking noise and a rumble as a good bit of the trash dropped off the floor and walls. I wedged a marlin spike into the drum end of the winch so the cave would not suddenly return like a rolled-up window shade without completing my cleaning effort.

In my caravan, I had four garbage trucks, two per cave side. They proceeded the length of the cave, hoisting mattresses, auto parts, cans, and bottles into their maws. Volunteer cavers picked up and tossed in any spills. I worried that the litter beneath the cave might be left behind, but I was assured that once the walls of the cave were cleaned and the marlin spike removed, the cave would sink back into to its former position, leaving the bottom trash in a neat windrow.

The mobile auto-wash unit was fitted with three revolving brushes on a hydraulic gantry arm. So, I could power up the brushes, lower them over the exposed cave walls, and drive the length of the cave. What cleaning solution should I use? The wrong solution could spoil the cave forever by poisoning the biotic scum clinging to the walls.

It is not generally known, but I discovered many years ago that the principal agent forming limestone caves is not weak carbonic acid but microbes. George Moore in the 1950s noted that microbes covered the walls of limestone caves in the "zone of discharge," a vertical band located between the highest flood level and the lowest groundwater drought level. I concluded (without proof) that these critters gobbled up the limestone grain boundaries, leaving a limestone paste behind to be washed out at the next flood. The seasonal torrent would scour away the limestone paste, leaving bare limestone to be turned into paste again.

MY FIRST CAVE TRIPS

I vividly remember my first cave trip at age five. I was visiting my cousins in Cleveland, and we went on an excursion to Put-in-Bay on South Bass Island in Lake Erie. I wore my "ice cream" suit, white shirt and white shorts. I remember seeing the Lake Erie Victory Monument, a single Doric column about three hundred feet high, as our steamboat approached Put-in-Bay. We boarded a horse-drawn wagon and went to a cave.

Crystal Cave was exciting to me because its walls and ceiling consisted of giant white crystals. The guide held a small wooden template to the crystal facets to show the angle made by the crystal faces was identical for all the crystals. I even remember the guide identifying the crystals as "strontium nitrate." He said it was used in fireworks. The cave was a one-room affair, with nothing else to capture my imagination.

We boarded the wagon and drove to another cave, not like Crystal Cave. It was a wide room with stalactites and stalagmites scattered around. A small lake in the middle was said to be at the Lake Erie level, indicating a connection with the big lake. As our tour passed a broken stalagmite, those ahead of me rubbed their hands over what looked like a fried egg sunny-side-up. I rubbed my hand over it thinking it was wet and smooth. I shivered from the cold in my short pants. *Where do those dark passages off the big room go?* I wondered, but we hurried on and marveled at the blast of hot air when we emerged from the cave. Another scene from that trip was the view from the top of the monument. I cut my knee on a pay-telescope base and was paid $200 to shut up about it. My aunt placed my younger cousin on the parapet to get a better view, and jumped when the kid began to crawl toward the edge!

My second cave trip was in 1936, at six years of age. My mama suggested we go to Mammoth Cave in Kentucky. We drove forever and arrived at a frame hotel. Which trip to take? I said, the All-Day Trip. My mom suggested a shorter trip because my "little legs" might tire. Tire, hell! I had saved to buy a flashlight for this trip, and only the All-Day Trip would do. At that time, the guide handed kerosene lanterns to the tour members. There were no electric lights in the cave, but the guide threw flaming torches into pits and high alcoves as we walked.

I shined my light into a dark lead and asked the guide, "Where does that passage go?"

He stopped the party and said, "Little boy wants to know where does that lead go? It doesn't go anywhere—it stays right here!" Most of the party laughed, but I was unhappy because he did not answer my question. (My mom sued later under the Freedom of Information Act and obtained a million-dollar settlement that paid for my college tuition and expenses.)

Hours later we ate lunch in the Snowball Dining Room, sitting at white picnic tables and eating a ham sandwich and orange out of a white cardboard box. There was a bathroom there, and I wondered how the water got there and the sewage got taken away. I puked on the floor.

At the end of the trip, we came to "Frozen Niagara," which was a curtain of flowstone. I had seen Niagara Falls when I was six, and this was not as impressive, but I could see the resemblance. Once outside, the heat of the afternoon was wilting. The guide said if I wanted, I could go a little way up the hill over the entrance and feel the cave air. I was mad to see for myself. A little way up the hill was a wooden box sticking out of the ground with a blast of cold air coming out. I learned years later this was a locating hole drilled to spot the entrance from which we exited. I thought of closing the hole to let bad air build up in the cave.

You may think this was not much of an introduction to caves, but I assure you it set my mind on fire with possibilities. The caves were utterly fascinating with distinctive stone walls and ceilings, nothing like manmade buildings. Mysterious corridors beckoned, leading in all directions. Where were we in relation to the surface? Who explored these caves? How could anyone *not* explore them? How could I make endless money from selling my expertise?

I visited other caves—Carlsbad Caverns, Wind Cave, and wild caves in Ohio and Indiana. I found out that ordinary people could explore caves, get muddy, get wet, and find new vistas. The burning desire to know where I was in relation to the surface was fulfilled by seeing that relationship in small Ohio caves.

Since those early days, I have been drawn to caves everywhere and have become wonderful due to my absorbing every clue and piece of information: a sponge soaking up truth. I became a gold mine of cave information. When I learned to survey caves, my imagination raced over the resulting maps, recreating in my mind's eye what I had previously seen underground. I could visualize caves in three dimensions! Many girls were charmed by my brave heroics.

Teaching others about caves, knowing what had interested me from the beginning, and helping cavers to discover those secrets electrified my imagination. I knew more than others about caves! I became an authority—a wonderful authority. One day, I entered the Cave Wonderful Contest and won first prize! A fitting tribute to my superior knowledge, I told others. Was it boasting? *No*, surely not. It was the simple truth—stranger than fiction. I realized that cave lore was true if interesting, especially if I presented it with hand-waving and breathless fluctuations of my voice.

My whispered secrets and universal proclamations assumed equal validity. "Ask Ergor!" was the answer to every cave question. Only the ignorant or stupid questioned my information or counsel. Just as I am entitled to the right answers, others are free to hold the wrong answers. Stupid people pay for my advice. Pride has nothing to do with it.

Would I recommend my experience as a good way to introduce people to caves? Yes, indeed, train the child, vector the caver. The wonderful part of being the foremost expert caver is the influence I have had on other cavers. Some corrupt youth; I develop them in truth! If Ergor says it, you can believe it. It could pay off big.

CAVE OF THE LONG DAGGERS

Most cavers have heard of the Cave of the Crystals, that deep cave in Mexico that contains immense selenite crystals. The crystals measure several meters in length, the longest at eleven meters. I am sure tourists would love to see those speleothems were it not for the fact that the cave is deep inside a silver, zinc, and lead mine and the temperatures are as high as 113° F (47.1° C) with humidity levels of 90–99 percent. Explorers must don air-conditioned suits made of unobtanium with self-contained air. Their time limit is ten to fifteen minutes, after which they melt like candle wax and gum up the suits.

I had applied to the Mexican Department of Tourism and the Sparite de Mexico LLC for permission to explore the cave. They turned me down because they said if they let in one of the world's leading cave explorers, they would have to let them all in. I immediately Googled "caves with gigundo crystals" and learned of a nearby cave with big crystals. I telephoned Sr. Jose Guacamole, owner of the cave, and he welcomed my visit as the world's most famous cave explorer. "*Venga* by yourself," he said. "We do not want riffraff cavers. See you mañana." He hung up before I could learn details of what equipment to bring, whether the cave was hotter than the Cave of the Swords, and how much he wanted to be paid to let me in.

I booked a flight to Guanajuato the next day and packed a duffle of conventional caving gear. Sr. Guacamole said he would meet my flight. At the arrival gate, I saw a cluster of grubby guys standing around a man with a sign saying GRINGO SUPERIOR. Not knowing much Spanish, I assumed he meant me. The other grubby guys must have been cavers too, for they said they were similarly attracted.

Cave of the Long Daggers is halfway up a new volcano, spewing smoke, fiery bombs, and choking ash. Sr. Guacamole said I must pay a thousand pesos in advance and sign a release form before entering the cave. "*Muy peligroso*," was his quaint description of the cave, which I assumed meant it is very pretty. I asked for a receipt, but he indicated he did not understand. He said the preparations required eating spicy food. The small peppers were new to me, but I was knowledgeable enough to recognize the wasabi and horseradish. When I was growing up, a housekeeper said the secret of eating spicy food was to keep it in the front of my mouth, just behind the front teeth. Under no circumstances shift the wad to the rear of the tongue. So, I took a big bite and parked it behind my incisors. My eyes began to water, and a stinging, burning sensation paralyzed my tongue. The room started to spin and grow dark. My cheeks became numb, and my throat felt like I had swallowed razor blades. Guacamole pointed to my ears and said, "Esteem, esteem." I found that 911 does not work in Guanajuato.

Any cave hotter than Sr. Guacamole's fiery meal would be a furnace indeed. The following day, I packed my cave gear and trudged up the steep banks of the volcano to the fumarole where the Cave of the Long Daggers yawned. Fortunately, I had brought my goggles, worn by all smart cavers, so the smoke was only a minor irritation. Stepping inside I beheld sharp, dagger-like crystals of every color of the rainbow, glistening and gleaming in the beam of my Sten light. I had set the switch on turbo to make sure not to miss anything. I thought I must take photos of this Eighth Wonder of the World del Sur. I knew when *National Geographic* saw my pictures and sent a rejection slip, they would dispatch their own photographers to take 250 pictures from every angle except the one I had chosen. But, such is the stuff of sharing Earth's grandeur with one's fellows.

The cave was so hot my candy bars melted, my gorp turned to black popcorn, and my water bottle contained only steam. My nylon rope dripped from my shoulder as it dissolved in a hot puddle of goo. "No exploration without survey" has been my training, but the compass needle bent over and melted at both ends. I could at least make a sketch. The survey notebook paper ignited like a magician's flash paper. Clearly, I was at the thermal endurance limit, prior preparation notwithstanding.

I staggered back down the volcano, leaving the Cave of the Long Daggers for another day. What could I do? My return flight was scheduled for the following day. I packed hastily and obtained a seat on the top of a bus back to Guanajuato. The chickens and passengers on the roof made me feel humble and glad to be alive . . . still the greatest cave explorer in the world today.

Thanks to Photoshop, the Cave of the Long Daggers is captured in brilliant colors in my PowerPoint show. Just look how small that caver looks next to that gigundo red crystal! The yellow and blue crystals are found in no other cave in the world. And the longest green crystal is longer than Mammoth Cave. In the interest of cave conservation and in furtherance of white-nose syndrome eradication, I shall keep secret the location of the Cave of the Long Daggers. The names of cities, countries, and Sr. Guacamole have been changed to protect the innocent. All this adventure and risky caving is in the interest of cave conservation, or my name isn't Corker Burger.

VEGETABLE BAT ADVENTURE

I thought I knew all the things worth knowing about the many varieties of cave bats. My research had extensively covered Mexican fruit bats that, during the night, raid maraschino cherry trees, date palms, fig bushes, and grape arbors. But on one of my trips to Guatemala, I was introduced to the little-known and seldom-studied vegetable bats. I met Sr. Rodriguez Jimenez Mendez, famed biospeleogist, at his office in the Grande Speleologico Instituto de America del Sur. I was enthralled with his stuffed bat collection that hung on strings from his ceiling. "Careful," he said, "some of the bats are alive but appear dead. They may defecate on your head." I admired his rhyming cleverness as I scraped off tiny black, rice-like substances from my hair.

As a fellow bat aficionado, we exchanged a few Latin terms to establish our creds with each other. He wondered if I wished to accompany him to Cueva Negro in the Sierra de Guatemalan Andes. He wanted to study the vegetable bat. I had never heard of the vegetable bat, so I casually said, "Related to the fruit bat, right?"

"No," he explained, "entirely different! The vegetable bat eats turnips, parsnips, and rutabagas. No fruit!" Naturally, I accepted his invitation to study the vegetable bat in its habitat. (Clever rhyme, no?) Fortunately, my cave gear was already packed. He requested I not bring my bat net, as the vegetable bats could only be caught by a special gossamer hair net, finely woven by Lake Titicaca fisherwomen in the winter season.

Nothing prepared me for the bumpy ride over deeply rutted roads that clung to the mountainside as we wound our way upward. Boulders cascaded from above, bouncing on the road ahead of us and over the sheer drop to the valley below. We pulled off at a wide place. A cave entrance yawned in the cliff. Since it was daylight, we saw no bats flying. I had been thinking about the tidbit of dietary information Sr. Mendez had shared. "Don't the natives miss their produce when the vegetable bats eat their harvest?" I asked.

"We do not know. Here comes one now. We will ask." I looked in the air for a vegetable bat but saw only a farmer astride an ox headed down the mountain. Sr. Mendez approached the farmer and engaged in a hand-waving exchange that I could not overhear. Later, "He says the bats do *not* eat the vegetables, but the crop of tubers has been disappointing for the past twenty years. Farmers plant turnips, parsnips, and rutabagas along with potatoes, carrots, and lima beans. When they harvest, there are never any turnips, parsnips, or rutabagas, just potatoes, carrots, and lima beans." That puzzled me, as the latter are vegetables, not fruit. Why did one crop fail while the other thrived? Clearly, Dr. Mendez wanted to know, too.

Upon entering the cave, we could hear the bats fluttering and squeaking. I knew the squeaking was not ultrasonic echolocation, which is inaudible to humans. But we must have disturbed them with our conversation. I asked Sr. Mendez about the contradiction. He had said that vegetable bats eat only turnips, parsnips, and rutabagas, but the farmer said the bats did not eat those specific vegetables. "How do you know what they eat?"

"I have analyzed the bat scat," (another rhyme) he replied. "It is rich in tuber fiber, but not carrot, potato, or lima bean." Ah, maybe Ergor could make a scientific breakthrough and solve the mystery. I brushed some droppings out of my hair since I had not yet put on my hard hat. I had expected to see black rice-like pellets, but instead saw brown dirt. Could it be a clue to the mystery?

I asked Sr. Dr. Mendez where the farmers lived. He told me they live on a terrace farther up the mountain. Their huts ring their gardens, and they have invested in metal roofing to build rain catchments since there are no wells at that elevation. "They are largely self-sufficient and use ox carts for transportation. They bring their produce to market on weekends and bring back cerveza. Subsistence economy." We plunged deeper into the cave, and the overpowering odor of ammonia assaulted our senses. Crunchy mud on examination turned out to be cockroaches scurrying over bat feces. "This—how you call it—shit, is what I placed under the microscope to determine the vegetable bat's menu."

Drat! More brown dirt falling on my hard hat. I suggested we go outside for lunch, but Sr. Mendez said we must trap a specimen first. From a matchbox, he extracted a fine net, which when unfolded measured about six by nine meters (we scientists like to use metric terms). He extracted from his pack what looked like mechanical pencils, but I saw they were lightweight telescopic tent poles when he extended them. With the net erected at the entrance, we returned to our vehicle and ate lunch.

On our return, we found a vegetable bat struggling to free himself from the net. Success!

With Mendez's approval, I carefully removed the bat from the net. His wingspan was roughly two-thirds of a meter. What immediately struck me was a brown stain around the bat's mouth. White-nose syndrome? "We do not have white-nose in Guatemala!" said Mendez.

He seemed to take personal offense at my observation, like some cavers I know.

"I am calling this brown-nose syndrome," I said, marking down the term in my science notebook. Mendez seemed nonplussed. "It looks like the brown dirt that has been dropping on my head." Mendez shook his head in disgust.

"No bat burrows in the ground like a pig for truffles!" He was hot. He registered his displeasure at my observation by abruptly

GRR!

packing his gear and stomping off toward the cave entrance, making a squishy sound as he went. I followed. He was fuming, and he refused to speak to me as he wheeled his SUV around and down the mountain road.

On the airplane home, I had an "Aha!" moment. The vegetable bats were eating the turnips, parsnips, and rutabagas when those vegetables protruded from the ceiling of the cave! No wonder the farmers were disappointed when they harvested their produce. Yet, the mystery remains. Why did they *not* eat the carrots and potatoes?

CELEBRITY CAVE TRIP

The least likely people in Hollywood to go in a wild cave are the celebrities who are celebrated for being celebrities. The Kardashians, Hiltons, Kleptos, and Druggies come to mind. They sure don't act like they want to get dirty, and their clothes would catch on every helictite within sight of their expensive Scurry-On lights. I never expected to see one in a cave, let alone be asked to take one on a cave trip. But I received a call on my private cell number from a Hollywood agent.

"Hi Ergor, Ron Dolay here. I'm the agent for Smiley Cactus, that hot new singing and acting sensation that's taking Hollywood by storm!" I sat down because I had never been called by such an enthusiastic person in my life. The fact that I had never heard of Ron or Smiley was not important—people achieve fame and fortune overnight in Hollywood thanks to social media like Tweep, Faceplant, and Score. "Ms. Cactus is the celebrity daughter of Prickly Cactus, famed Hollywood character actor Oscar nominee in 1973, and his fifth wife, Cardashian Cactus!" Ron said. "And we'd like to have you, Ergor, take her wild caving!"

"Just her?" I asked.

"No, there would be press . . . and publicists . . . and security . . . plus Ms. Cactus! We'd fly to wherever you say and give you four hours to take a photogenic cave trip!" Ron was emphatic that four hours was all the time Ms. Cactus could spare between publicity events at the Hollywood Bowl, the Queen Mary, and

Disneyland. I asked why she wanted a cave trip. "Her image! She's seen as too much wussy and too little survivor! You know, she needs Hunger Games, killer self-sufficiency, reckless risk-taking, guitar shredder!"

"What's your budget?" I asked.

"Under $10 K … plus expense! She can only go next Saturday!" Ron gave me his unpublished 24-7 cell number to call him back with details of the trip.

Did I *really* want to do this? After all, my impeccable reputation as the best and most famous caver could be sullied if this event were seen as a mere publicity stunt. My machismo might need a transfusion if this trip was perceived as too wimpy by my worldwide caving admirers everywhere. However, I could use the money. So, the next step was to pick the right cave. The three-thousand-meter Death Drop in Mexico seemed a little tame. The Goolag Suckhole Sump Cave in Ukraine was probably too far away for a four-hour window. Maybe Clothes Shredder Cave in Arizona, 23.3 miles from Ft. Stanton Cave, could be the right cavern. Smiley Cactus might catch her cave suit on a few gypsum formations and reveal a little skin—maybe more skin! I'd have to tell her that the cave was 69.5°F warm so she would need to buy red mosquito netting coveralls and wear as little underwear as possible. I telephoned Ron within the hour with all the details.

Clothes Shredder Cave is on BLM land, so I called the cave specialist in Arizona and explained the trip we planned to take. "No camping in the cave," he warned. I told him this would be a short scientific visit, and our purpose was to do scientific stream tracing with fluorescein dye. (I could picture the bright green water being complementary to Ms. Cactus's skin and red suit.) "Bad news, Ergor, there's no water in Clothes Shredder Cave. And it's only three hundred feet long," said the specialist. "You'll need a better scientific purpose than stream tracing, and you will need to fill out our seventy-two-page form." He said he'd fax me the form. This was fast becoming a lot of work for $10,000, plus expenses! But I soldiered on.

On the form I listed our scientific purpose as measuring the ratio of radon gas to unobtanium gas due to the half-life decay of boron nitride molecules in the bedrock. I said that would enable us to fix the age of the cave, plus or minus several million years. I faxed the form back to Arizona and sent an email to Ron Dolay about what gear Ms. Cactus should bring.

Our entourage met at the Ontario, California, airport at six on Saturday morning. Smiley Cactus was accompanied by Ron Dolay, a video cameraman, sound boom man, three photographers, and a large mafioso with dark glasses and an earpiece. Smiley's guitar was hooked up to an amplifier on wheels atop a large speaker. We were airborne in our Gulfstream in twenty minutes and alighted on the Arizona tarmac in another twenty minutes. Rodrigo Gomez, the BLM cave specialist, met us under the windsock and handed over the approved form and cave key. I had booked a bus to take us to the cave.

At the cave entrance, Smiley set up her amplifier and plugged in her guitar. The sound techs moved in. She began a loud melodic intro as the boom man hovered over her. The recordist raised his hand in the air to stop the performance and the video man lowered his camera. "Too dead. We'll overdub in the studio later." She turned the knob off on her guitar and silently strummed away as the video guy took various shots at cool angles.

The bright rocks behind her backlit her red suit enough to cause Ron to shout, "Yesss!"

Time to go caving. I unlocked the gate and sent the sound guy in first. Ms. Cactus and I would enter as the videographer made establishing shots, then scooted around us to shoot our entry from inside the cave. "Smile and roll your eyes . . . show fear, then resolve!" I thought Ms. Cactus followed directions rather well. I took out my all-glass impinger and drew in a sample of cave air. Ron beckoned me to hand the impinger to Smiley. She bravely pulled the plunger filling the impinger body with invisible cave gas. We crawled deeper into the cave.

A sudden ripping sound pierced the air! Clothes Shredder Cave had claimed another victim! Her red suit was torn from neck to waist, knee to ankle. She modestly clutched the tattered fabric to her chest. The cameraman scampered from one cool angle to another as poor Ms. Cactus turned this way and that. Later the boom man recorded several tearing takes, until poor Ms. Cactus was severely underclad. I removed my Cordura jacket and handed it to Smiley, whose lips formed a soundless *Thank you*.

Now that Smiley Cactus's photo adorns the cover of *People* magazine and her caving clip has been shown in both *Entertainment Tonight* teaser promos and in a two-minute segment of that show, I guess she's the next world-class caver! Alas, they never mentioned me. Whoopie, they never mentioned me!

SUPERCAVES AND SUPERCAVERS

The editor of *Outhouse Magazine*, the foremost outdoor adventure monthly, asked me to pack my bag and fly to Oaxaca, Mexico, to interview Bob Rock, the famous supercaver. He was preparing to break the world cave depth record of 7,432.6m set in that unbelievably deep hole, Gruta Phreefall, (twice the size of the Petronas Towers in Malaysia) that had been bottomed by a Kurdistan caver team just last year. The fact that none of them survived made it impossible to interview them.

As I stepped off the AeroMexico 747 onto the tarmac, I was met by a smiling Bob Rock, tanned, chiseled face, and with an imposing seven-foot, two-inch frame. He thrust his hand down and forward and squeezed mine like the Boston Strangler. "Hola, Ergor, *tanto tiempo sin verte.*" We reminisced about our caving together in Cenote del Muerto several years before. We were waved out of the way because the afternoon plane was circling to land.

As we jounced and hacked our way through the rainforest in his eight-wheel drive truck, Bob told me how the expedition was going. "We have thirty-two ropes in place, sixteen camps staked out, and three hundred kilos of beans staged," he recited. I asked about the golf bags in the bed of the truck. He said they are not golf bags, but descending rack bags. "We use twenty-five-bar racks on these deep boogers," he said, "and the bars are sodium-cooled titanium to withstand the heat when we whiz down to the bottom of each pitch."

At the expedition's camp, which hung from hammocks in jungle trees "to keep the tapirs away," I met a striking and statuesque redhead named Consenta. An expedition member told me she had been the champion pit rigger of Kazakhstan in 2008 and was the current *esmeralda* of Bob Rock. The 27-pound, gas-powered bolting hammer that swung from her waist caused her to list to port about fifteen degrees. She gave me a wink and a 48-karat smile, a little nudge, and a palm-scratching handshake. I did not want to get too close as she inched perceptibly toward me, for fear her bolting hammer muffler had not cooled down sufficiently.

"Stash your gear, get some grub and some shut-eye," Bob said, "because tomorrow we are going 6,272.6 meters down to Camp Sixteen." I learned later from Consenta that Camp 16 was suspended by parachute cord from a soda straw and was constantly pelted by plantain leaves showering down upon it. Consenta said the crunchiness of the leaves made lovemaking a noisy affair at Camp 16.

After washing down a rasher of huevos ranchero, beans, and plantain seeds with two gallons of free-trade coffee, we entered the yawning maw of the cave. It was so large you could park three 747 tires in the "Sala Grande." Guácharo birds swooped and dive-bombed us with a curious paste-like substance that did not taste good, either. We descended a five-hundred-meter fixed rope. I was a little concerned because the electrical tape was coming unwound where they fixed it. At each stainless-steel bolt and re-belay, I dangled and thrashed, hooking my cow's-tail over each bolt, traversing sideways and sometimes upside down. At the bottom, near Camp 15, I asked about the numerous windows we passed on the perilous descent. Bob said, "We don't screw with them. They are horizontal caves, and who cares about horizontal cave? Depth is where it's at. Depth!"

Camp 15 was laid out on blue tarps over six inches of quick-sand. I could not hear any of the preparation briefing at Camp 15, as the blue tarp crinkled and crackled so loudly as to drown out conversation. I imagined the noise would make amorous activity less private.

The coffee was getting to me about then, and Bob motioned for me to use the pee bottle. These deep supercavers are fastidious and take out of the cave everything they take in. Last year in the dreaded Santa Anita d'Eques, Manuel Labour lost his right leg when it was shredded in a jumar, and dutifully carried it 5,326 meters back out of the cave. When asked whether it hurt, he replied, "Only when I laugh."

Lunch at Camp 15 consisted of tubes of guácharo butter, double-fried beans, and Ho Hos. Bob started to lecture me on carbohydrate loading, but I told him to stop as my PhD is in Nutritional Science and Arts. The lunch was not very good.

A couple more six-hundred-meter drops, and we were at Camp 16, the jump-off for the two-km sump through twisty little passages that all looked alike. The super-cold water was at 0°C, and I was handed an ice pick in case the liquid turned solid on my transit. I was fitted with a self-contained breathing device and told that so long as the green LEDs were glowing, I had nothing to worry about. I sank into the depths and picked up a clothesline that wound through and around boulders, drowned speleothems and speleogens, and one Volkswagen.

Emerging in a gigantic hall, I pulled myself up on a shale beach and awaited the other divers. Bob Rock was next. He said the others had decided not to dive when their refried beans took to outgassing and floated them to the ceiling of the sump in a "bad air bell." We scrambled along the beach in a tube 432m in diameter, slanting downward at eight degrees. We passed the bloated dead bodies of the Kurdistan dive team arranged in a circle, heads to a butane stove, long since out of gas.

Bob said, "Poor devils, they had just set a brass elevation marker at their world-record depth when their butane tank leaked. Without methyl mercaptan, they could not smell the deadly CO gas concentration when their stove blew out." We stood still a moment in their memory, then proceeded to the brass cap:

Gruta Phreefall
World Depth Record
7,432.6m
Kurdistan Deep Speleology Team

Bob whipped out a trowel and a length of measuring tape. He dug a hole in the floor at that point 1.4 meters deep. "Now, I have set the depth record of 7,434 meters!" I said he could have dug a deeper hole. He said, "That's three years from now. I already have seven million dollars lined up for my expedition to Brazil next year. And I'm taking Amazonia. She's the best caver in Brazil."

FIRST FLIGHT REVISED

There is ambiguity about the first flight by the Wright brothers at Kill Devil Hills, Kitty Hawk, North Carolina. One account says Orville made the first flight on December 17, 1903, staying aloft twelve seconds and traveling 120 feet. Another account said Wilbur was at the controls of a powered flight on October 10, 1902, in which he stayed airborne fifty-nine seconds and covered a distance of 852 feet. Which account is correct? I decided to go to Kittyhawk and find the truth once and for all.

North Carolina has many cavers, so I contacted Sloan Zurn, Ben Dover, Ali Bye, and Helen Brown (she looked like the Helen Brown I had met at the 1995 Spelunkers Convention). We met for breakfast at the Flying Albatross Restaurant in Kittyhawk. I explained the discrepancy. According to a North Carolina Geological Survey report on the state's stratigraphy, the River Bend Limestone lies six to thirteen feet beneath the beach sand in that area. We wondered if the River Bend featured karstic characteristics—caves, sinkholes, etc. Such solution features might have changed surface distances over the last 120 years since the record flights.

We drove to the site of the supposed first flight(s), now under control of the National Park Service. A uniformed guide conducted us on a tour, pointing out the takeoff point part way up a low hill, and a monument marking the end of Orville's first flight 120 feet away. Ali Bye asked the guide, "What about the 852-foot flight in 1902? Didn't Wilbur's flight come first?"

The guide pulled a field manual from his back pocket and leafed through it. He found the place, and said, "We have been instructed to describe the 1903 flight and not mention the 1902 flight. I'm sorry, but those are my orders." Clearly, our North Carolina cavers were not impressed with this "official" explanation. We decided to return after dark when the NPS personnel had gone home, to check a few things.

Sloan Zurn showed up with a six-foot pole. Ben Dover had found a thirteen-foot pole at a fishing supply store. We parked in the vacant parking lot and fanned out along the flight path of the Wright brothers. We formed a line from start to finish. We pushed the six-foot pole into the sand until its tip was flush with the surface. Then pulled the pole out and passed it to the next caver. In every case, the pole sank in the sand until its top was flush with the surface.

Next, we pushed the thirteen-foot pole into the sand. It would only penetrate about eight feet into the sand until it struck an impenetrable object—probably the surface of the Odorous Limestone. Successive probes yielded 9.4 feet, 8.7 feet, 8.3 feet, and 9.1 feet. Then the thirteen-foot pole vanished! Swallowed up by the sand with no resistance.

At 45.6 feet from the start of the flight, the thirteen-foot pole's loss ended our probes. We all gathered around the spot where the pole disappeared. Helen cried out, "A sinkhole is forming! The sand is pouring into a hole just like the sand in an hourglass." Sure enough, sand was draining away, as if it were pouring into a void below. We had to step back from the widening rim of the sinkhole as the sand around us began to move toward the new deepening hole.

After about twenty minutes, the hole stopped spreading. Ben Dover noticed the end monument had moved closer to the flight's origin marker. We stretched the measuring tape. The distance was not 120 feet—it was 98.9 feet! That astounding revelation confused us, so we adjourned to the Flying Albatross Restaurant (they close at 11:00 p.m.) to decide what to do next.

Over delicious lasagna, we discussed the possible inaccuracies of our survey. Had we read the wrong end of the tape? Read numbers upside down? Transposed numbers? Tape readers had taken precautions to report accurate readings by having a second member of the party verify the measurements taken and verify the numbers written in the survey book. We decided there must be a cave below the thirteen-foot pole. As the evening was still young, we motored back to the site. Ben and Ali broke out the shovels, and Sloan checked the headlamps while Helen uncoiled the rope for descending into the cave, if we found a cave.

By 2:45 a.m., we had uncovered a cave entrance at the bottom of the sand funnel. We drew straws to see who would descend. I drew the short straw, so I adjusted my harness and clipped onto my short brake bar. I backed down the sand slope and braced on the rim of limestone that was now exposed. I then descended about 32.5 feet into a limestone-walled chamber, about sixteen feet in diameter. On the floor was a jumble of monuments. Inscribed on them was "First Flight." A few older monuments bearing the patina of age read "Second Flight." Sand lay around the monuments, half burying most of them. I surveyed the cave room and called the dimensions up to Helen who copied them into the survey notebook.

Since we did not have permission to excavate the site, we shoveled back the sand and smoothed it over so there was no trace of our footprints or discovery. We concluded that the first flight had been in 1902 and had been 852 feet in length, but the end monument had moved toward the flight origin point that winter, spring, summer, and fall, so when the real second flight took place, the new monument was placed 120 feet from the origin. That monument had subsequently moved toward the sand sinkhole and was now 98.9 feet from the origin. Thus, we proved that history is dynamic rather than static, as most historians believe. While monuments may mark events that occurred, there is no telling if their position is still accurate.

We submitted our new findings to Wikipedia. The editor wrote back that we needed several citations to verify our account and five sworn eyewitness reports of individuals who were not members of our expedition. Alas, our only evidence is the North Carolina Stratigraphic Survey of the Odorous Limestone, our cave survey notebook, and the smoothed sand that looks like nothing happened at the Wright brothers' site.

CAVING ROBOT

I understand that Bill Rock, a well-known caver, was awarded a ten-million-dollar contract to develop a robotic cave explorer for use on Mars. If Mars has any water, it is deep underground in caves, so Rock's robot can function in underwater caves. Last I heard, he was testing the contraption in a Florida sinkhole near the Woodville Karst.

Rock knows a lot about rebreathers and underwater exploration, and I know plenty about underground caves and mouth-breathers—cavers who are allergic to mold. The hazards to be expected in caves include falls where the robot topples over a cliff or into a vertical shaft, or where rocks fall on the robot burying it under a heavy pile. Robots notoriously run out of battery, so power loss is an inherent risk in designing a caving robot. Since robots have evil enemies that are often equipped with weapons such as claws, trip-hammer smashers, saws, and flame throwers, a properly designed caving robot will need offensive and defensive weapons to survive the competitive realm of Mars cave exploration.

I built a prototype caving robot to test that I think shows a lot of promise. It is roughly conical in shape like an ice cream cone, but to the average evil person or robot, it resembles a big stalagmite. If rocks fall on it, they will slide off since its walls are made of fiberglass-reinforced Teflon. Should it fall into a pit, it will land heavy-side down. So that it will not burn, I have made the inside of damp campfire wood. It uses eight tiny feet for locomotion so that four of them are in contact with the ground at all times. A flypaper dispenser is the weapon. Fuel is carbide, the most dependable source for cave lights, and it carries five gallons of water to drip on the carbide. No batteries to deplete. Photos are out of the question because it is dark in Mars caves, so no camera will bring back pictures. I know this will disappoint the evening newscasters, so I have attached a Go-Pro camera to a railroad train pointed at the ballast next to the rail. The resulting moving video will be broadcast continuously from the robot during its exploration and will convey the appearance of real progress.

For its maiden test run, I took my caving robot to Mammoth Cave, Kentucky. I started it at the top of the Historic Entrance. It looked cute climbing down one concrete step at a time with its little cone head tipping precariously as it moved off one step onto the next. At the bottom, it trundled off into the cave. Alas, it was stopped by a locked metal door—you can't think of everything, you know. Several hours later, the first tour guide opened the door, and the robot marched in along Houchins Narrows. The national park superintendent who was watching the monitor commented that the robot was picking up images of rocks—hard to explain since the path in the cave was paving blocks. I pointed out that the feed from the robot showed macro-lens photo enlargements of minute dust and lint particles that just looked like rocks.

The robot was programmed to make the complete Historic Tour of Mammoth Cave, but when the tour exited, my robot was nowhere to be seen. I decided to wait for it before calling out a recovery mission.

Eighteen hours later, it tapped on the closed metal door. I had to wait until the next morning's tour group arrived and the guide unlocked the door. I was sorry to see that the carbide was nearly spent and most of the five gallons of water had been used. I picked up my caving robot and examined it closely. Some vandals had scratched the letters J.L. on one side and the other side had B.A. carved into the Teflon. That was a hazard I had not anticipated in a caving robot. I picked up my conical robot and cradled it under my right arm as I climbed the steps past the waterfall. At the platform at the top, I was met by a seasonal ranger.

"Whatchoo got there?" he demanded, pointing his Taser at my robot.

"It's my cave-exploring robot prototype, back from a successful trial," I explained.

"I'll just bet it is," he said with a hint of sarcasm in his voice. "Looks like a stalagmite to me, and there's a ten-thousand-dollar fine for taking speleothems out of the cave!"

I explained to him that it just *looked like* a stalagmite. "See," I said, "stalagmites don't have initials on them."

He unfolded his investigational magnifier and peered at the J.L. and B.A. inscriptions. "I think you put those initials on there," said the ranger. He was speaking into his lapel mike. "We need a bus to transport a vandal to Bowling Green . . . yeah, the US magistrate's office." He took my robot and placed it into the back of an electric vehicle; then he turned and put handcuffs on me. "Fines for graffiti artists are doubled in this park, buster, and I think you just ran your bill up." I protested that the robot was a science experiment, and the park superintendent could vouch for my project. "Better get the superintendent up top. This vandal says he has the super's okay to steal a stalagmite and carve his initials on it."

We met the park superintendent back at the visitor center just as the paddy wagon pulled up for my trip to Bowling Green. She told the ranger to release me at once. "This is Ergor Rubreck, world-famous caver who has been testing a caving robot explorer. It's okay." Those cuffs had nearly rubbed my wrists raw, but I thanked the park superintendent for rescuing me, and she said the ranger would undergo reeducation by Resource Management to learn the difference between a stalagmite and a robot. She apologized for the inconvenience. I said I'd send her the robotic sensor download.

In retrospect, I believe I'll equip my modified robotic cave explorer with a lock-picking device and run further tests. But not in a national park.

ITHACA FRACKING ADVENTURE

I received a call late at night from Hilary Lambert, former Steward of Cayuga Lake. She lives in Dryden, New York, near Ithaca. She said that her dog, She-Ra, had been whining at night without any explanation. Hilary tried giving her dog a biscuit, but that didn't quiet the dog. She looked out the window with her night vision binoculars, but the green scene produced no movement of coyotes or weasels. Then she remembered that dogs' hearing can detect lower frequencies than human ears. In California, some dogs alert to impending earthquake shocks and tip off their owners by whining. Could that be the offending trigger? The second night after the mysterious whining, Hilary borrowed a stethoscope from a health clinic in Ithaca. She applied the instrument to the concrete foundation of her house and recoiled in horror.

"I heard a low-frequency grinding noise, like a large drill, very faintly. When the mechanical sound stopped, She-Ra stopped whining. When the strange noise resumed, She-Ra alerted with her ears up and head cocked to one side. She howled mournfully," said Hilary.

I asked her if there were any caves beneath her house on Ripsaw Road, a little distance from downtown Ithaca. Since I am the world's most experienced and wonderful cave explorer and speleological expert, that would toss the explanation ball directly into my court. She said no caves were known, not even any sinkholes! I Googled "Ithaca industries." A list of companies scrolled by. Then I saw it! Cargill Salt Mine, operating miles of galleries beneath the lake and nowhere near Dryden. Cayuga Salt & Mineral Corporation (CS&MC), recently defunct, was the next listing with no information on their operations. One of their products was salt, apparently mined from a deep salt lens that underlies a northeast belt from Detroit through Cleveland, Buffalo, Lockport, and as far east as Schenectady, New York. Cargill's mines are twenty-five hundred feet down, and the salt bed in the Salinas Group is located *between* the Marcellus shale above and the Utica shale below. Both shale formations contain natural gas.

My guess was that what Hilary had heard was drilling in the old CS&MC salt mine beneath her house. Room-and-pillar mining is practiced in the mines beneath the larger cities—Detroit, Cleveland, etc. Drilling may occur for a shift or two, followed by blasting to loosen the salt. In Louisiana, they pump water into salt domes and pump brine out to spread over evaporation beds. I flew to Ithaca with my caving gear and borrowed She-Ra for a stroll past the location of the defunct CS&MC.

The mine was located in a seedy part of town, next to an auto-wrecking yard. An ancient CLOSED SIGN dangled in the front door window. The windows were so dirty and dark that I could not see any signs of life. Yet She-Ra was sniffing vigorously at a closed gate to a driveway next to the dilapidated building. A shutter hung at an angle and swung gently in the wind. She-Ra investigated a puddle in the driveway. The mud in the bottom had fresh tire tracks as if the abandoned salt works had been visited recently! The dog and I retreated to my rental car and hunkered down to wait. Fortunately, I had brought a small bag of Purina Lamb & Rice, together with my bologna sandwich.

Around midnight, a small yellow school bus with blacked-out windows pulled up to the gate. I couldn't make out the license plate number from our hidden vantage point, but the driver swung open the gate and drove through. Inside the yard near the mine headframe, a dozen or so men streamed out of the bus and into the mine building. The elevator wheel at the top of the headframe turned. The school bus backed up, turned, and drove out, the driver locking the gate behind.

The old salt works were silent, apparently still abandoned. In an hour, She-Ra began to whine. We left our car to check around the perimeter fence. High grass and junk made the going rough, and my helmet lamp guided us through the thickets. Near the back corner adjacent to the auto junkyard, my feet felt something soft. The ground was freshly dug. A recently filled trench extended from the mine premises into the heart of the junkyard. Crushed, old auto bodies had been piled one on the other into a high wall. She-Ra and I followed the trench into the junkyard, and behind the auto wall, we saw tanks and a large pond glistening in the moonlight. None of this would be visible from the road.

Suddenly, I heard a chilling low growl. A junkyard dog tore out of the shadows and leaped at me! She-Ra leaped in the air, crashing into the attacking dog. Both fell heavily to the ground in fierce combat at my feet. She-Ra delivered a smashing blow to the mongrel guard dog, who slunk away with tail tucked. "Good dog," I said, giving her a good head rub and two biscuits.

I now had the information I needed. A stealth fracking operation was going on in the old salt mine. Since fracking had been outlawed in all of New York, the frackers had resorted to secret exploitation out of sight. Apparently, they believed if they could drill up and down and in all directions from inside the abandoned mine, nobody would be the wiser. I returned She-Ra to her owner the next evening.

Hilary Lambert activated the anti-fracking chain as well as the infamous lawyers who had started the effective push to ban fracking in Dryden and the environmental champions. Together, they descended on the city council with video from my Go-Pro camera. The council viewed the evidence and ordered the city solicitor to file a writ of hocus pocus and a permanent injunction against the Greater Northeast Energy Exploration, LLC.

Upon investigation, the evidence showed the bandits were drilling upward into the Marcellus shale and downward into the Utica shale, extracting petroleum and gas from high and low. I am told that the officers of that organization would have been sentenced to ninety-nine years in the electric chair—if only New York had not outlawed the death penalty. Instead, they were sent to Attica for thirty days and fined $500. I further learned that Hilary gave She-Ra a juicy filet and even provided a chair for her at the table.

FEAR!

Charles Harvey Jr. lost for
thirty-nine hours in Mammoth Cave

Non-cavers imagine that every cave trip is fraught with fear—debilitating, pants-wetting, shake-in-your-boots *fear*! That is true, of course, if you ask Charles Harvey Jr., seen below courtesy of Colleen O'Connor Olson and Charles Henion, authors of *Scary Stories of Mammoth Cave*. He spent 81 percent of two days quivering like Jell-O when he lost his way in the longest cave. When his rescuers found him, his hair was white. (It was white before he entered the cave.) Caves are not necessarily as scary as some folks think.

People sometimes ask me if I have experienced fear in the hundreds of thousands of caves I have explored. Would the world's greatest cave explorer conquer the kind of fear all other cavers have felt? You can count on me to remain fearless. Scared shitless sometimes, but never fearful.

Once in a cave, I had crawled into a body-size hole in the floor. The lead headed downward at a twenty-degree angle. I was crawling "down the scallops." Real cavers will recognize that this means I was following the ancient watercourse downstream. Tight walls pressed against my pockets, squashing my candy bars. The floor glistened with quartz pebbles weathered out of the Caseyville Formation. In ten feet, I found my face three inches from a trickling stream, and the stream passage I had intersected issued from a five-inch crack that lowered to a four-inch crack downstream. The beauty of cave minutia like that transfixed me for several minutes. Time to leave.

I dug in my toes to gain purchase and pushed with my gloved hands in the stream. No go. I tried again with more force. Still no movement. I was trapped! Less experienced cavers might have thrashed and hunched. Instead, I closed my eyes and tried to visualize every inch of the route down that tube so I could retrace it millimeter by millimeter (international cavers use the metric system for extra drama).

My painstaking analysis recalled that the shallow side of the scallops had enabled me to slide down without much resistance. But now I was encountering the steep side of the scallops—the upstream side that stopped my retreat like a locked ratchet. Second, the candy bars, now flattened, nevertheless contributed to my volume and helped fill the passage. I slid my hands into my pockets and using my fingers like chopsticks I extracted the remains of the candy. I popped the goo into my mouth for increased energy and hypothermia protection. It would require micro-movements of toes and fingertips to back out of the tight tube.

I prayed for deliverance, and my body extruded itself upward. There was no time to indulge in fear as I employed each panicked spasm in a consciously upward direction. After a few feet, the purchase for my toes improved. My morale improved with each incremental movement. It took ten minutes to get into that hell hole and an hour to get back out. My companions had assembled at the hole when I backed out.

"Wow! You must have discovered a bunch of caves. You've been gone over an hour," one said. "What did you find?"

"I didn't reach the end. It will take a small person (Tiny Tim?) to go farther than I did." I described the quartz pebbles and the glistening trickle of water between them. Talk long enough, the cavers will drift away and not ask embarrassing questions.

Charles Harvey Jr. has a bad day.

Here's my recommendation for conquering fear.

1. Close your eyes—it immediately removes the sight of fearful things and replaces it with the comfortable state in which you spend about one-third of your life.
2. Change your underwear ASAP.
3. If somebody is making a movie, be sure to look back— the monster strikes when explorers stupidly move in one direction for a long time or step blindly around corners without looking.
4. If you really are in the grip of fear, *scream bloody murder*! Or yell, "*Fire!*"

A farmhand once fell into an old cesspool behind the barn. The farmer in the barn heard the cry, "Fire! Fire!" He raced out the back door of the barn and peered into the cesspool at the struggling farmhand.

"Why are you yelling 'Fire!'" he demanded.

The farmhand said, "Do you think if I yelled, 'Shit!' anyone would come?"

REPORT ON EAR BATS

Previously, I reported on vegetable bats in Guatemala—eaters of turnips, parsnips, and rutabagas. As an internationally known and admired authority on cave bats, I'd like to correct some misapprehensions about bats and reveal some new information. Many people think fruit bats are the largest members of the bat community because of their reputation for carrying off whole watermelons and bananas. However, fruit bats do not tangle in your hair, as some women fear. Louisville Slugger bats are not flesh and blood bats. Bats live in caves but not indoors—unless they live in hollow-core doors.

While leading a caving expedition in Bhutan, I discovered ear bats, which are undoubtedly the smallest of bats. Most are solitary bats, although some are colonial bats. How can bats live in human ears, you may ask? Bhutan is high country, not to be confused with Bessarabia (formerly), and the altitude is unfriendly to most species. Diminutive species survive best because of their low energy requirement. The average adult ear bat measures 0.015 mm, so many can live at once in the average ear, particularly at such high altitudes.

Ear bats exhibit a reverse cycle. Whereas most bats forage at night for insects, ear bats reverse this cycle, sleeping at night and venturing out on feeding excursions in the daytime. That is why they had never been detected before my discovery of them. How many doctors look in people's ears with an otoscope at night? In the daytime, when ENT medical exams take place, ear bats are absent.

For many years, ear bats were suspected to exist but never proven. "She has bats in her belfry," goes the anecdotal phrase, or "He is acting batty." The excreta of ear bats is termed "ear wax." Bats in many parts of the world exhibit white-nose syndrome. Ear bats experience runny-nose syndrome. If you have suffered from runny nose at any time, rest assured, your ear bats are suffering worse

Our expedition entomologist, Dr. Seymore Avians, PhD, first called the creature to my attention. "Dr. Rubreck!" he exclaimed one day at the dial of his audiometer, "I detect a high-pitched sound at 72,500 Hz. and 0.0013 decibels." I left my dowsing station in Bishop's Cave and hurried to his post in Level 5. Could it be the sound of a mite peeing on a washcloth? The source of the sound was too small to be seen in my microscope, so I switched to the binocular microscope and there it was—a precocious juvenile male ear bat emitting his first mating call to attract females.

Since then, I have discovered ear bats in practically every cave and caver. In North America, histoplasmosis immunity has been found in most inhabitants of the American Midwest. Their initial introduction to histoplasmosis was probably dismissed as twenty-four-hour flu. Ear bat victims have just assumed they had a runny nose, never suspecting their ear bat infestation. When they blew their nose, they never realized they were bringing entire colonies of ear bats to the knife edge of extinction.

Fortunately, ear bats have no deleterious effect on humans beyond the benign symptoms of nose drip and ear wax. A possible exception: Did the impressionist painter Vincent Van Gogh slice off his ear as a result of hearing fluttering ear bats? Unlike their larger brethren, ear bats do not eat insects, cross-pollinate crops, or carry fruit and blood from place to place. They may have no use.

Acarologists have told me that their study of mites has revealed untold millions of hitherto unclassified varieties, such that one might earn a PhD before lunch investigating but one new species. Mites are as small as ear bats, so it is no wonder they have not been exhaustively investigated. An exhaustive investigation of ear bats might poison them with carbon monoxide. Probably not a good idea because of the well-known scientific principle of serendipitous co-prosperity sphere of living.

Since I have not yet submitted my paper, "Ear Bats of Bhutan's Bishop Cave," to a peer-reviewed journal, I can relate here some particulars of our expedition. The caves of Bhutan are little known and not well studied. Local folk wisdom holds that both of Bhutan's caves are cursed and that entering them dooms their explorers to death. The history of Bhutan, as found in a monastery library, confirms that in 1811, two teams of explorers entered Bishop Cave and Knight Cave. By 1911, when the history was written, all the members of both teams were dead. Undaunted and bereft of superstition, I applied for and received a UNESCO grant of €235,300 to mount the subject expedition.

I recruited Dr. Avians, entomologist; Ms. Klima deRope, vertical specialist; Sr. Pablo Escobar, pharmaceutical investigator; and Ms. Shrill Scream, media relations—all internationally famous and wonderful cave exploration experts—to accompany the Ergor Rubreck Expedition to Bhutan. We left New York on February 28, 2004, landed at Thimphu Municipal Airport, and returned the following November 31, 2004. We surveyed and mapped both caves and made several notable discoveries. This first report on ear bats is one of those. The second was the existence of light water on Level 5 of Bishop Cave (the subject of a forthcoming report of water in the form of cotton candy), and crystallized skulls of cave bears.

Those wishing to join my next cave expedition are invited to download an application form from www.WTFexpeditions.com (World Traveler Fame Expeditions) and include a PayPal fee of $85 US for S&H (shipping and handling).

THE LONGEST ICELAND CAVE

Iceland is the island of fire and ice located just below the Arctic Circle between Greenland and Scandinavia. Situated on the Mid-Atlantic Ridge where two massive tectonic plates meet, geothermal features such as volcanoes, geysers, and hot springs compete with ice fields and glaciers for the most bizarre environment. The lava has spread over hundreds of square miles of land and comprises 90–92 percent of all of Iceland. Sedimentary rock only accounts for 8–10 percent and is limited to silt and sandstone. You would expect lava tube caves to exist on the island, but certainly no karst or caves. The best time to see ice (glacier) caves is October to March—in winter when the ice has stopped melting.

Iceland is not large, about the size of Kentucky. Its main industry is tourism. Literally hundreds of tour companies compete for tourists. Some specialize. For instance, seventy-nine ice cave tours and forty-seven lava cave tours are currently available. I sent emails to several tour companies indicating that since I was the most wonderful cave explorer, I wanted to discover the longest combination lava-and-ice cave. I heard back from Floyjed Colljins, a speleologist who worked for a small, obscure, specialized tour company in Reykjavik.

Floyjed said he would be honored to accompany me in a record-setting effort to map "the longest cave in Iceland." He said, Blackener's Cave is a two-plus-mile-long lava cave, but nearby is an unexplored lava cave that features a hot-spring drain input that ends at an ice field. "If we go in January, the hot water may melt an ice cave that could go a long way. This explains why a summer trip is out of the question."

I told Floyjed I would bring my Disto-Z equipped with Bluetooth and a digital recorder with a Go-Pro video camera. We'd map the cave in real time as we moved through it and print out the map at the end of our expedition. He needed a $745 deposit to secure a reservation for January 10.

We met at the Reykjavik Icelandic Airways arrival gate 32. He held a sign saying WONDJERFULL! so I knew it was Floyjed who was there to greet me. He was accompanied by a young woman he introduced as Matilja Magnesonj, the government's official record keeper. "Floyjed has told me about your expedition, and he invited me to join you. I keep statistical records for our country which is occupied eleven percent by glaciers. I am sorry we will not go to the lava tunnel Raufarhólshellir, which is thirteen hundred sixty meters long, up to thirty meters wide, ten meters or more tall, and formed fifty-six hundred years ago."

I checked over our trekking supplies: meals for three days under lava and ice. Our Super Jeep navigated a snow-covered paved two-lane highway 130 km west to Blackener's Cave. Just two kilometers beyond, we pulled into a turnoff and parked. To our right, a hot spring bubbled merrily away, draining under the road and trickling into a snowfield. The steam from the stream was blown away to the north by a fresh breeze. We followed the stream 1.3 km to a sinkhole in the snow. "I am afraid we are stymied," said Floyjed, "Normally the entrance of the cave is here but then the ice field was melted when I discovered this cave."

Uncoiling the 120-foot eleven-meter diameter static rope I had brought for just such occasions, I lowered it into the drain hole. I secured the end to a lava spire jutting out of the snow. "Follow me!" I said. Judging by the looks I got from Floyjed and

Matilja, they had never rappelled before. I had to teach them how to use the brake bar rack.

"Only rock-climbing guides know how to rappel in Iceland," said Matilja. We descended rapidly into the vertical shaft cut by the warm water flowing into the ice. About thirty-two meters down, I stepped off into a vividly blue-lit cave mouth. The others joined me as we turned on our lamps and plunged ahead into the dark lava cave.

The lava tube was roughly 3.2m in diameter with no side leads. We trekked for many hours, stopping for meals only briefly as we had no idea how long the cave might be. My Disto-Z indicated we had traveled five kilometers when we popped into a blue-lit continuation of the passage as an ice cave beneath the glacier. The stream had cooled down by this time. After 460m, the ice cave opened to the outside on the toe of the Vatnajökull Glacier. A sign identified the glacier, and where the lagoon ended, several Jeeps were parked.

"We have set the Icelandic cave length record of fifty-four hundred sixty meters! We have mapped the longest cave in Iceland," I declared.

"No, we have not. You see, in Iceland the ice caves disappear in April, not to be formed anew until November tenth or twelfth. So this cave will be missing soon. As for lava caves, there are hundreds of them, who knows how long? They have housed sheep, goats, and ancient people for thousands of years. If you take the Archaeology Tour for eight-hundred sixty-five dollars, you will see some of these caves," said Matilja.

I begged Floyjed to overrule Matilja, but he said he was reluctant to do that for fear his tour guide license would be revoked by the government. I bargained: "The rappel training alone was worth hundreds of dollars."

"I'm afraid Icelandic laws are very strict," he said. "The best we can do is give you a certificate suitable for framing that attests to the fact you explored an unnamed cave on your vacation."

The certificate was delivered to me at the departure gate, rolled in a protective tube. I have yet to unroll it to look at it, because they probably misspelled my name as Ergjor Rubrjeck.

They always do.

CAVES FROM OUTER SPACE

A surprising fact is that not all caves were developed here on Earth. A few caves originated in outer space and arrived fully formed. These remarkable marvels of science are asteroid caves. Earth scientists know that from the Big Bang at which our current universe formed, our planet has been bombarded by a variety of extraterrestrial objects—meteorites, space dust, asteroids, moonbeams, sunshine, cosmic rays, and northern lights.

A few asteroids produced cataclysmic results when they struck Earth. A Siberian asteroid that exploded over Tunguska in 1908 leveled trees for 772 square miles and charred an additional 38 square miles. The Cretaceous–Paleogene extinction sixty-six million years ago that marked the end of the dinosaurs was caused by a comet or asteroid that struck the earth in what is now the Yucatan Peninsula. The comet or asteroid was estimated to be 6.2 miles in diameter and formed what is called the Chicxulub Crater, which is 93 miles across and twelve miles deep. You have no doubt heard of the caves of Yucatan—including the Sac Actun Cave System (at 215.6 miles long, it is the longest underwater cave on Earth)—and thousands of other caves, cenotes, and karst features that spalled off the Caribbean asteroid in the collision and explosion.

Do asteroids have caves? Astronomy has never proved that they don't! Asteroids are made of rock. If you took Geology 101, you know that there are only three types of rock: sedimentary, igneous, and metamorphic. Caves occur in all three kinds of rock. Odds are that a certain number of rock asteroids already contain caves. When they fall to Earth, their caves fall with them.

Asteroid caves are not documented. No geomorphology textbook describes them, and speleological journals are utterly silent on the subject of asteroid caves. Maybe it is because I am the only speleologist in the world who has studied asteroid caves, and my in-press paper has been temporarily withheld at the request of a super-secret government agency. They asked me not to reveal my findings lest they strike fear and despair into the hearts of world leaders and trigger a doomsday scenario of nuclear exchanges that would wipe out civilization. You can see that, while I am skeptical of that scenario, I am nevertheless prudent enough to save humanity.

What do asteroid caves look like overall? I feel I am not revealing any national military secrets by giving cavers a few generalities. Natural caves on Earth form in a limited number of patterns. Most numerous are three-dimensional dendritic (tree-like) pattern caves. They resemble most river systems, although they may be modified by geologic structure to form trellis, angulate, radial, or network patterns.

Asteroid caves are different: They form in the natural galactic pattern called orbital elliptic, meaning asteroid caves resemble three-dimensional ellipses in plan form. Some cave passages in terrestrial caves have elliptical cross sections, but this is related to phreatic passages formed below the vadose zone of drainage—not related to the orbital movement of astronomical features like galaxies, stars, planets, asteroids, comets, and space junk.

Just as planetary orbits have no beginning or end, asteroid caves have no entrances or exits. This could be another reason why they haven't been reported before—nobody but me has found them! The late Rane Curl, PhD, calculated that the number of caves with no entrances was roughly ten times the number of caves with one entrance.

However, his calculation did *not* include asteroid caves since none had been found at the time of his paper. About the only way one can discover an asteroid cave is through a fortuitous intersection with a tunnel, mine, or preexisting cave.

I have now informed you of asteroid caves—caves from outer space. But have you ever wondered about missing caves? Have you ever considered that caves you used to hear about or found in your youth but are missing now are not figments of your fading memory? I am convinced those missing caves have become asteroid caves. They are no longer on our earth but are part of the vast celestial belt of orbiting debris whirling around us. The caves of yesteryear are part of the cyclonic maelstrom orbiting our planet. We can't find those caves because *they are no longer here*!

As evidence of this startling conclusion, I cite speleologist Bill Copeland, a distinguished member of the Cave Research Foundation. For twenty years, Bill has specialized in finding, mapping, and describing the reported six hundred smaller caves in Mammoth Cave National Park. He will be the first to tell you he has not found six hundred caves. Although he is a competent and skilled cave finder, he has searched in vain for caves that seem to be missing. I know because I have accompanied him on some of his search excursions. We did not find some of the caves we were seeking.

I am hereby informing him that he will never find them because some of them are not there anymore. They can only be found by going into space where they are part of the orbiting mass that surrounds our solar system. Some of the small caves have been picked up by tornadoes and other high winds and whirled at terminal velocity out of Earth's gravitational reach. Momentum has a death grip on some caves you can't find. If you are out in the field searching for a cave and can't find it, remember the phrase, "Suck it up." You're not crazy.

Most caves are too big to be pulled into orbit or outer space. Mammoth Cave would make a spaghetti-like cave trail 430 miles long as it was unceremoniously yanked up beyond our atmosphere. If that were to happen, only a billionaire astronaut could tour Mammoth Cave.

What's it like inside an asteroid cave? The one I am sure I have visited is Lower Ruby Cave in Lookout Mountain, Chattanooga, Tennessee. It was first intersected when a railroad tunnel was dug and penetrated the bottom of the cave. The second intersection was the elevator shaft sunk to Ruby Falls that penetrated to the cavern below, Lower Ruby. The cave had no stalactites or stalagmites. All the surfaces were covered with thick soot. My guide said it was locomotive soot from the old trains, but now I am not so sure. It was a never-to-be-repeated experience.

TOWER OF PISA FIX

The urgent message was my second invitation to Italy. The first was to explore the caves of Venice. This time it was from Cardinale Capodipesce Garibaldi of Pisa, Italy, the prior of Pisa Cathedral. This cathedral is the site of the famous Leaning Tower of Pisa, the fifty-six-foot high, eight-story campanile that leans about four degrees from vertical.

The problem was *not* the tower, as I surmised, but the cathedral's *battistero*. The round marble baptistery building sits in front of the cathedral, and the leaning tower is behind the cathedral. The baptismal pool inside is fed by a natural warm spring, and its overflow drains into a sinkhole at the edge of the building. The problem, according to Cardinale Garibaldi, was bats. During an evening baptism, a cloud of bats issued from the drain sinkhole, circling as they rose, and exited the building through a high open window.

"It scared the daylights out of a baptismal party. And since we had never conducted baptisms in the evening, we never noticed the *pipistrelle* before." Il cardinale sounded upset. He said it had taken 199 years to build the cathedral, starting in 1173, and nobody noticed bats until now. I thought of telling him to place a basket over the drain but held my tongue because that is not a green solution to the problem. So, I listened further.

"Since you are the most famous and wonderful international *speleologo*, we are turning to you to advise us on what to do. *Il*

Papa suggested we place a basket over the drain, but I asked for a second opinion. *Le Sacre Scritture* has no remedy." Cardinale Garibaldi said he would pay my expenses plus an honorarium if I would interrupt my busy schedule and fly immediately to Italy. I gave him my answer: "I'll drop everything and come at once!" Scaring babies and their parents is never good PR, and bat defecation on a bat flight exit or return cannot be hygienic. I packed my kit and gear, passport, and investigational instruments. I thought of asking my neighborhood priest to bless the kit and kaboodle, but time was too short.

Italy was lovely as I landed. Il cardinale had arranged for a black Maserati to pick me up at the airport. We sped to the cathedral where I was awestruck by the gleaming white marble duomo, battistero, and *torre pendente* glowing in the dazzling sunshine. Il cardinale unlocked the bronze doors to the battistero and led me into the pool. The building had a magnificent echo—which would have been exquisite for solemn Gregorian chants—but the echo defied my understanding of il cardinale's echoing explanation. Fortunately, his Italian heritage prompted him to use his hands and arms liberally as he pointed to the spring, sky, pool, drain, and marble fonts. I nodded in assent, ignoring my urge to yodel a jolly acknowledgment.

The nearly ponded drain was about eighteen inches in diameter. I dug at the edges with my Palmer putty knife and enlarged it to about two feet. I lighted my lamp and dove headfirst into the drain. Norbert Casteret had discovered a Neanderthal cave that way.

Almost immediately, I surfaced in a pool at the top of a waterfall. I braced my feet and hands against the dark walls of the shaft and descended to a dry paleo-drain that I would explore later. About five meters lower, I found an underground river in a wide passage two meters high by ten meters wide.

From the above-ground site layout, which I had memorized at a glance on my way in, I saw the general direction of the cave was toward the duomo. Some 175m later, the river trickled into a pile of breakdown rocks. I retreated the way I had come and chimneyed up to investigate the dry paleo-drain, a passage two meters wide by one meter high. At a distance of 121m, I entered a room five meters in diameter and strongly smelling of ammonia. Bats covered the ceiling, their pungent urine odor nearly overwhelming me. I strapped on my respirator and checked out the walls of the room.

The right-hand wall was actually composed of a breakdown of rocks. The left wall was solid. I calculated that this room lay directly beneath the leaning tower! If I could place a heavy-duty screw jack under the ceiling at the point of collapse, it might be possible to restore the tower to a vertical position and thus repair it.

I had read that the tower weighed 14,500 tons, so I'd need a super jack to fix the lean. Outside the cave, I visited the library. I found the tower had started to lean while being built—soft earth, they said—and they jiggered the plan to compensate. In 1990, the tower leaned 5.5 degrees, A comprehensive engineering program between 1993 and 2001 stabilized the tilt at 3.97 degrees.

I summoned Cardinale Garibaldi, who summoned the Sindaco di Pisa, the *presidente del consiglio regionale*, and the duomo staff. Even the *direttore del tourismo* was there for my report. In the crowded cathedral, I told the hushed audience of my discovery and my proposed fix to restore the famed tower to its intended vertical position! I was totally unprepared for the reaction: "*Bestemmia!* (Blaspheme!) *No, no!*" Negative shouts echoed from the ceiling of the great duomo. "*Never . . . No way!*"

"Nobody will come to see *la Torre Retta di Pisa*, the *Straight* Tower of Pisa! It will be the economic ruin of Pisa! We all shall starve!"

I could take a hint. So, I left a sign outside the baptistery bronze doors to protect bats: Edificio Chiuso dalle 17:00 alle 5:00 (Building Closed Daily 5:00 p.m. to 5:00 a.m.) My excellent plan to fix the leaning tower was clearly unpopular. Live and learn. However, I *did* save the bats!

TANK TUNNEL BENEATH US ROUTE 66

A top-secret World War II document was released three months ago revealing an astonishing secret. During the early prewar days prior to 1939 and the Second World War, President Roosevelt asked Major Dwight Eisenhower and General George Patton to construct a top-secret tunnel beneath US Route 66 to be used to rush army tanks to any place between Los Angeles and Chicago in the event of an invasion of the United States.

Some background: In 1937, then-Captain Dwight D. Eisenhower conducted an army mobilization test to see if tanks and an armored division could move quickly from mid-America to California. Unfortunately, the test was a disastrous failure when the army column became mired in mud from spring rains at Fort Riley, Kansas, only a few miles from its base. Disaster sealed the go-ahead for the secret project.

The secret tunnel project, constructed mainly during nighttime hours, was completed in thirteen months, a record for tunnel building at the time. As part of the Great Depression recovery program, thousands of young men from the Civilian Conservation Corps (CCC) and the Works Progress Administration (WPA) were organized to pave US Route 66, and to construct the top-secret tunnel beneath it as it grew. Fortunately, the long tunnel was never needed or used after its completion in late 1938. Information about the project remained more secret than the Manhattan Project.

Upon its declassification, I made it my business to investigate, even though I am a cave explorer, not a tunnel explorer.

I decided to start my investigation in Missouri, knowing cavers there could be counted on to help explore this mystery tunnel. We met at five in the morning at a street manhole on the south side of St. Louis. I selected this as the closest potential underground access, based on its proximity to Route 66.

The manhole ladder led downward about thirty-five feet. Suspiciously, there were no water or sewer pipes, no electrical lines, nothing but a horizontal brick wall. The wall looked as old as the manhole itself. I pounded on the wall, and a brick moved, cracking loose and falling into a space behind the wall. Eye to the hole, I could see a small chamber. We took turns pulling bricks out of the wall and soon crawled into a brick-lined tunnel about six feet wide by seven feet high. Could this be the 1937 tank tunnel? I sent three of the Missouri cavers to the left, while I took the other two cavers and headed to the right.

In a half-mile, I came across an army tank filling the tunnel wall to wall. The tank was an M1917, one of about nine hundred manufactured in the US in 1918 based on the Renault FT-17 (FT char) two-man light tank. We barely squeezed beside the turret, where a 37mm cannon projected. Another tank was located three feet behind the first tank. In all, we found six tanks in a line. Why had the tanks been abandoned? I opened the top hatch on the first tank and shined my headlamp in. I was *shocked*!

There was a human skull and below it a skeleton clad in a brown wool army uniform. Clearly, our discovery had suddenly moved beyond our pay grade. We needed to notify the police at once!

Back at the manhole, we met the cavers who had gone left. They had not found any tanks but had turned back at the time limit we set.

Once on the surface, we called 911. We explained the situation briefly and asked that the coroner be dispatched with the first responders.

The record revealed that on the eve of the tunnel completion, a squadron of six tanks had departed from Fort Lincoln in Illinois into the tunnel in the dead of night. The postmortem evidence was that the tank crews had been overcome by carbon monoxide poisoning. Nothing further was heard of their secret trip, and they never arrived in California. Twelve unlucky tankers died making the inaugural entry of the tank tunnel because the tunnel had not been equipped with a ventilation system as it advanced beneath Route 66 day by day.

But why was the disappearance not investigated? General Patton realized that the tunnel was too narrow for the tanks that were then on the drawing board in 1938, and he had the army order 250 railroad flatcars that could transport larger tanks anywhere in the USA. Thus, the tunnel was obsolete even before its completion and a profound embarrassment to the Roosevelt administration. It was not the first government boondoggle, nor would it be the last.

Meanwhile, Dwight Eisenhower had been promoted and was then in the War Department in Washington, DC. I understand that as part of the government cover-up, the remains of the hapless twelve brave soldiers were recently and secretly transferred to one of General Patton's flatcars, specially painted black, and quietly moved by rail to Dover, Delaware. They were interred in a secret night ceremony in Arlington Cemetery with full military honors.

Yesterday I checked with my Missouri caver friend, Scott House. The six tanks have mysteriously disappeared from the narrow tunnel, and Scott reported a new concrete patch in the old concrete pavement on Route 66 just south of St. Louis.

I am sure this account will be denounced as "fake news," but I believe all patriotic Americans need to know the full story.

POST-HISTORIC CAVE PAINTINGS

Most people are aware of the prehistoric cave paintings in southern France. Ancient explorers depicted wild animals, such as wildebeests, yaks, tigers, and gazelles. Two characteristics of those decorations stand out: 1. Artists never signed their names or dates, and 2. They only rendered pictures of creatures with beating hearts. You never see cave paintings of automobiles, locomotives, or cruise ships. Obviously, those subjects have no beating hearts so were entirely skipped by Neanderthal and Cro-Magnon artists. I'm convinced that prehistoric cave paintings endure because the cave environment is uniform, dark, and non-abrasive. . . .

I mail-ordered the Famous Cave Artists Course and received Lesson 1 plus paints, a palette, brushes, charcoal sticks, fixatif, kneaded rubber eraser, a practice cave, a flimsy collapsible easel, and several sponges. Lesson 1 was *Painting Mammoths*. It called for burnt umber and burnt sienna colors and the charcoal stick for sketching the outline. I drew a curve like a rainbow and two tusks, a trunk, and wiggly wool sides. It looked like an elephant with a hairpiece.

Upon reading further, Lesson 1 said to compose your cave picture well, keeping in mind art composition tricks such as the triangle, inverted triangle, and Hogarth's curve of beauty. For Chinese cave painting, it suggested the tri-part Man, Heaven, and Earth configuration of oriental flower arrangement. The more I studied ancient cave paintings, the more I discovered there was *no* composition evident—Ergor's first significant discovery! Ancient cave explorers *never* composed anything!

I only glanced through Lessons 2 through 10, but I could see the Famous Cave Artists were trying to teach me to ape ancient animal painting. A waste of the $699 I paid for the course. When cavers would see the first cave I painted in, some caving loud-mouths would denounce me for counterfeiting prehistoric cave art. They would certainly heap scorn on me because I intended to not make the ancient mistake of no name or no date.

So, I decided to create my own original post-historic cave art. I needed a cave that was accessible so cavers could view my art with suitable awe, yet not a pristine cave like Lechuguilla where there are very few flat walls and nobody is allowed in. I chose Sinks of Grindstone in Kentucky. Some years back a group of desecraters set sixty-six dozen tea candles around the big room in that cave and lit them all. Maybe I could bribe them to repeat the desecration for my unveiling.

I elected that my first underground painting would be a cruise ship. Since it was a cave, I figured a cruise ship like the boats used for many years in Mammoth Cave (the Howe Caverns boats were too beat up). Since the guides propelling the Mammoth Cave boats were variously Caucasian and African Americans, it figured that a modicum of diversity in my post-historic painting would not sully my reputation. Yes, Stephen Bishop would be a suitable oarsman. I could have him singing. I could letter the words of "My Old Kentucky Home" in a balloon over his head. A friend, hearing my idea, said I should not depict Stephen singing "My Old Kentucky Home" because first, he hated that song, and second, I might run into copyright litigation that could tie me up in legal snarls when I'd rather be painting caves.

My scene of Stephen cruising on Echo River included several fine ladies with pink parasols and feather boa hats and gentlemen with top hats and silk waistcoats. One little girl trailed her hand in the water, and I painted a cave blindfish nibbling at it. One man held a derringer and was about to loose a gunshot to demonstrate the echo properties of the watercourse. I was proud of the finished picture and returned home to think about what kind of frame to paint around it.

I returned to Sinks of Grindstone weeks later and, to my horror, I discovered graffiti superimposed on my painting. Stephen had been desecrated with an unspeakable appendage, and there were initials and hearts in white paint. An ugly "UK" was painted in blue and the numeral "14" beside it all over the cruise boat. Greek letters glowed Day-Glo red. One NSS number marred a lady's parasol. My name and the date had been sprayed over with black paint. In short, my twenty-four-foot by twelve-foot painting was trashed beyond recognition. It was heartbreaking after the months of work I had invested. I could see why Michelangelo painted the Sistine Chapel Ceiling so vandals could not reach to trash it. I nearly gave up post-historic cave painting because it obviously encouraged graffiti taggers. Too much temptation.

Then I hit on an innovative alternative. I would paint beautiful, well-composed paintings, then roll on a layer of water-thinned latex paint to match the original walls and ceiling. I tested several formulas in a Weather-O-Meter (accelerated severe weathering simulator) and found a paint formula that would fade and disappear in fifty years, leaving my painting resplendent in all its grandeur. Future visitors would enjoy my fine art, even if present cavers were denied the privilege.

I spent two years painting sixteen pictures in sixteen caves. If you visit any of those caves today, you will not see my paintings. That is, unless you visit the one where I inadvertently rolled latex paint over a bat colony—it's the lumpy patch near the ceiling. But fifty years from now, you will be able to see "The Grand Canyon at Sunrise," "Vintage Corvettes at a Drive-in," and my masterpiece, "Portraits of Thirty-Seven Vice-Presidents of the USA."

DISCOVERY OF CARLSGOOD CAVERNS

New Mexico has some remarkable caves, but I have discovered the best of them all. In 1951, I was exploring the Guadalupe Mountains seeking caves. One day, I noticed a column of ascending bats that came from a draw. I guessed they were five miles away. When I reached the location, I was astounded to see that what I had taken to be bats was, in reality, smoke! Smoke from a hole in the ground can mean only one thing—fire in the hole. I made camp next to the entrance and wrote the location in my journal. I thought of the name "Smokehole Caverns," but a reference in the *Gurnee Book of Show Caves* indicated that name was already taken. So, I looked up *Carlsbad,* a nearby town, and found that name was taken also. I decided "Carlsgood Caverns" was good to go!

Early the next morning, I set off with my hard hat and carbide lamp, a 120-foot-long rope, and two peanut butter sandwiches. The smoke issuing from the Carlsgood Caverns made my eyes water, but fortunately, I had my cave goggles (an essential for every caver). The smoke was no worse than many smoke-filled rooms where I have played cards, so I thought of the prehistoric Indigenous people who explored Salts Cave in Kentucky and toughed it out. The entrance passage, five meters wide by four meters high, slanted downward about fifteen degrees and was decorated with soot-covered flowstone resembling organ pipes. I figured the atmosphere was too smoky for bats, and the temperature was probably also too warm.

After 430 paces, I came to a large room, which I named The Big Room. There were majestic columns—Ionic in style—reaching upward into the gloom. Festoons of a wispy white growth similar to Spanish moss hung down from the tops of the columns, giving the place a distinctly southern feel. A log cabin stood in the center of the room. How could a log cabin be built in or under a part of the country where there is no significant number of trees? On closer examination, the "logs" were solid flowstone. The structure was made of horizontally laid-up stalactites and columns. The pitched roof was not cedar shakes but exfoliated stone from cave walls trimmed into rectangles by hand.

I knocked on the door of the stone cabin, expecting no answer. Instead, I heard a croaking voice say the words, "Come in." Had I imagined it? No, the summons repeated, "Come the hell in." I opened the door, and my lamplight fell on the crags and fissures of an ancient-looking face and numerous scars and tattoos.

"Congratulations! You are the first outsider to find this cave! Ed Black is my name," he croaked. "I am a Texas guano miner." I judged the speaker to be in his nineties from his visage and croaking voice.

He told me he had lived for years on canned baked beans from a semi-truck that had crashed out on the main road.

"How. . . ?" I began.

"How what?" he asked.

"How old are you?" I had a thousand questions, but that one seemed appropriate given the man's weathered-leather appearance.

"I am thirty-one years old," he said, then pushed me back into a stone chair, and continued. "I accompanied Jim White when he found Carlsbad Caverns, but he cut me out of the bat guano mining profits, cheated me, that's what." He motioned for me to sit down. I was reluctant to sit because, with a captive audience, Ed might pour out the whole tale of injustice, double-dealing, and lost dreams.

Where does the smoke come from? And how had Ed been able to live all these years in dingy, smoky surroundings? I changed his subject from how Jim White and his family had cheated him over the years to Ed's living conditions by asking him where all the smoke came from. "As for where the smoke comes from, I don't rightly know. We could go see." Ed stood up and beckoned toward the door.

We followed the main cave out of The Big Room for about two miles. Ed looked at the walls and ceiling as if he had never seen them before. "I never saw any of this before. Light's too faint from my torches. Your light makes it bright enough to see." Ed seemed to enjoy cave exploring and waited patiently while I made scientific notes in my Spelunker's Notebook.

Around noon we came to a pile of smoldering refuse. A hole in the ceiling opened to daylight. Just then I heard the unmistakable sound of a dump truck beyond the hole, and a deluge of unburned refuse, garbage, offal, furniture, jetsam, flotsam, and junk poured down onto the fire, which immediately blazed up and then died down to a billowing cloud of smoke. By my cave reckoning, we were under the Carlsbad, New Mexico, landfill and unsanitary waste disposal dump. They had been dumping municipal trash in that hole for years, and the smoke had given away the location of Carlsgood Caverns.

I led Ed by the hand back to his cabin because he said the smoke hurt his eyes. I offered to bring him out to the entrance I had discovered and back to civilization. I said a new day was ahead when he could collect a guano miner's pension and when municipalities would convert to sanitary landfills instead of burning dumps. It would be a jubilee of smoke-free days, a return to health, pure air and water, and green landscapes.

Alas, he refused my offer. The most I could persuade Ed to share was a peanut butter sandwich. He bolted it down with relish. As I turned to leave, he said, "Ergor, by any chance you got any cigars?"

FINDING THE BEST CAVING VEHICLE

Thirty years ago, I thought the ideal caving vehicle would be a four-wheel drive (4WD) Jeep with a winch. Its drawback would be its small load-carrying capacity. Three months ago, I opened the latest *Consumer Reports* to find a major article, "Nine Caving Vehicles Rated." Nearly all of them achieved a high rating except the Mack Truck Model 95000, which guzzles diesel fuel at the rate of two gallons per mile. I thought they covered the waterfront with such vehicles as the Dodge Ram 4500, Ford 190, International Road King. Cadillac Escalade, and Range Rover. But the Cummins Cave Master 7000 caught my eye. I called up the factory and told them who I was—Ergor Rubreck, world's most famous (deservedly so) and wonderful cave explorer and that I'd like to evaluate the Cummins Cave Master 7000 and write a review for the "Spelunkers Action Digest."

They instantly recognized my name (or maybe nobody else applied) because they said I could pick one up at their plant in Columbus, Indiana, on the first of the month and have it back by the tenth. I showed up on the first of the month. Since they did not stipulate the tenth of *which month*, I naturally allowed enough time to ring out the vehicle in Mexico.

Several Texas cavers answered my query to help field-test the new caving vehicle. Bill Iron had four thousand feet of Blue Line static rope, a month's supply of burritos, and directions to an off-road cave that should be a rugged test for this specialized vehicle.

With Bill beside me and eight other cavers in the back seat of the double cab, we decided to compile the statistics while the vehicle was still in tip-top shape. These are the statistics we recorded:

Cummins Cave Master 7000

- Cost (as equipped with front winch): $54,970
- Dry weight: 51,750 pounds
- Fuel capacity and mileage: 150 gallons diesel, two mpg
- 0 to 60 mph: 5:34 min. (We did not record the 0 to 100 mph as we would have had to drop it from the back of an aircraft to reach that speed.)
- Stopping distance from fifty mph: 375 feet
- Stopping distance from sixty mph: 482 feet
- Turning radius: 580 feet
- Cargo capacity: 31,350 pounds
- Grill: Wall-O-Steel
- Lawns run over while turning: six
- # police cars responding: four
- Winch capacity: 387 furlongs per fortnight
- Smoke mortars: six (three each side)
- Transmission: three ranges, thirty-two speeds, transmission cooler

With our passports in order, we crossed at the obscure Mexican town of Piedras Negras, then south on Route 57 to Monclova. From there, we headed west cross-country into the Sierra Madre Oriental. Our Cummins 7000 handled the mountains beautifully and seemed at home in roadless areas. The steeper the better.

We saw a native with bandoliers slung over both shoulders, a large sombrero, and two Colt 45 revolvers at his belt beckoning to us from the middle of a trail ahead of us. We stopped and asked if he would be our guide for a suitable price. He said, "Si," which I took to mean, "I'll see." He climbed aboard the bed of our Cummins 7000 and began to plunk chickens with his revolvers as we pitched and bucked our way ever deeper into the wilderness. He must have had many friends in the area for soon we had a trail of enthusiastic natives running after us yelling, "Alto, alto." The pitch of our engine was more of a bass-baritone than an alto, and we soon lost the pursuers.

A raging mountain stream crossed our path. The torrent would have swept away even our Cummins Cave Master. Our guide alighted and gestured toward the winch hook on the front. I let out the clutch, and he pulled out three hundred feet of slack cable. Taking the hook in his teeth, he plunged into the raging river and emerged dripping wet on the far bank. He wound the cable around a spire of rock and signaled for me to energize the winch. Slowly we crept toward the rushing water, raised our windows, dipped our front bumper in, and then submerged completely! We moved inexorably across the stream underwater and climbed up the far bank. Water poured from the bed, and our burritos floated sadly in the ebbing tide.

Ahead of us, I could see our guide's many friends running toward us with machetes raised on high. They must have crossed the swinging suspension bridge just below our crossing. I thought our guide would be happy to see so many of his friends rushing to greet us in such high spirits, but I was wrong. Bill Iron, a veteran of Mexican caving expeditions, shouted a warning. Their intent was hostile, not friendly!

I slammed my hand on the mortar button and instantly we were engulfed in choking smoke. I shifted the Cummins 7000 into eighteenth gear and roared off in a cloud of gravel and smoke. I crested the mountain ahead and slalomed down the far side, alternately gunning it and hitting the brakes hard.

"We're at the pit," said Bill, peering at the GPS. I applied the brakes and within three hundred feet, we rolled to a dead stop at the brink of a deep sinkhole. Vultures circled the abyss. Wisps of vapor wafted out. I was glad we had tested the stopping power of the brakes. I did notice something peculiar when I looked out the rear-view mirror. There were two smooth tracks where before there had been no track at all or even a goat trail. Then I realized that the Cummins 7000 vehicle weight was heavy enough to crush the larger rocks and deliver a smooth ride, unrelated to the suspension system.

Suddenly a brigade of heavily armed Federales appeared surrounding our vehicle. Those soldiers pointed their weapons at us. Bill Iron suggested we get out and parley with them. He talked with the captain in low tones with many negative side-to-side head movements at first, then gradually nodding up and down as if approving. Bill pointed to the bed of our vehicle. He and the captain shook hands as if to seal the deal. Bill reported that we could have safe passage back to Monclova if we would make a small donation of rope—two hundred feet per man. That just about used up our supply of four thousand feet of cave rope. I fired up the Cummins 7000 and gunned the engine until the chrome headers glowed cherry red. We cut the rope with a machete and sealed the ends on the hot muffler pipes. Each of the eight cavers coiled a two-hundred-foot section of rope into a coil to fit over the shoulders of the twenty soldiers. At last, the Federales retired, and we were free to go. Clearly, the bribe had deprived us of the rope to explore the bottom of any significant pit in Mexico, so we voted to return home, soggy burritos and all.

I left Bill and the eight Texas cavers in Austin and headed for Columbus, Indiana. Bill was a good sport about the lost rope, "We have ten miles of it in our caving warehouse left behind by the Polish caving team," he said.

Back at the city limits of Columbus, we were met by several police cars with blue lights flashing. They escorted us back to the Cummins factory where I turned the vehicle in. I was a little uneasy about how the cops held their hands loosely on their firearms. Mr. Cummins greeted me as I drove in. "Where have you been?" he demanded.

"You said be back by the tenth—and here I am, back on the eighth."

"Yes, but I meant the same month. Why did it take you two months to evaluate our Cummins Cave Master Seven-Thousand?" he said.

"I gave it a full-scale evaluation—in Mexico. You cannot evaluate cave vehicles without taking them to Mexico where they encounter rugged conditions, high mountains, and scorching heat. No caver would believe it if we just drove it around the block," I said. "You wanted a *real* evaluation, didn't you?"

"What are you going to write?" he said hesitantly.

"I am going to tell cavers this is the *best* caving vehicle *ever* manufactured. *Every* caver should have one. Of course, I must be objective—tell the bad with the good."

"Bad? What could be bad?" Cummins was clearly worried.

"For one thing, the CB antenna spring makes a funny twanging sound when we drive under low trees. Second, the Cobra CB radio only picks up profanity—in three languages: English, Tex-Mex, and Spanish. Maybe some Apache and Pueblo, too," He seemed to take the bad news rather well.

"That's it? The CB is the only bad thing in your evaluation?" Cummins said.

"Yes, that's *all* the bad news. As I say, *every* caver should have one!"

WARNING: TAG COLDSPOT

Geologists know that the Yellowstone hotspot is a stationary volcanic hotspot over which the North American plate has been migrating. It appears the hotspot formed approximately seventeen million years ago, and the North American plate has been moving over it ever since—four hundred miles so far! When the Yellowstone hotspot first formed, the area of the North American plate that was directly over it was where the Oregon–Nevada border is now. Presently, Yellowstone National Park is over the hotspot, and that is how the Yellowstone hotspot got its name. The Yellowstone hotspot has erupted with catastrophic results at least ten times over the last seventeen million years and is expected to erupt again—maybe at any moment.

Less well-known is the TAG coldspot. This is an area that cavers know as TAG (**T**ennessee, **A**labama, and **G**eorgia), home of thousands of vertical shafts—called pits—a place where sudden disaster may occur at any moment!

The problem in the TAG coldspot is *not* volcanic eruption. *No!* The problem is the potential sudden collapse of a 95–122-km-diameter piece of three states that may sink into the earth's mantle. This large "island" in the TENALGA plate boundary contains the largest aggregation of underground vertical shafts in North America.

The vertical shafts in TAG create a "perforation hazard," which in plate tectonic terms means the USA may be ripped on the dotted line and suddenly sink into the mantle below. Everybody knows how coupon or check perforations create a zone of weakness where the coupon or check tears off easily. In this case, a circular area of landscape about 120 km in diameter with vertical shafts perforating the earth's crust is ready to rip. It would let go like an apple core on the last cut of a curved knife. Fortunately, this circle has few large cities within it, as the death toll could be many times larger than will occur in rural TAG.

What could trigger such a geologic disaster? For one thing, too many cavers at once rappelling into TAG pits. I have not calculated the exact critical number of cavers that can cause the rapid detachment of the area from surrounding rocks. From personal experience, I know that Saturdays are especially dangerous because hundreds of cavers are likely bouncing in these pits on their day off. Their combined weight, concentrated on a few rope anchors, is likely to sunder the fragile remaining rock bonds, plunging the entire mass down into the mantle. The splash of hot mantle material squirting up the broken face of the mass will probably kill the cavers instantly as the massive island lets go. All cattle, sheep, and all other life on the surface near the boundary are likely to be incinerated by molten mantle splashes.

If there are heavier cavers on one part of the circumference of the loosened TAG island, the corresponding mantle splash may cover many more hectares of land on the heavy side compared to the lighter side.

I call this TAG area a coldspot because there is no present volcanic activity present there . . . yet. However, there is one mysterious location in Tennessee that cannot be accounted for by ordinary sedimentary rock formation. Igneous rocks there suggest an extraordinary tectonic or volcanic event that I have yet to investigate. If the Big Sinking Event holds off for a few years, I may get to apply my enviable expertise and report on that anomaly.

What should TAG cavers do in the face of this danger? I suggest several precautions: 1. Scheduling; 2. Para-rappelling;

and 3. Leave instructions back home. I will give you my best advice in the face of such a profound risk.

1. Scheduling: If you plan to descend a pit on the north boundary of the TAG area, get a buddy to descend a pit on the south side edge of the area at the same time on Saturday. That will balance the weight evenly to prevent side-overload with its probable disastrous result.

2. Para-rappelling: Vertical cavers are well versed in common single rope technique (SRT) descending. A few friction descenders such as brake bars, figure eights, and proprietary devices, to name a few, are in wide use. To these, I suggest adding a parasail pack. In the event the TAG area collapses along the vertical-shaft perforation lines, the descending caver is likely to plunge downward or not depending on which side of the shaft the anchor is secured. A whoosh of air is expected to reverse the caver's direction and hurl her or him into the air. At the apex of the caver's trajectory upward, the ripcord would be pulled, and the caver may steer and glide to safety on the intact side of the breach.

3. Leave instructions back home: In other words, leave an up-to-date will where your loved ones can find it. (Suggestion: Name the Rubreck Foundation as your beneficiary if you don't know anyone else.)

Naturally, safety first is the most important consideration now that I have identified the perforation hazard incipient in the TAG area. But what about public safety?

I have drafted a Public Safety Protocol, as any responsible caver would. I propose that road signs be erected at the boundary where each local road crosses onto the TAG island: STOP! OPEN CHASM AHEAD. DO NOT DROP IN. Then paint a 24-karat gold stripe across the road at that point. If the sign doesn't stop drivers, the gleaming gold will. Second, around one kilometer within the restricted boundary erect signs: Gun Confiscation Zone, Prepare to Surrender Firearms 500 Feet Ahead. Third, contact all the roadmap publishers and have them place a restricted zone shading over the TAG area. Garmin and Google Maps will be asked to provide similar shading on their digital products. Fourth, post signs at the edges of all pits in TAG. No Dumping. Overloads May Cause Collapse and Death! Undoubtedly, state highway authorities will devise other measures to mitigate possible accidents.

We are all in this together (except me—I'm not going near TAG!), so if you have a warning suggestion for cavers or the public, please submit it to me: Ergor Rubreck, Wonderful Caver, PO Box 69, Sinking Springs, OH, 45432. Enclose $50 for S&H.

CAVING WITH SCOUTS

When I was a boy in Shelby, Ohio, I joined the Cub Scouts at age eight and the Boy Scouts at age twelve. I rose through the ranks to Star Scout, at which point I succumbed to the "fumes" that used to terminate Scouting for adolescent boys—gasoline fumes and perfumes. As everyone in caving knows, I, Ergor Rubreck, became a paragon of trustworthiness, loyalty, helpfulness, and many other modest attributes of character. Naturally, as the world's greatest cave explorer, I felt a debt to those volunteer leaders who patiently taught me such lifelong skills as bookbinding and semaphore communication. So, several years ago, I contacted the local Boy Scout leader in town and volunteered to talk to the kids about cave exploring.

I talked to a joint meeting of Troop 192 and the Venture Scout Troop a week later. Regular Boy Scouts range from ten and a half to eighteen years of age and Venture Scouts—men and women—fourteen to twenty-one. I was told this was a select group interested in caves—those who had signed up to attend the "High Adventure Caving Base" in Big Cave National Monument next summer.

It was a little older audience than I remember because it included a number of boys with beards and girls with bulging merit badge sashes. After my ninety-minute PowerPoint lecture and equipment demo, they asked some good questions: Is the air good to breathe? Are caves vadose or phreatic? How do you keep from getting lost? Can you contrast dendritic pattern caves with network caves? Since I could not answer their questions fully in the allotted time, I invited the Scouts to join me in a caving expedition the next weekend at Doom Cave, Indiana.

The leaders accepted, and we rendezvoused the following Saturday morning at Aunt Assid's Restaurant in North Vernon. Following the motto "Be Prepared," the Scouts were equipped with hard hats, electric lamps, old clothes, ankle-high boots, and a ditty bag of candy bars. I delivered a safety lecture, mentioning all the rules of caving and with a dramatic reference to Floyd Collins—which I thought evoked tears from several Venture Scouts. We made a list of participants and left it on the dashboard of one of the SUVs. So, when any Scouts failed to return, we would know who they were.

Doom Cave's river entrance required wading that elicited some yodeling in base, tenor, and soprano registers. At the confluence of the Mud River and Clear River, I stopped the party to answer their question about air being good to breathe. I asked them to take several deep breaths. There was a faint stink about the place, which we later determined came from a ripe deer carcass trapped behind a bar in the Mud River. I pointed out the scallop marks sculpted into the walls and taught the Scouts that the steep side of the scallop occurs on the upstream side of the paleoflow. A couple of Scouts yelled that several scallops indicated flow in the opposite direction. I told them that a former Scout never lies, and they must take *my* word for it.

My plan was to lead the Scouts up the Mud River, through Crossover Canyon, and into Colossal Dome. There, we would have the teams of Scouts survey and explore. If any surveyed through the drain, they would follow the Clear River and immediately recognize their location back at the confluence.

In Colossal Dome an hour later, we relaxed with a candy bar break and assigned the Scouts into exploring teams to survey the leads. It became evident that none knew how to survey—there was then no merit badge for cave surveying—so I had to teach them the rudiments. Three hours later, several Venture Scouts wanted to leave the cave to retrieve any text messages. I ordered them back to their teams with an ultimatum: *Survey out or die!*

Mutiny in a cave is no laughing matter. Once in a cave in Mexico, I witnessed a mutiny of cavers equipped with machetes. I did not stick around to the end, but I think that may account for the many human bones in some Mexican caves.

Peer pressure resolved the mutiny threat. The older party leaders menaced the miscreants with flat rocks. I decided to attach myself to the Clear River survey party since the other teams would soon enough come to dead ends or too low cracks. Those other parties would experience the hard reality of caving: a cold, muddy, tight, crawling passage that pinched with no hope of real discovery. We, on the other hand, would survey through a four-foot-high passage with twenty-four inches of fast-flowing water.

After four hours of surveying in Clear River, our soaking-wet party arrived at the confluence of Mud River. Time for another candy bar. We waited two hours singing campfire songs until the party shivered with incipient hypothermia. We left Doom Cave to await the other parties back at the SUV.

Five hours later, the three other parties banged on the door of the SUV. They were surprisingly fresh and over-animated. Each party had chosen an abandoned drain from Colossal Dome, and each had surveyed over a thousand feet in an ever-enlarging borehole. One party found gypsum crystals four feet long. The second found three human skeletons, their heads facing a long dead campfire. We had talked about leaving archaeological remains undisturbed. The third party found a connection with the ten-mile-long Hidden Beauty Cave in the next county. It was just dumb luck—our party found crap while the others all scooped booty!

At the end of the summer, I learned that the Scouts who had stayed with me had dropped out of Scouting and caving altogether and were serving time in reform school. The others became stellar

GLORY

leaders at the summer session at High Adventure Caving Base in Big Cave National Monument. Three of them were inducted into the coveted Out Arrow Society for wonderfulness in Scouting leadership.

Now that the sting of that experience has subsided somewhat, I have left my phone number with the local leaders of the Brownies and Cub Scouts, offering to lecture on caving to those younger, more impressionable kids. It has been two weeks and they have not yet returned my calls.

DIVING THE BERMUDA BLUE HOLE

A blue hole is a karst feature, a hole either in the ocean floor or on land, that brings fresh water up from a karst aquifer below. When viewed from the sea, they stand out as circular, deep-blue areas in a green or lighter-blue sea. Prominent among blue holes are the following: Bermuda Blue Hole on the north coast of Bermuda; Abaco Blue Hole in the Grand Bahama Islands; Belize Blue Hole off the coast of Belize; and, in the past, the Blue Hole in Castalia, Ohio. The latter stopped being blue when agricultural runoff polluted the upland groundwater basin and changed its color from pure blue to murky gray, but it has since recovered its deep-blue color.

The Abaco Blue Hole was explored by speleologist George Benjamin in 1968 and is surrounded by dozens of blue holes on the island and in the sea. An Abaco commercial scuba diving resort industry has developed there in recent years. The Belize Blue Hole is being explored as I write.

Few people know about the Bermuda Blue Hole. Bermuda is a British island located 1,780 miles off the US southeast coast, discovered in 1503, and made a British Crown Colony in 1707. The Bermuda Blue Hole is about 300 meters in diameter and about 125 meters deep. Its 400-foot depth discourages most scuba divers but is an easy dive for scientific submersible vehicles.

I was called by famous British explorer Sir Upp of Maypole, who was preparing to dive the Bermuda Blue Hole in his new submersible ANKOR. The caves of Bermuda have been studied ever since geologists discovered that Bermuda's climate was summer year-round. Its Blue Hole bottom had not been fully probed because of its daunting decompression depth. Sir Upp, a billionaire, had built his high-tech submersible vehicle to get to the bottom of it. Naturally, he called me to head the in-water part of the karst investigation since I am such a wonderful cave investigator. I studied what was found at the bottom of other blue holes: many marine creatures but often a flooded cave system with beautiful stalactites and stalagmites, crystals, big rooms, and fresh water.

Aboard the bright yellow ANKOR, we were shocked and surprised by what we found at the bottom of the Bermuda Blue Hole. Scientists on three continents were astonished, baffled, and confused—a totally unforeseen outcome that flabbergasted and horrified British speleologists and historians alike. But I'm getting ahead of myself. Nobody could have predicted what we found.

What I could see through the round porthole after a twenty-minute drop to the bottom was a rowboat. I could make out an oarlock in the gunwale. As our submarine ANKOR slowly turned, I could see another oarlock, then another and another. We motioned the pilot to take our sub a little deeper to inspect the hull. Clearly, the hull was clinker-built—like the overlapping wooden siding on a house. The rowboat was much longer than a conventional rowboat. It was a lifeboat about thirty feet long. Our movement stirred up some of the marine growth on the side of the lifeboat, and it disappeared in the obscuring cloud.

The next day when we submerged, the water was crystal clear again. The light blue changed to a darker blue as we floated downward, so I switched on our powerful light. Suddenly I could see several submerged lifeboats, ten in all! How could ten wooden lifeboats litter the bottom of the Bermuda Blue Hole? The mystery gave no ready answer. We glided over the graveyard of scuttled lifeboats seeing oars randomly distributed between them. Tropical fish darted from between the hulks, and we saw several crustaceans extending their claws.

When I spoke to the harbor master the following day, he

could hardly believe what we described 450 feet down in the Bermuda Blue Hole. He said, "One lifeboat I can imagine. But ten lifeboats suggest a colossal disaster at sea. Our Bermuda history records no such disaster."

The reference librarian in town offered to help. She provided a history of the White Star Line, a British steamship company. Fortunately, the history had been indexed and annotated. Listed under "lifeboats," I found the following entry in the "1911 HM the King George V Marine Proceedings, Aberdeen, p. 326."

The RMS Titanic design in 1909 originally included a complement of twenty lifeboats, each clinker-built, 9.2m in length. As the 1911 launch approached, White Star's marketing director contacted the chief marine engineer and told him the Titanic was unsinkable. He feared that news of twenty lifeboats would reduce the credibility in the unsinkable claim. Rather than risk the loss of passage bookings, the management decided to reduce the number of lifeboats to ten. Accordingly, White Star attempted to cancel the original lifeboat order, but they were too late. The twenty lifeboats had already been built by a subcontractor. White Star quietly sold the ten excess lifeboats as surplus to a resort in Bermuda. After one year of attempts to rent the lifeboats to tourists, the rental business went bankrupt. Nobody wanted to rent a boat holding sixty-five passengers. The lifeboats were subsequently abandoned and scuttled in a deep-sea hole near Bermuda.

That reference solved the mystery, but the shocking realization was the sickening consequence: had the extra ten lifeboats been installed on the Titanic, the death toll would have been reduced. Of the 2,240 passengers and crew on the Titanic, 1,500 lost their lives. Only 740 survived. An additional ten lifeboats might have saved another 740 souls. To be sure, an additional ten lifeboats would not have saved everybody—760 of the remainder would have died instead of 1,500.

It astonished me that we had revealed what remained hidden in the murky past for so long. Imagine the horror of 760 individuals floating in hypothermic waters and sinking into a cold death for no good reason other than greed. Maybe they should make a movie.

APPLE PAYS TO NAME A CAVE

The public relations head of Apple Inc. wrote to me on company stationery asking if I would be interested in finding a cave in a prominent place that could be named "Apple Cave." I called to learn details of his unusual request. Finding caves is relatively easy, but finding caves in prominent places is tougher than a permanent wave in frog hair.

"We have a company anniversary coming up, and we'd like to discover a major cave in a major location to commemorate the occasion. I tried to pay Mammoth Cave a million dollars to change the name to Apple Cave, but they refused," said Johnnie Sapseed, VP for PR of Apple.

"I'm not surprised," I said, "Mammoth Cave changes the names of tours all the time, but it's way off in the boonies in Kentucky—not a prominent location at all!"

"Yes, that was a big drawback. Ideally, we'd like the cave to be under the Capitol Building in Washington, DC, or beneath the Tower of London or Big Ben."

I told him, "I doubt we can find a long cave like Mammoth Cave at 415 miles long, but since location is everything, I can look for the right cave *and* the right location for a hundred thousand per mile of cave passage including expenses." Apple agreed but wanted to know the location first before cutting a check. I thought about prominent locations. The Eifel Tower in Paris sounded about right. But there are catacombs and old sandstone quarries under

Paris, so that seemed too remote a possibility. How about Times Square in New York City?

Times Square is called "The Crossroads of the World" and "The Great White Way," plus the annual New Year's ball drop is conducted there, and the billboards are the fanciest in the world. Wow! A big *SEE APPLE CAVE* billboard! But could there be a cave beneath Times Square? A Google search on the subject revealed that on June 8, 2018, a rumbling sound was heard beneath Ripley's Believe It or Not Museum in Times Square. It may have been in conjunction with sewer construction, but a sinkhole and cavern opened. That was all I needed!

The bedrock geology of Manhattan Island shows metamorphic rock (sedimentary rock modified by heat and pressure). But in the vicinity of Times Square, there is a lens of Ordovician-aged marble. A cave indeed—albeit a small one—but big enough to rename Apple Cave? Better yet, *Apple Caverns*?

Investigating anything around Times Square is a hassle, due to Homeland Security. I contacted the New York City Movie Production Assistance Department and filled out their form requesting permission to photograph the cave at Times Square. Armed with the approved form, I headed uptown.

Times Square is a busy place at all hours of the day and night. I looked around to get my bearings. I recognized the Flatiron Building built in 1902, an early skyscraper. Ripley's Believe It or Not Museum was there, as well as an entrance to a tunnel between Rockefeller Center and Times Square and connecting to the subway. How to find directions to the cave? A shabbily dressed guy wearing a yellow hard hat approached me. "You from outa town?" he asked. "Be happy to show you around . . . but first, gotta ten? I haven't had brunch yet." He said his name was Broadway Joe.

I said I'd take him to brunch if he'd help me find something. "Sure thing!" Over brunch, I told Broadway Joe what I was looking for, the cave under Times Square. "We'll start with the tunnel near Believe it or Not. I live there at night, so I know all about it." We descended a staircase near the museum. We walked down to the subway, put two tokens into the turnstile, and went to the end of the platform.

There my guide jumped down onto the track and led me into the gloom. "Don't hit the hot rail!" he yelled. Flashlight on, we came to a ladder going down. We were in a large sewer tunnel, maybe twenty feet in diameter with a narrow walkway on one side. In another thirty feet, we stepped sideways into a niche. "Welcome to my home!" He kicked aside a pile of sleeping bags and blankets, revealing a manhole cover. Under it, a ladder led still lower.

The walls paralleling the ladder were rougher than concrete. It smelled moist, like cave air. At the bottom of the ladder, we stepped off into a cave. The circular cave room was about sixty feet in diameter by five feet high. A tiny stream trickled across the floor and disappeared into a crack at the far end of the room. With my Disto-X I shot rays into all parts of the cave. The room measured about fifty-three feet in diameter and 832.5 square feet in volume. I told Broadway Joe I'd pay him 25 percent for his help.

I called Apple on Johnnie Sapseed's private cell number. "I found Apple Caverns. That's the good news. The bad news is that it's only fifty-three feet long with a volume of eight hundred thirty-three square feet. But the location *is* under Times Square. It's a hundred-thousand-dollar location." I reminded him that it is "Location, Location, Location."

Johnnie Sapseed replied, "It's one percent, one percent, one percent . . . I'll send you a certified check for one percent of a hundred thousand. That's a thousand dollars." My expenses: $620 airfare, $250 finder's fee for Broadway Joe, $20 for two breakfasts, $200 for hotel, $3 subway fare = $1093. I was out $93 for my contribution to Apple! No wonder Apple is so big and so rich!

Caving does not pay!

THE LONGEST QANAT

Fresh water is scarce throughout the Middle East. Petroleum is plentiful. Water- and oil-well drilling require abundant water to lubricate the diamond drill and to flush out loose tailings from the deepening well. Deep-well drilling provides developmental water in northeastern Saudi Arabia, Kuwait, Iraq, and Iran. Potable water for drinking has been necessary forever.

Hafar al-Batin is a city located at the northeast end of the Arabian Gulf near Kuwait. A cave two kilometers from this Saudi city intersected a qanat. What is a qanat? There is abundant fresh water in the Iranian plateau northwest of this area. Ancient Persians in the first millennium BCE—predecessors to Iranians—developed underground aqueducts to carry fresh water as much as seventy kilometers from the plateau to cities. Some fifty thousand of these dug subterranean conduits were constructed. Today, about thirty thousand qanats still carry potable water from upland caves and springs. These water tunnels were hand-dug in an A-shaped cross section, carefully leveled so water would flow downhill by gravity. Vertical access shafts were dug every thirty meters or so for the initial excavation, where dug-out material was hauled out by leather bagfuls and for periodic maintenance.

Alibaba Cave, outside of Hafar al-Batin, is developed in limestone. A dry cave, it contains many stalactites and stalagmites, draperies, cave onyx curtains, and flowstone—all bone dry. In the farthest recess of the cave, the passage intersects a vertical shaft into a qanat carrying flowing water. Our expedition's objective was to map this qanat and discover the water source.

Ours was an international expedition. I will use anglicized names: Mark from KSA, Ata from Iran, Hugh from the UK. I was the only American caver. We knew from ancient manuscripts that the vast qanat network covered a wide area of Iran, Kuwait, and Saudi Arabia, so we had packed supplies for a multi-week cave surveying expedition. I had brought two sets of Disto-X survey instruments, a tablet computer, and an automated pen plotter for drawing the map. These instruments and related equipment would give us real-time cartographic capability underground and above.

Heavily loaded with gear and supplies, we entered the cave, moving past beautiful cream and orange dripstone formations. The temperature was about 85° F. After one hour, we arrived at a shaft dropping into the qanat. We tied a rappel line onto a column and descended approximately ten meters into a shallow stream flowing from northwest to southeast. The passage was A-shaped, seven feet high at its peak and six feet wide at the streambed. Pick marks on the wall revealed the hand-dug origin of the qanat. I spotted a cave blindfish in the stream, indicating a cave origin for the water.

We could survey rapidly since the cross section was mostly uniform. I figured we could go for ten or twelve hours before making camp. Our supplies would last for weeks.

The stream passage was uniformly pitched at an incline of +1° upstream and straight on a heading of 38° (NNE) with occasional departures of 1–2° from the 38° orientation. Honestly, this cave surveying was the most boring I have ever experienced because we racked up two-hundred-foot shots in a straight line hour after hour after hour. Every fifty meters or so, a dark shaft led upward. After approximately 106,000 feet (twenty miles) of survey, we calculated our rough position as under a corner of Kuwait. Here we found three remarkable objects.

Item 1. A T-shaped wood structure with a hole in the base of the T. Both pieces of wood were about one meter long. We knew the technology of qanat construction was an ancient mystery—how to maintain the direction and how to maintain the one-degree pitch so water would flow downhill?

Ahaa! The device we found was a primitive clinometer. It was held upside down with a cord strung through the hole and a plumb bob at the end of the cord. When the base was aligned with the passage floor, the clinometer would be tilted one finger width—one degree—down.

Item 2. We found nearby a wooden stick a half-meter long with a hole at either end. When the construction team laid out the route of the qanat, they placed rocks thirty meters apart on the surface in a line directly pointing at the destination. Each rock marked where the next shaft would be sunk. The stick with two holes was aligned with the next rock on the surface and the stick lowered down to the tunnel. That provided the direction for the next horizontal dig. We had solved two ancient mysteries!

Item 3. The last thing we found was a reservoir (anbar), a stone-lined tank or chamber, ten meters long, wide, and high that holds water for a town or farm above.

The qanat continued on the other side of the anbar. We camped for the night and plotted our map. We were headed straight northeast into Iran toward the mountainous plateau.

Many days later, we had surveyed well over two hundred kilometers of the qanat, and, by my calculation, we were directly beneath Ghar Perau, a 751-meter-deep cave in the Zagros Mountains of Iran. Our way upward was blocked by a breakdown choke, but a waterfall merrily splashed through the rock choke. We realized we had not only solved the mystery of how the qanats were constructed, but how that famous cave—thought to end by a British expedition—actually delivered sumped water into our qanat. We decided to keep the length we had surveyed secret so we could return to survey the downstream qanat from Alibaba Cave, and then reveal the length.

We would have presented a learned professional paper on our sensational findings, but Mark warned that we were not equipped with the official visas to allow such an investigation. Immigration authorities from Kuwait and Iran would become enraged, and arrest and incarcerate us for ninety-nine years for incursive trespass. It could cause a United Nations scandal!

Sadly, we have kept silent about our discoveries until now. The international statute of limitations has run out, so we are revealing the world's and the century's most significant, stupefying, and wonderful speleological triumph.

LOST BOOK OF ZOLTAR

The dazzling white crystals of Rho Yerbote Cave left me breathless with excitement. My heart palpitated in wild astonishment. Could anything so bright exist in nature, except the noon sun viewed without eye protection? Three-dimensional white toothpaste commercials pale by comparison.

Those were my exact feelings when I first parachuted into Yucatan's impenetrable rainforest to check out a LiDAR trace of a dot next to some linear structures—probably walls—in a remote region of Mexico. I chose this mode of entry because Bill Steele had hired the helicopter for his Sistema Huautla expedition that month. The JN-4 "Jenny" biplane, a relic of World War I, was affordable at a thousand pesos (one way), but it limited me to caving alone (never safe). I checked my gear: helmet, three lights, rope, inflatable boat, UV lamp, snakebite kit, MREs (Meals Refused by Enemy), and GPS. The dot was a cenote some twenty-four meters in diameter with water at the bottom.

Naturally, I read the GPS while pumping up the boat and donning my gear. Unsurprisingly, the round cenote belled out to thirty-eight meters at the water surface, and a main trunk passage led in a NNE direction. An hour of steady paddling glided me past smooth walls of limestone to a subterranean beach of pure white sand. High on one side of the beach, I saw the blackened embers of an ancient campfire surrounded by the bones of three individuals with bird of paradise headdresses on their skulls and decked with lavish lapis lazuli necklaces set in gold medallions. I left the skeletons in situ as archaeological remains are best studied in place rather than in a museum.

Beyond the beach lay a canyon two meters wide by four meters high. The left wall was covered with the white crystals I told you about. Fortunately, I had brought my sunglasses and could see their facets reflecting white light in every direction. A typical crystal measured forty-seven centimeters from wall to tip. A thick sheet of these crystals packed together covered the wall from floor to ceiling and extended as far down the canyon as I could see. The canyon's right-hand wall was black and undecorated. Nothing to see here, folks.

Imagine my feeling of awe and shock as I gazed at this gleaming display of natural grandeur for thirty minutes! Each crystal glinted more dazzling and unique than its neighbor. Then I remembered my UV lamp. All mineralogists know that when UV light falls on calcite crystals, they glow even brighter but with an eerie blue-greenish hue. When the UV lamp is switched off, the glow continues, emitting stored photons for thirty seconds or more.

Bathed in teal-colored light, I caught a glimpse of a glow behind me in my Rolex wristwatch crystal. I turned around and was so startled I wet my pants!

On the plain black rock wall behind me, I saw glowing picture writing. It was in pre-Mayan characters, a continuous coda of stanzas. I switched off the UV lamp, and the glowing characters soon disappeared, leaving only the plain smooth black right-hand wall of the canyon passage.

How could it be? An unmarked, plain rock wall one minute, and the next, a veritable torrent of glowing characters? It was no accident. With ordinary cave headlights, the wall was plain, but under UV illumination, the characters glowed.

Three questions consumed me. Why hadn't I brought a change of pants? What was the message? Had pre-Mayans made a solution of calcite and water and painted the characters on the wall, invisible when dry? Fortunately, I had studied the Mayan language prior to my departure. The characters were not pictographs or representational artwork. And the characters were not individual letters.

Mayan characters are words. But the pre-Mayan language was largely unstudied. I could see a proto-serpent, I thought. And maybe an eye. I moved to the first character revealed by the UV lamp. (Maybe it was the last—many languages read right to left or bottom to top.) It was a delta. A delta could be the end of a river or the last fin on a fish. If the word was FINIS, that would be the end of the message, not the beginning! I took a chance and ran along the canyon to where the UV lamp revealed the beginning (or end?) character.

There was a suggestion of a human figure moving right to left. START? No, that would call for a left-to-right direction. RETREAT? maybe. How about BOOK? The second character resembled a fan of cards. Or a rainbow? An arch? (Not yet invented by Romans.)

A flash of a childhood experience—age six—hit me. The carnival came to my town every year. In the penny arcade, a glass case held a swarthy figure swathed in silk and wearing a turban. If you inserted a nickel, lights inside flashed on, and the closed eyes of the figure would open and stare at you. His bosom rose and fell. Then his hand would sweep slowly from left to right several times as his head turned to follow his hand over the fan of playing cards and crystal ball before him. Suddenly his hand would stop. His eyelids closed. And a printed card would fall out of the machine. His name: ZOLTAR. The fortune on the card I got said, "You will travel far and have good luck!"

Could that be it? BOOK of ZOLTAR? Since I had found it, maybe the LOST BOOK OF ZOLTAR? My UV lamp began to falter. I had lost track of time, so I hastened back to my boat and paddled back to fading daylight. I ascended and pulled my boat up after me. I knew it would be a long hike through the jungle to Cancun.

My trip report reached the Central Museum in Mexico City. A year later, I called the curator to find out what had become of my discovery. Sr. Rodrigo Gonzales said, "Glad you called, Ergor. We've translated the first four pages. It says, 'You will inherit money.' 'You will go on a journey.' 'You will have good luck.'"

I apologized for the interruption and thanked him. "Sorry, I have a call I must take on the other line." I said I would call him back. I was now almost certain I had found the LOST BOOK OF ZOLTAR.

CHINESE CAVE SEDIMENTS

The call from the Chinese embassy was from the chargé d'affairs. They wondered if I was an expert in the science of cave sediments. I asked why they wanted to know. They said they needed a cave sedimentologist and had only a ten-thousand-dollar consulting budget. I said I was the caver who had trained all the expert cave sedimentologists. The embassy said they would forward the paperwork, and I should prepare to come to China.

I called the only cave geologist I know who specializes in cave fill. "Rachel, what can you tell me about cave sedimentology?"

She replied, "The fine stuff is on top, and the big rocks are on the bottom. That's ninety percent of it."

I packed my cave gear and read the contract sent by email from Beijing. The air ticket was delivered later by courier. The smooth international flight brought me to the airport where I was met by Chinese cavers in a Range Rover 4WD. In perfect English, the leader said we were headed directly to the cave, stopping only for Chinese takeout.

Our destination was Mount Li (Lishan) outside Xi'an, Shaanxi, China. This karst region of springs and sinkholes was a source of jade and gold in the hills and mountains. Its history dates back to Qin Shi Huang, the first emperor of a unified China (221–210 BCE). I was told there was an interesting museum in the region, but a visit would have to wait until we investigated Shii Zoung Cave.

The entrance to Shii Zoung Cave was a crescent I estimated at 250 feet wide by thirty feet high. In the zone of darkness, the cave floor was perfectly flat. If there had ever been a river or breakdown, all trace was gone. "This is the sediment we seek your expertise on," said leader Won Zon Fuz." I paced from the left wall to the right wall and corrected my original guess—the cave was 248 feet wide. There was no elevation change in the red, sandy floor; no stream banks, valleys, or canyons. "Notice the fine sand on the floor. We should expect successively more coarse sediments as we go deeper." Several of our cave party took notes, and one woman took pictures. I indicated where we should start digging our test pit.

At a depth of six feet, the shovel struck something hard. We switched to the trowel and brush to prevent damaging anything. The sand made digging easy, and we soon uncovered a terracotta head wearing a red helmet. I explained, "That is a headlamp on the helmet." I no sooner said this than the red paint began to flake and spall off the helmet. The ensuing panic caused the leader, Won Zon Fuz, to rush out of the cave. I was told he was contacting his headquarters.

We halted the excavation, wondering when we might continue. The following day, a large helicopter bearing a red star windmilled down, carrying a sling holding a thirty-foot shelter. The shelter was connected to an in-cave environmental pod that would maintain a constant temperature and humidity. We could continue digging beneath the shelter pod, since the damaging dry air would be replaced by controlled air, saving the paint. We could continue digging with the environment stabilized.

How did the leader know to order the environmental pod? The leader explained that in 1974 farmers in a nearby field had found terracotta warriors—eight thousand of them—along with 130 chariots, 520 horses, and 120 cavalry horses all buried in a field. The terracotta figures were all painted bright colors that began flaking within a few minutes of being exposed to dry air. Humidification preserved the paint. The terracotta figure was orange, the color of fired field tile or bricks.

Over the next week of digging, we found figures with yellow, red, orange, blue, black, and white hard hats—all with headlamps. The full figures varied from sixty-eight to seventy-five inches tall. All eighty of the terracotta men and women wore kneepads, removing any doubt that they were anything but cavers!

At the feet of the figures was a simulated cave stream of mercury. Wading cavers!

Several planeloads of archaeologists arrived as we found caving artifacts—terracotta compasses, cave bags, and survey notebooks. Chang-ton, an archaeologist fluent in English, explained that the Chinese had invented the compass. (They also invented fireworks, but we found none of those.)

At the end of the month, a major scientific conference was held in the nearby warriors' museum. Briefly, some wood from the excavation had been radiocarbon dated to 132 BCE, placing the figures during the time of the first emperor of China, Qin Shi Huang. He was the first spelunker. Being in line for a royal future, Qin Shi wanted to prove the concept of his terracotta warrior funeral monument, so he experimented with a terracotta replica of his caving club, eighty strong. The prototype was a success, attested by the eight-thousand-strong army created later.

I was asked to address the conference on the fuel used in the headlamps. Since the lamps were not metal, but terracotta, they were not hollow and therefore contained no fuel. I saw the audience of scientists nod approvingly. Did the Chinese invent calcium carbide? Snake oil? Electricity?

When the first discovery of the terracotta warriors became known, every museum in the world wanted to host an exhibition. The warriors set attendance records in museums worldwide. The precursor experiment of eighty cavers by Qin Shi would not attract such crowds, but I was sure every caver would buy a ticket.

That was what I had been paid to find. (I never did find the bigger rocks Rachel said I would find.)

NETHERLANDS TREASURE CAVE

I'm as interested in treasure as the next person. I also wondered why nobody had written about the caves of the Netherlands. My search led to a blurry photo of a ticket office in Maastricht, Netherlands, where a map of a vast cave system adorned a high wall over a ticket counter. I learned that this Dutch city had a cave of some eighty kilometers in length beneath part of the city near Fort Saint Peter. Located in the southeastern section of the Netherlands, the city is close to Belgium.

Another account said there were two hundred kilometers of underground passages with twenty-three thousand passage junctions. That startling statement required expert investigation, and I was the only expert to have the week off. I flew to the airport seven kilometers north of the city of Maastricht and taxied into this picturesque major city. Historically, the city is extremely old. The museum contains dinosaur bones and Neanderthal artifacts. Vikings arrived about eight thousand years ago. Celt occupation dated to 500 BCE. Roman occupation dated from 375 AD. Wars and battles were frequent, and remnants of fortifications attest to a long military use. In World War II, citizens transferred paintings from the museum to the caves for safekeeping from bombing. The Germans occupied the city in 1939. The caves served as bomb shelters, and it is said Dutch partisans hid arms in the cave. I went to the north entrance, Grotten Noord, and purchased an eight-dollar ticket for the English language tour.

Our tour guide was Hans Andfeet, a Dutch caver who spoke perfect English. He told us the caves were not natural caves but underground tunnels used to mine limestone, which started in Roman times to produce building stones. The form of limestone is marlstone, easy to cut. The passages were later connected to forts around the city and were used to store cannon balls and powder. I asked if Hans had explored all the passages. Hans answered, "Indeed not. The map is hundreds of years old, and I suspect nobody has examined all the mines."

Hans showed us the part of the mine where paintings were stored during World War II. I was struck by a set of twisty little passages, all different, off to one side of the gallery. Using a penlight, I ventured a few feet into one branch and discovered a dip in the floor with a loose pile of rocks in the dip against the left wall. I had seen no breakdown before this, so I was naturally suspicious that the breakdown may have hidden a continuation of the mine passage. Hans allowed as to how he had never seen breakdown in the mine, but of course, he had seen breakdown many times in caves.

I asked Hans if he and some companions might be interested in an "off-book" trip into the cave to examine the breakdown. He winked and said, "Your reputation precedes you, Ergor! My two friends and I will meet you tonight at ten at the front entrance."

At five minutes to ten, three figures materialized from the darkness dressed in cave gear. Hans produced a key. We darted into the ticket office and down the stairs into the mine. There I was introduced to Pierre, Ingrid, and Alfonse. We exchanged pleasantries about how I became so wonderful and famous as a caver. We trudged to the twisty little passages and the breakdown. All agreed it was *not* natural. (Indeed, nothing was natural in the mine except the 11° C constant temperature.) For two hours, we moved breakdown and slowly revealed a buried wooden door with iron hinges and an iron latch. Excitedly, we entered a part of the mine not seen in ages. It was filled with paintings in wooden racks, as fresh as the day they had been hidden.

The first painting was a giant oil, three meters tall by twelve meters wide. Shown were 130 full-rigged sailing ships on a sea, each with cannon ports open, and top-gallant sails flying. The flags of Spain stood out straight in the strong breeze. My Dutch caver friends wondered what it could be. I told them it was the Spanish Armada that set sail in 1588 from Spain under the Duke of Medina–Sidonia. The fleet had sailed through the English Channel with eight thousand sailors, eighteen thousand soldiers, fifteen hundred brass guns, and a thousand iron guns. They intended to invade England and defeat Elizabeth I, putting an end to the Protestant religion and returning England to the papacy. Storms ultimately devastated the armada, although the English sailed against the armada with two hundred faster and more maneuverable ships. All were painted in exquisite detail. The painting had disappeared in 1613.

Our next painting treasure was an oil two meters tall by four meters wide of a lowlands landscape with windmills. Fluffy white clouds floated over a bright blue sky. But the windmills had no blades! Where the blade hubs would have been there were tiny holes. Behind the painting, we found twenty-nine sets of painted windmill blades, each with a clock-wheel on its axle. There were intricately forged chains and a central clock mechanism with two heavy weights attached to the chains. I guessed that the painting was the first animated landscape of the Netherlands with operating windmill blades powered by the clock mechanism behind the painting. At the beginning of the day, the janitor would raise the weights to power the chains that turned the windmill blades all day for the astonishment of museum visitors.

We found dozens of other paintings: Hans Brinker with his left hand in the dike breach that almost flooded the Netherlands. (The story said his finger plugged the dike leak, but the painting told the real story.) Winter ice skating on the Zuiderzee—the forerunner of modern ice hockey. The tulip and cheese market in Amsterdam in 1712 was displayed in bright colors. There was a massive portrait of Napoleon Bonaparte and his twenty-six marshals appointed between 1804 and 1815, with each whisker and epaulet in place. In short, we discovered a missing treasure trove of European art. I was sorry there had been no Vermeer or Rembrandt paintings, but despite that, our find was termed "the cave discovery of all time," by the Amsterdam *Daily Trombone.*

Our discovery was reinstalled in the Maastricht Museum of Art and was previewed by the crowned heads of the European Union. Hans Andfeet was at the gala event. He sidled over to me and said, "The management wanted to thank you for discovering this magnificent treasure and wanted you to have this." He handed me eight dollars and a lifetime pass to the caves of Maastricht.

VACUUM CAVE

A caver friend of mine suggested that I visit an inflatable cave. He said, "You can bounce around in it, collide with the stalactites and stalagmites, and never get hurt." I imagined how hollow, rubberized stalagmites would penetrate your skin like a black banana. A fall down a pit would feel like a fall onto a feather comforter. What is worthwhile about that? It strikes me that crawling in a pneumatic cave would be the reverse of real caving. Caving is the antithesis of mountain climbing—going down instead of up. But the antithesis of a cave would be a non-cave.

Caves are hard places made of jagged rocks, pointy speleothems, gritty gravel. Yes, I know there is soft squishy mud. But isn't risk part of the real caving experience? What's the risk of bouncing in a rubber room? Maybe if you launched your Zodiac inflatable boat in the Niagara River and had to bounce your way out *before* going over the falls, that would be a risk!

Since a cave is a void—an absence of rock and not a solid thing (like an inflatable cave), it is different from most tangible things in the world. The old riddle asks: What gets bigger the more you take away from it?* Think about that and you will understand what I mean—an inflatable object just *cannot* be like a cave.

An analog of a cave would have to be a vacuum cave. I could not visualize how this would work, so I made an appointment with

---

*Answer: A hole

a physicist at a nearby university. Dr. Kray Z. Gloo, PhD, welcomed me into his faculty office lined with shelves full of physics textbooks. "Publishers send them to me all the time, hoping I will require my class to buy them for a hundred twenty-eight dollars apiece. They're too expensive to throw away, and I already know everything about physics that's worth teaching," said Dr. Gloo. "Why do you wish to see me?"

Extending my hand, I introduced myself as the world's most wonderful caver and authoritarian on speleo-ephemera. I sketched out for him the inflatable cave problem, and he agreed it would just not be right to recommend the representation of nothing with something. "According to the laws of thermodynamics, you must represent nothing with nothing. Come down to my laboratory, and I will show you," said the physicist.

We descended several flights of stairs into the dimly lit second basement. His high-ceilinged lab was lined with racks of electronic instruments. A vessel of blue plasma pulsed and danced in one corner. A Van de Graaff generator sent long crackling sparks up slender rods; a pendulum as big as a bowling ball traced a track across a giant circle. He directed my attention to a giant Hoover vacuum cleaner, perhaps ten feet high.

"Our budget was severely cut," he said pointing to the huge vacuum cleaner, "so we had to improvise. The giant Hoover vacuum cleaner was left over when the New York World's Fair was dismantled in 1942. It gathered dust in a warehouse in Queens until I bought it for my antimatter experiments." Dr. Gloo was clearly pleased with his machine, his broad smile left no doubt. "Best of all, it works!"

I do not know anything about antimatter, so Dr. Gloo's explanation lost me with the words, "The Coriolis effect explains why water spins clockwise in the northern hemisphere, anticlockwise in the southern." Even my yawning did not slow nor halt his lengthy discourse that extended some thirty-two minutes by my watch. (Also, the Coriolis effect has been discredited.)

He showed me a live chicken in a cage. He placed the chicken in a tray beneath the business end of the Hoover. He threw switches to turn on various generators, fans, and compressors. Then he dramatically flipped the switch, and the chicken began to turn inside out. White feathers flew in all directions obscuring my view. The cloud of feathers shrank, and I could see that the chicken was no longer there!

"You may think the chicken has been sucked into the Hoover," he said, waiting for my response. My face registered sufficient wonder, so he proceeded: "The anti-chicken is still there but invisible. I have rearranged its molecular structure, replaced matter with antimatter, and created a fully functioning vacuum chicken!" I reached into the seemingly vacant tray and felt a strong peck on the back of my hand. Ouch!

"But Doctor Gloo, will it work on a cave?" My idea was to challenge Dr. Gloo to produce an anti-cave or vacuum cave, even if it became an invisible cave.

"Bring me a cave and I will convert it to an antimatter cave that you may take home and explore to your heart's content," The size limitation of his machine loomed as an insoluble barrier. Where could I find a cave small enough to fit into his converter?

Weeks went by. Where could I find a small enough cave for the professor's experiment? The answer came to me while examining my fossil collection. I found a "button," a piece of a crinoid stem weathered out of limestone of the Mississippian Period. An island in the Green River in Kentucky has a beach composed of lifesaver-like miniature donuts that were part of the stems from ancient sea animals. The largest were about a half-inch (thirteen mm) in diameter with a hole through the center. I picked out the best specimen. It measured about one-eighth inch (three mm) thick. I hurried off to Professor Gloo's university office. A sign on his door told me he was not there but was in his laboratory. I descended the stairs two at a time.

In the gloomy subbasement, I heard the unmistakable sound of the spark generator—ZZZZZ, ZZZZZ, ZZZZZ. The door was ajar, so I pushed it open and entered. The doctor bent over his notebook. He wore large ear protectors and thick safety goggles. I cleared my throat several times, and he finally stopped writing and looked up. The plasma still pulsed in the background. "It's you," he said. "Did you bring me a cave?" He removed his earphones and glasses.

"A small one," I said, "but one that will fit in the tray of your antimatter reducer." He picked the crinoid button from the palm of my extended hand. He removed a jeweler's loupe and screwed it into his right eye.

"Are you sure this is a cave?" he asked.

"It is pure limestone of the Mississippian Period, a fossil crinoid button, but both the material and natural hole in the middle are exactly the same natural material as Mammoth Cave. There is no objective difference, since the limestone members containing Mammoth Cave—the Girkin limestone, Ste. Genevieve Limestone, and St. Louis limestone—are all made from microscopic fossil remnants of ancient sea life. Calcium carbonate, $CaCO_3$, through and through. It *is* a cave." I thought Dr. Gloo would be impressed by my superior scientific knowledge.

Very well, place the cave in the tray and stand back." Dr. Gloo switched on the associated compressors, fans, and generators. Then he fired up the mighty Hoover vacuum machine. There was a loud "*Foop!*" and the tiny cave disappeared before my very eyes. "You may approach now," he said removing his protective equipment.

I placed my thumb and forefinger in the tray. I felt the invisible thing and picked it up, only there was literally nothing to see. "Congratulations," he said, "you now own the only antimatter vacuum cave in the world!" He generously said I might keep it. So, I thrust it in my pocket, thanked him, shook his hand, and left his laboratory.

I carried my vacuum cave around for three weeks. It turned out to be magnetic, not just for all metals, but for pocket lint, hair, gum wrappers, pens, rubber bands, and trimmed fingernails. It soon resembled a hair-covered bowling ball with all manner of rubbish and junk magnetically sticking to it. Worst of all, it grew larger daily! If I tried to show it to friends, it attracted their dandruff flakes, barrettes, pencils, pens, earrings, chewing gum, cigarettes, eyeglasses, and rings. Those objects literally flew to my vacuum cave and sometimes caused pain when they hit the growing ball with unexpected force. If it reaches medicine ball size, I am afraid I can no longer carry it around.

I will happily trade my vacuum cave for an inflatable pneumatic cave, sight unseen and no questions asked—or answered. Would you like to hear my take on the law of unintended consequences?

FORT HEELBLISTER CAVE AND THE MILKY WAY DISCOVERY

In 1875, a decade after the Civil War, the US Government detached the 3rd Battalion from the army's 47th Regiment to establish an outpost thirty-two miles NNE of Fort Stanton, New Mexico. Fort Heelblister was named in honor of Lt. General Reginald S. Heelblister who led the 47th regiment in a battle against the locust swarms that plagued the desert southwest. The campaign was a failure because the soldiers of the battalion were outnumbered by the billions of locusts. The locusts were united in a strong and very organized battle formation that completely humiliated the soldiers.

The fort was located near a water source, a sinkhole that was incorporated within the stockade's perimeter. Opening off the sinkhole's bottom was a cave, coincidently enough named Fort Heelblister Cave. From inscriptions on the wall, we know soldiers visited the cave with their wives on Sunday and Monday, and with their sweethearts on Saturdays. Some 4.62 miles of the cave were surveyed by Sgt. G. Brick but without cross sections or a north arrow.

I was contacted last year by US Bureau of Land Management (BLM) State Director Sage B. Rush, to resurvey the cave to contemporary standards and offered a no-bid contract for $15,238, which I accepted. Since solo surveying is not safe, I recruited local cavers John McMac, Barb Wyer, and Lew Skinflint to round out my mapping team. We arrived at the cave late on a Thursday in June, set up camp, and inventoried our caving gear. McMac was six feet nine inches with red hair, freckles, and a red bandanna over his face. Lew was four-foot-two, white haired, and covered with tattoos of all known western cattle brands and figures of line-dancing cowboys. Barb wore a broad smile and a merry twinkle in flashing blue eyes. They were reputed to be renowned cavers.

The next morning after a hearty breakfast of Spam, eggs, pancakes, waffles, bacon, sausage, biscuits, gravy, and two gallons of coffee, we elected to delay our entry by two days. We reached a stopping place at a terminal breakdown, known to be so by its name on the old map—Grand Central. I calculated the error of closure at two-tenths of a foot while John, Barb, and Lew cursed and moved rocks on the left side of the breakdown. The ensuing wind blew out all our electric LED lamps, leading us to believe a tornado whirled outside the cave or a borehole beckoned beyond the breached breakdown.

We celebrated our breakthrough beyond the breached breakdown by eating three Mr. Goodbars apiece, three Paydays, and a Nature Valley Granola bar for health reasons. Two days later, we resumed our survey into virgin cave

Barb's trip report best describes our survey progress: "We were all armed with Disto-Zs so we could move briskly along the 47.8-foot-wide by 62.3-foot-high canyon, profusely decorated with conifer-sized stalagmites and VW-sized stalactites, glittering giant crystal chandeliers, and pipe-organ-sized flowstone walls in cream, orange, beige, mauve, and rosy-red velvet. Each successive room was larger or smaller and more or less decorated with bigger or smaller speleothems. helictites, angel hair, crystals as long as pole vault poles, and cave pearls like bowling balls. It was pretty unbelievable and vice versa." I admired her restraint and understatement.

One side lead angled down and promised more going-cave. We surveyed along a zigzag course and entered a passage with a glittering ceiling of stars, planets, and asteroids punctuating a black ceiling. It stretched around a curve far away, shedding sufficient light to read an apartment rental contract. Indeed, we had found the Milky Way underground. John said we must name it Milk Dude, but Lew said that sounded too much like Milk Duds. Nothing milky or dudish about that passage!

Barb asked to name it Snowy River. I said that sounded too much like Snotty River, and besides, Fort Stanton Cave already had a Snowy River. They'd never forgive us. I was paying the bills, so I said the name was Milky Way, in honor of the part of the galaxy that we could see under the New Mexico sky.

The following day, we left a note at the entrance and started the survey of the Milky Way. The passage headed more or less straight south, shot after shot. We were glad we had brought sufficient candy bars for a thirty-six-hour trip. Camping would have required logistics, so we agreed on a continuous survey. The "stars" on the ceiling of the passage continued to appear exactly as the Milky Way would have appeared on a night outdoors.

At the thirty-six-hour point, we stopped for candy bars. We had surveyed 12.9 miles (20.4 km). A stronger than normal breeze sprang up, and an owl hooted a spooky dirge. The new moon loomed on our right. Moon? "What the?!" Barb screamed. "We're outside!"

Outside? Yes, indeed. We were so fatigued by our repetitive two-hundred-foot-long shots and the 120-foot-wide passage hour after hour that we surveyed our way out an exit and had mistaken the real Milky Way for the cave ceiling! How long had we been outside? Did anyone notice coming out of the cave? Had we exited in daylight, I'm sure we would have noticed. Distant sirens caught our attention. Flashing red and blue lights bored into our little candy circle. Heavily armed swat troops in black coveralls, bulletproof vests, and black helmets surrounded us.

"Drop your bars!" they yelled through bullhorns. "Face down on the ground. Anyone who moves gets it!" Lew didn't move fast enough to please, so the lead trooper forced him upside down with his Koch & Heckler MP5 submachine gun. I heard radio traffic. "Yeah, we got 'em all. ten-four, ten minutes tops." We were zip-tied and dumped into the rear of two black SUVs.

At an underground sally port, we were stripped, read our rights, separated, and waterboarded. Finally, we were blindfolded, prodded into a blacked-out minibus, and delivered to Fort Heelblister as the sun was rising in the east. We were never told where we were or why the black ops didn't use black helicopters. And we don't know where the cave ended and the outdoors began, so we don't know the real length of the Milky Way passage.

MY (SECRET) CORVETTE ADVENTURE

When the floor of the Corvette Museum in Bowling Green, Kentucky, collapsed into a sinkhole in February 2014, the story was widely reported. The forty-foot-diameter cavity was located directly beneath the dome of the museum. The floor fell in, dropping eight classic Corvettes into a thirty-five-foot-deep sinkhole. That sort of collapse happens frequently in Bowling Green, so it should not come as a surprise.

Credit: National Corvette Museum

George Philips, a West Virginia caver who is not as good a caver as me, suspected that I had something to do with it. "Sounds like something Ergor would be involved in," he said.

My caver friend Roger Brucker, who is also not as good as me, suspected my connection with the Corvette story. Roger said I had mud on my upper lip. Shifty eyes, too. I said I would take the Fifth before saying anything publicly. I swore him to secrecy. But I think he betrayed my trust. Since he spread the secret story widely, I am still swearing my readers to secrecy. Here's my story (to correct the outrageous rumors that are circulating).

I discovered Storm Trooper Cave (not to be confused with State Trooper Cave under Dishman Lane in Bowling Green) in 2010. The entrance is a shallow sinkhole on the property that used to be the I-65 southbound rest area northeast of Bowling Green. I made a series of trips with Ellie Babba and Sid Badd (names changed to protect my companions). We surveyed our way to the Corvette plant, plotting the survey to end just at the end of the production line door where they drive away the finished Corvettes. We found a breakdown there; according to our map, it was in the right place to intercept the next few autos off the line at the end of their night-shift break. Our aim was to equip ourselves with new Corvettes. I poked at the breakdown with a long bar. Soon the whole thing collapsed just as I jumped out of the way to safety. I thought we had hit the jackpot as several Corvettes appeared in a blinding blur as they descended.

Ellie Babba, Sid Badd, and I picked our way through the muddy pile, seeking the new Corvette of our color choice. Imagine our shock when the cars in the pile were *old* Corvettes, not the new ones we hoped to appropriate! Zounds! A screw-up!

We retreated to a secret basement in Bowling Green and discovered that survey decimal-point errors had taken us 1,523 feet beyond the end of the production line, across the road and under the Corvette Museum. Rats!

The reason you—and you alone—are sworn to silence is it would never do for it slipping out that we made stupid survey errors. I am, after all, the world's foremost cave explorer, a reputation dearly earned and deserved through vivid writing. It is common for caves to plot out short, but almost unheard of to goof on the long end of the cave! My friends Ellie Babba and Sid Badd say that unless I deliver to them a promised new Corvette of their color choice, they will never cave with me again! You can help me save my reputation with them by sending me $256,000 in small bills.

Roger Brucker said he was not sure he believed my story. He thought I had sabotage in mind from the beginning. If he sent the money I asked for, he feared he would be tarred by the same sloppy survey brush. I was shocked! Shocked, I say, that he would think ill of me!

One of those Eastern cavers, Danny Brass, could not understand how a cave could be plotted long or short. I had to explain to him that we had misplaced (omitted) survey-distance decimal points when making the map. That did not satisfy skeptical Danny! Most cave surveys plot out to show the cave that really exists, neither too short nor too long. If the survey book pages stick together, I can see how a cave might be plotted too short. And I can see that if you plotted the same pages twice, the cave would look too long.

First, you need to know that I, Ergor Rubreck, am a wonderful cave survey expert. So expert in fact that I measure shots to thousandths of a foot. Second, the note taker (not *me*) misplaced the decimal points in the book. So, 49.879 feet became 498.79 feet. Any fool can easily see that a few such errors would make a cave plot long. No, I did not draft the map of Storm Trooper Cave, so nobody can accuse *me* of survey incompetence.

I hope readers who really appreciate precision surveying will send money so that my so-called friends Ellie Babba and Sid Badd will go caving with me. They are not as good as me, but if I don't receive enough money to buy them new Corvettes, I fear they will never cave with me again, and they will spread hateful stories about me.

Mum's the word.

CAVING IN TAG: PLUMBING THE DEPTHS

The caves of TAG (**T**ennessee, **A**labama, and **G**eorgia) are some of the deepest caves in the United States. I wanted to try some of the most challenging of those caves since I had already conquered—or attempted to conquer—deep caves in Mexico and Ukraine. I called Fumbler Nerdwell, NSS #29453, a veteran deep caver in Birmingham, Alabama, to see if he would take me to Fern Cave. "Nah, you don't want to tackle that. It's a wimp cave. Every Boy Scout in these parts has gone down it on a clothesline. *You* want to go to a *real* cave!" Fumbler said, whetting my interest immediately.

"What do you have in mind?" I asked. He told me he was leading a survey trip in two weeks to the brand-new Bottomless Cave, and he'd be honored to have me along. Since I am famously known as the most successful and wonderful caver of all time, I wondered if he was playing to my well-deserved reputation. I generally know the difference between sincerity and flattering B.S. (a few detractors say I am an expert at one or both of those), but he sounded so sincere.

We agreed to meet at a Baptist church near the cave in Nosebleed, Georgia. (Most of the caves in TAG are less than 300 feet from a Baptist church.) Two weeks later, I pulled into the parking lot of the Free Will Flaming Pillar of Fire Baptist Reformed Tabernacle, where various caver cars were parked. Surprisingly, Fumbler was small for his size. I had imagined a seven-foot giant with rippling muscles, but Fumbler was about four feet seven inches. "My mom and pop were short," he explained.

A short walk through a pine and old-auto-body forest led to a yawning sinkhole. There, Fumbler wrapped a new five-hundred-foot rope around a live tree and tied a figure-eight knot in the end. He cast the rope into the pit entrance. "You can have the honor of being the first down. We don't know how deep she is. You can tell us," Nerdwell said. With a name like Bottomless Cave, I was concerned whether the rope had indeed reached the bottom. With everybody watching, I wound the rope through my sodium-cooled eight-brake bar rack. I descended in a shower of dirt and rocks and subsequently through an ice-cold water cascade. The dark was so thick, I could not see the walls, floor, or ceiling. I passed through the rusted engine compartment of an old Blue Bird school bus lodged on a ledge. Thank heaven there was no engine in it, and the hood was open. My feet contacted a flat rock just before the knot at the end of the rope.

As I turned my light on to the highest turbo setting, a note fluttered down from above. It read, "Yell if you want us to come down. We can't hear you, so we are coming down anyway. Watch out for falling stuff." It was signed Nerdwell Fumbler, NSS #29,453. I scooted back under a protective ledge as four cavers successively slid into view.

"You scope it out yet?" Fumbler asked. I told Fumbler I had eaten a Snickers bar and found a six-inch-high drain, but no leads. "No leads? Hell, you city slicker cavers don't know Shinola about TAG caves. You got to bring the leads with you!"

Fumbler broke out his candy bar stash—mini-Mounds, M&Ms (peanut), and Hershey's Kisses. Short rations for a short caver. He had a half-pint jar of burgoo that he downed with one gulp. I had expected he'd bring chitlins and pickled pigs' feet, but that was just my stereotypical expectation.

"How do you *bring the leads with you*?" I wanted to know. He held out his survey notebook and showed me a column of two- and three-digit random numbers: 27, 136, 84, 15.3, etc.

"Run your finger down the column and pick one," he said, holding out his notebook. I ran my muddy finger down the column of numbers, stopping near the bottom. I had selected 72.6. "That's your lead—Ergor Hole—she's seventy-two point six feet deep." Fumbler seemed elated. "You city cavers usually pick Shinola leads, like three feet or twelve-point-six feet." The three other cavers had reached the bottom of Bottomless Cave. "How deep did you make it?" queried Fumbler. The others said 461 feet from the rig point to the bottom. "Okay, five hundred thirty-three point six feet it is," said Nerdwell, "including Ergor Hole."

Shouldn't we take some pictures?" I suggested. "Newsletter readers will want to see what we found."

"Nah, t'weren't nothin'. A wimp cave. Not worth Shinola," said Fumbler, tossing his head. That smarted a little—after all, *my* lead had extended the original depth of Bottomless Cave!

It was time to leave Bottomless Cave. Jim-Bob Jackson went first, then Billy-Bob E. Lee. Cissy Nerdwell, Fumbler's sister, was next in line. When she had been gone twenty minutes, I clamped my ropewalkers on the dangling Bluewater line. The jerking rope told me the others were still ascending. When Fumbler Nerdwell reached the top of the rope, we packed the gear and drove to the Eat & Get Gas Restaurant for a big bowl of burgoo, crackers, pickled beets, and eggs. I bid farewell to my newly found TAG caver friends and said I'd never forget their generous invitation.

About a year later, I heard that Fumbler Nerdwell had died a horrible death. The account was in *American Caving Accidents*. He was leading a Boy Scout trip to Bottomless Cave. On his way out of the cave following the last Scout, the hood of the school bus slammed shut, severing the clothesline and plunging him to the bottom of the so-called Bottomless Cave. I was glad the account left out the name of the only lead, notwithstanding my sincerest sympathy for Fumbler's family.

SIJU CAVE ADVENTURE

In my search of the globe for unexplored caves that could challenge me, I saw that India has many caves, but most are carved out of rock by religious Buddhists. On the other hand, Siju Cave near Napak Lake in the northeast state of Meghalaya, India, is more than four kilometers long. Found in 1927, Siju Cave is also known as Bat Cave. In addition to stalactites and stalagmites and thousands of bats, Siju is described as having passages filled with water (the photos show water on the floor of a passage to a depth of about one foot). The most startling comment was, "There are many unexplored caves in the region, mostly filled with water." Unfortunately, the length of the unexplored caves is not given. Nor is the depth of the water.

I booked tickets to India with a bus trip to Balphhakram National Park—the place nearest Siju Cave. Naturally, I did not want to cave alone, especially in a wet cave, so I sought the assistance of the Delhi Speleological Society. They said they had an "away team" of three cavers ready to go caving at a moment's notice. I contacted them by phone and verified that all of them had scuba divers' wetsuits. They were eager to join my expedition to the undiscovered cave system near Siju Cave.

The team's leader was Bagshesh Shesh Kabab, a tall man about twenty-five years old who had led cave trips all over the Middle East. The second caver was Anishshesh Shestemic Foulard, a former Indian bush pilot, about twenty-two, who always wore khakis. Sheshbigorie Ashish, an attractive woman caver from Hyderabad in the south of India, was the third. She is a PhD biologist who wrote her thesis on Indian bats.

We departed the bus and organized all our equipment for the survey trip into a new spring cave named Sheshbesh Shaloom. This was next door to Siju Cave. I knew that for flowstone speleothems to exist, there must be an upper level to this new cave system. We waded into an oval opening four meters wide by six meters high with ankle-deep water. At the second lead upward, I suggested departing the river passage and surveying any upper levels first. We climbed a ten-meter pitch and crawled into a window that led to a trunk passage after fifteen meters. Stalactites, stalagmites, draperies, and columns were everywhere. Hundreds of bats clustered on the ceiling, chirping loudly. We stripped off our hot wetsuits.

I squeezed into a small lead in the wall and found myself stuck. A rock had fallen on my left leg. The others fastened a rope around my torso and pulled until I screamed in agony that my ribs were breaking. Fortunately, Sheshbigorie had a flask of palm oil. She poured it down my left leg until my toes felt soggy. Then the others pulled again, and I popped out like a champagne cork.

Our next problem occurred when we came to a narrow spot in the passage interrupted by a deep pit. A ledge led around the left side. I carefully crawled across it on my hands and knees. The others followed. As the last caver crossed, the ledge gave way and plunged into deep water at the bottom of the pit thirty meters below. The last caver was safe, but there was no retreat—we were cut off! Since we had come this far, I argued that we should continue to survey to at least leave a record if there was no way out. Our dead bodies would mark the place where our survey ended. Fortunately, in 120 more stations, we exited on a cliff about 220m above the entrance.

Safe, but not safe. We had brought a thirty-two-meter length of rope that proved one-seventh as long as necessary to rappel to safety. Daylight was fading fast, and we were trapped in an unexplored Indian cave, poking our heads out of a perched entrance on a cliff 220m up on a sheer wall. Our joint cries for help in six different languages summoned nobody.

I told the party that our lives depended on finding an alternative route to the entrance level of the cave. We ate our last meal of chicken masala and scrambled back to the passage we had surveyed. At the brink of the pit—where no return route existed—we aimed our lights into the pit. About thirty meters down, there was a dark shadow on one wall. Was it just a shadow? Or a lead? Vertical shafts often have paleo-drains that are abandoned as the shaft deepens itself. Without any alternative, I decided to rappel into the pit to check the shadow. If the dark "lead" was any lower, I knew we'd be sunk since that was the full length of our rope. I drove a bolt into the wall, tied the smallest anchor knot I could to the bolt, and prepared to descend.

"Tie an overhand knot in the end of the rope," yelled Bagshesh. I snugged it tight to prevent falling off the rope's end, then backed down the pit wall. My feet moved away from the wall, then arced into the lead. It was an abandoned drain, just as I suspected. The others rappelled down, but we had to leave our only rope dangling from the bolt at the top of the pit.

We were moving through a tall canyon maze, heading lower into the system. The walls were wetter now, and the floor was muddier than printers' ink. The ceiling lowered over a pool that sumped within one meter. Too bad we no longer had wetsuits. There was no airspace and a passage only a half-meter in diameter. I said I would try to penetrate the sump even at the risk of drowning. On the other hand, if I made it through okay, I'd signal the others to follow. Sheshbigorie removed her knitted sweater and began to unravel the yarn into a single strand. I would carry the end as I dove the sump. Safely through, I'd tug the yarn to signal others to follow.

After holding my breath for one meter, I surfaced in air. I tugged the yarn, and the next caver emerged. All four of us were now on the other side of the sump but shivering with onsetting hypothermia. It was time to move or die! We did jumping jacks to revive our numbing bodies. In two hours, we had climbed down canyons, traversed ledges, and stuffed ourselves through a tiny hole in the top of a passage. There was a survey station—ours! We were in the entrance passage only a few meters from outside.

I told the crew we would resume our survey at ten o'clock the next night. However, they never showed up!

There's a great cave in India I'd like to interest you in. Sponsorship is still available.

EXPLORING THE CAVES OF ZANZIBAR

The kid looked like he'd just come to my lecture to embarrass me, as if he had done some obscure cave exploring that I had not already done years earlier. I know the type: vigorous hand-waving to be chosen to ask a question. Flashing eyes and a smirk to indicate his "superior knowledge." I, of course, called on him immediately, knowing that my wonderful knowledge of caves would eclipse his naive, trick question.

"Mr. Rubreck," he said, "You claim to have explored caves from A to Z. Lots of caves have names starting with A, but no caves have names starting with Z. So, I challenge you to tell us one cave you've explored that starts with Z."

I struck a thoughtful pose to catch the expected attention of my audience—and added a twenty-second pause to build maximum tension. "The caves of Zanzibar, son," I said. "In the year 1999, I explored the three named caves in Zanzibar—Kuza Cave, Tazari Cave, and the underwater-connected caves called Kiwengwa Caves." I described my snorkel tour of those caves during the next hour of my talk. As I was recounting my adventures, the audience diminished one by one until midnight when only the wise-guy kid was left.

Qatar Airways made my visit possible when they were setting up their global route network. They wanted to popularize some of the more remote destinations. Zanzibar Island is really many small islands and two larger islands located in the Indian Ocean fifteen miles off the coast of Tanzania in Africa. The PR head of Qatar Airways knew of my reputation as the most wonderful cave explorer and that I might report on the caves of Zanzibar for *National Geographic Magazine.*

Zanzibar has been populated for twenty thousand years and has been the object of studies by archaeologists and paleontologists. Natives developed pottery. Paleontologists have discovered old bones of a large crocodile and a giant rat. The islands are a source of many spices—cloves, nutmeg, cinnamon, and black pepper—but tourism is the principal economic activity.

Visitors don't go to Zanzibar unless they have plenty of money. I stayed in the Zawadi Hotel ($960 per night and up) and would not have survived except for the generosity of Qatar Airways. The warm, blue waters off the coast of Zanzibar, good for snorkeling, are the main tourist feature, followed by shopping among the quaint shops of natives selling their crafts.

But what about those caves? If you rate world-class caves on a scale of 0 to 100, then I'd rate the caves of Zanzibar somewhere near -100. A few of them have small stalactites and stalagmites that are mud-covered, dull gray, and unappealing. I saw water in several—sumps that could be dived with a mask and snorkel to a depth of ten feet. After one dive, the stirred-up sediment prevented me from counting my fingers. One cave has a pool that connects to an adjacent cave or two (I've been told) and is approximately at sea level. These caves are commercialized only because there is little else to do if you don't fancy drinking and snorkeling while further bronzing your suntan.

Why, then, is Zanzibar memorable? It may be valuable to a small circle of speleologists who are acquainted with a wild cave I discovered on an outlying island. I won't name the island because to do so would invite vandalism. I'll call it Ergor Cave (not its real name). The cave's distinction is having the largest cave pearls known to humankind. Most of the pearls are the size of basket-balls. The largest was the size of a medicine ball. You can see how such prize speleothems would soon occupy the mineral specimen cabinets of every university geology department worldwide. They'd be collected to extinction.

When I first entered Ergor Cave, I was astonished to see on the ceiling a colony of gigantic fruit bats some two feet long with a wingspan of six feet. Their guano covered the basketball-size cave pearls, so the mineral depositional forms were obscured by the organic depositional waste product. In other words, thick bat shit.

A few of the cave pearls were broken, revealing a solid interior with a core of a single sand grain. I estimated the weight of one pearl at fifty-nine pounds. I did not lift any additional cave pearls because that first one stained my new white coveralls an ugly dark brown that even Tide detergent could not erase. I didn't taste the bat scat. It might have contributed to Zanzibar's spice trade.

In the dead center of the 250-foot diameter round room was what looked like a stalagmite, but on closer examination it proved to be a sculpture of rounded forms resembling a giant fertility doll. It was lumpy, reminding me of the Pillsbury Doughboy, but nine feet tall. In the center of its forehead was what looked like a twenty-five-carat diamond that glinted and shot rays of reflected (or refracted) blue light onto the walls, floor, and ceiling of the room. I regretted I could not reach the diamond to bring it back so mineralogists or gemologists could analyze it.

Come to think of it, the gemstone was probably tanzanite, not diamond, since the island was only fifteen miles off the coast of Tanzania. Semiprecious tanzanite is worth roughly one-four-thousandths of the value of a similar-size diamond. Since my plane was scheduled to leave in four hours, I regret I could not survey the cave and take photographs. Please don't tell other cavers about Ergor Cave . . . it's our secret alone.

BODY-SLICK™ EXPERIENCE

All the cavers I admire have failed to squeeze through a crack that perhaps prevented the discovery of a lifetime. I am average size: 180 pounds., sixty-nine inches tall, thirty-eight-inch waist. Early in my caving career, I could fit through the Crack in the Ceiling in Floyd Collins's Crystal Cave. But since 2005, that crack has either narrowed, or I have increased in size. One day, I saw an ad in a prison trade magazine for BODY-SLICK™, a liquid-lube that would enable prisoners to squeeze through jail bars.

An example of reverse marketing, the BODY-SLICK company was trying to sell out its total inventory to jailers, to keep the liquid off the market and away from criminal escape artists. I called the manufacturer and spoke to the company president. "I could send you a trial bottle, Mr. Rubreck, if you will only use it in cave exploring and not jail breaking." He explained that BODY-SLICK works externally and internally. "Rub it on your body and you can squeeze through five and a half or six inches. Drink one ounce and it lubricates the bones so you can make it through even tighter squeezes." He assured me BODY-SLICK is non-toxic.

Below is my mixed review of BODY-SLICK:

It takes getting used to. After drinking a small quantity and rubbing the liquid on my clothes, I tried to eat lunch. My fork and spoon squirted out of my hand and flew across the room. Mac and cheese flew all over the kitchen. I swallowed tomato soup okay, but the bowl shattered into a hundred pieces when I set it down on the table.

In Crystal Cave, I slipped effortlessly through the Crack in the Ceiling. Later, in Cave City, Kentucky, I was walking to the Mexican restaurant when a dodgy-looking thug stepped out of an alley. He threw his arms around me. immobilizing my arms briefly. He growled. "Your wallet or your life!" I squirted out of his arms and shot twenty feet away to safety.

Having such slippery clothes had drawbacks, such as sliding around on the driver's seat of my car. So I experimented with lubricating my nude body with BODY-SLICK, then donning my un-slicked clothes. If I were stuck in a cave, I could peel off my coveralls.

I had not counted on being arrested, however. After applying BODY-SLICK to my body, I put on my regular clothes. In a shopping mall, I passed the perfume counter in a department store. The salesclerk—a spectacular young woman—beckoned me to approach. I did, and she squeezed the rubber bulb on a jar of amber-colored fluid. It was some kind of cologne that irritated my nostrils. I sneezed an enormous, loud effusion, attracting the attention of all the customers in that half of the store. The shock of my sneeze caused all my clothes to fly off in all directions, leaving me standing by the perfume counter in my altogether! Somebody called security. They set a world record for fast response, surrounding me and handcuffing me (I slipped out of the handcuffs forthwith). The city police booked me on a charge of indecent exposure.

It was two years before I summoned the courage to experiment with my remaining supply of BODY-SLICK. In Millard Fillmore National Park is Badaire Cave. The Crack of Doom in that cave is only three and three-quarters inches wide. A light shown into it reveals a large room beyond with speleothems. Nobody has been able to fit through that small space and solve the puzzle of what marvelous prize awaits the first caver to reach the room and see the beautiful crystals.

Cavers had applied to seek the room. They had all been refused. The park superintendent knew that the explorers would try to "shave" or blast their way in. But the use of explosives is prohibited in National Parks. I explained to the park superintendent that I would use only BODY-SLICK on my person, and it was not flammable.

Not wanting to cave alone, I took Sam Ovarr, a Russian caver, along to Fillmore Park. I lubed myself thoroughly with BODY-SLICK, and a guide led us to The Crack of Doom. "We used to have a light in there so visitors could see some of the crystals. But the bulb burned out in 2011. Nobody could fit through the crack to put in a new bulb. Maybe you can fish the old bulb back out if you make it." I was skeptical of my ability to squeeze through that three-and-three-quarter-inch crack, but since Sam, the guide, and I were alone, I peeled off my cave clothes. It *was* a tight squeeze. I nearly panicked partway through. Sam said I turned a vivid red just before I popped through.

The so-called Big Room was about thirty feet in diameter by ten feet high. White crystals of gypsum decorated walls, ceiling, and floor. The tiny crack had preserved their dazzling beauty over the millennia. I changed the light bulb and wormed my way out. The park superintendent presented me with a certificate suitable for framing because I enabled park visitors to see the gypsum crystals after so many years of darkness.

Several years later, the Screw-Dup Grotto was celebrating its twentieth anniversary and advertised its new motorized squeeze machine and a $150 prize for the smallest caver. I knew I could win, using the remainder of my BODY-SLICK.

On the day of the contest, the Grotto officers treated me to lunch. You'd think they had never seen a cave celebrity before. A caver demonstrated the motorized squeeze machine. He flipped the switch, and the motor drove the nuts down the screws, bringing the beams together slowly. He forced his body through just as the dial indicator atop the machine hit 3.74 inches. If he had been a few seconds slower, he would've been melba toast.

I anointed myself with BODY-SLICK, wearing only my Speedo swimming trunks. I dove into the descending machine, swishing sideways like a fish. I could not see the clearance dial from inside the machine, but I could feel the beams exerting increasing pressure. My bones displaced with an audible *click-click*. I extracted my left ankle at the last moment with a mighty lunge. The cavers cheered. I had cleared 3.625 inches using the last of my BODY-SLICK.

WHITEWATER CAVES

hitewater rafting is a thrilling, heart-stopping river trip in which even experts sometimes plunge into the boiling churn. Voyages down Class V waters in kayaks may be more dangerous. Personal flotation devices notwithstanding, high-risk hazards include being held underwater in hydraulics, becoming locked against rock barriers, and overturning in high-velocity rapids. But what about whitewater caves?

If you have been caving for just a few years, you may believe there are no whitewater caves. Trickles of underground water are commonplace. Deep, slow-moving pools at the base level are well-known in caves such as Lost Sea and its Lost Sea, Howe Caverns' River Styx, and Mammoth Cave's Echo River. Where watery cave trips have been discontinued, the reason for the discontinuation is less likely due to risky safety considerations than to the fact that the cleanup of mud after flood events is very expensive.

However, my vast experience includes whitewater caving. Some years ago, I explored caves in the Andes Mountains of Peru. These snow-capped peaks are full alpine uplifts with summits above twenty thousand feet, and, with spring thaws, their cols carry wall-to-wall raging torrents. Caves in these mountains sometimes also contain rushing whitewater in their underground rivers. One such cave is in Aconcagua, the highest mountain in the Andes at 22,838 feet. The cave in conglomerate rock resembles a tunnel more than a cave because of the scouring deluge of water at a steep angle.

Having floated my way up Hawkins River in Mammoth Cave using an inner tube, I brought along a four-foot plastic kayak to South America, seeking a cave whitewater challenge. Sr. Pablo Diablo, Director General of the Argentinian Speleological Society, took me up to the famous cave's headwaters.

I pushed off from shore in the dark cave, my headlamp illuminating the frothing turbulence ahead. The current caught me in a rocket-launching acceleration where only my consummate skill allowed me to deftly avoid jutting rocks and center my craft on downstream *Vs*. As I was hurtling downstream, I feared there might be a sudden waterfall or drop ahead. Around the next bend, the roar of rushing water approached the intensity of Niagara Falls. My sturdy kayak tipped vertically and plummeted straight down ninety feet into a plunge pool.

An early teaching unit in kayak paddling is the Eskimo roll. This is a left-to-right 360-degree corkscrew where the paddler spirals underwater and comes back up on the other side dripping. It was at that moment that I perfected the end-over-end roll, now known worldwide as the Rubreck roll. Most kayakers will not try this dangerous maneuver without being heavily insured. When I reached the beach at the end of that trip, I was sopping wet and paralyzingly cold from the sub-freezing temperature.

Had I been using a carbide lamp on my hard hat, I'd have made that trip in the dark. Instead, I wore my lithium battery Cave-O-Lite providing fifty thousand lumens — even underwater.

Another unique experience was when I inner-tubed in literal whitewater. This was not an adventure in rushing water — in fact, the water was barely moving. North Dakota has vast fields of wheat. These are harvested by giant combines, and the wheat is trucked to milling companies and animal feed producers. In Bismark, North Dakota, there is a lazy river cave beneath the city. Compared to Lost River in Bowling Green, Kentucky, the Mustang Cave river is no great shakes. As I was floating in this river, the Moody & Thomas Milling Company suffered an explosion, and Harvest

Queen flour was broadcast over a twenty-hectare area. A gentle rain alleviated any risk of subsequent fire, but it washed some of the flour into sinkholes and down into the Mustang River. Floating on that river was like floating in a milk bath. I believe this was the only instance of cave whitewater referring to the color of the water. (To my knowledge there have been no accidental releases of white shoe polish from the Shinola® factory.)

My only other whitewater adventure was one summer when I attempted to shoot the Niagara River rapids above Niagara Falls. It was a time when I had applied to examine the hydroelectric tunnel providing power to Canada. The manager of Canadian Hydro rejected my application, pointing out that the tunnel was normally running pipe-full and that if I got stuck in the turbine blades at the end, I'd be responsible for blacking out all the lights in Ontario and half of Quebec.

More out of both foolish braggadocio and sour grapes, I thought I could paddle my kayak over Niagara Falls and do the Rubreck Roll at the bottom of the falls. World acclaim! Nothing like it since Charles Blondin walked a tightrope over the Niagara Gorge in 1858. I deliberately did not notify the press of my attempt for fear of embarrassment if I failed. Imagine my surprise as I plunged over the brink of the American Falls and was blasted sideways by the wind!

The Cave of the Winds at the base of the falls has been a tourist attraction for many years. Ticket holders wear yellow slickers to protect against the misty spray. A strong updraft caught my falling kayak and whirled it to a gentle landing inside the Cave of the Winds. Since Cave of the Winds is not a solution cave in the normal sense, I was denied a world record. Neither cave whitewater title nor a title for the second cave execution of the Rubreck Roll had been created. My kayak looked like a bundle of blue plastic recycling rather than a vessel.

Neither the Smithsonian nor the Maple Leaf Museum accepted my offer to donate the remains of my kayak. I thought millions of young kids were thus deprived of their chance to see such an important part of world history. Barrels used by daredevils who went over Niagara Falls survive in some private museums, but not my kayak. I could see myself as a wax figure in my polypropylene underwear holding my paddle triumphantly aloft over blue wreckage.

A fitting memorial!

THE SHORTEST BIG CAVE

I have recently read about some big cave rooms in China. Everyone knows long caves, such as Mammoth Cave in Kentucky with a length of 426+ miles. And every month, somebody in Mexico or Ukraine claims to have the deepest cave, as if length doesn't matter. But *biggest* is a new description championed in *National Geographic Magazine*. Those caves in China have rooms approaching twelve thousand cubic feet, and articles about them never mention length or depth!

Shucks, if you want to talk about volume, Mammoth Cave has 140–570 million cubic feet (depending on the average cross section size you use). Tom Brucker used an average passage cross section size of four by five feet to calculate the volume of a Mammoth-Cave-sized elliptical cylinder to be 140,000,000 cubic feet. I used eight by twelve feet and immediately increased the volume of Mammoth Cave to 570,000,000 cubic feet! The rest of the world uses metric kilometers to increase the apparent size of caves, but doesn't that leave important questions unanswered?

Like, What is the Most Wonderful Cave? Or What is the Best Cave?

The caves I have explored are the most wonderful and the best, but they are also the Toughest Cave, The Baddest Cave, The Nastiest Cave, and the Shortest Big Cave. Most commercial caves call themselves the Prettiest Cave, but not one calls itself the Handsomest Cave.

The shortest big cave in the world might be the Cave of Swallows (Sótano de las Golondrinas) in Mexico. For a few years, it was the deepest cave in the world until they made nylon cave rope in longer unbroken lengths. There is no horizontal cave at all in the bottom of Golondrinas, so it would certainly qualify as a big, short cave (or a short, big cave), except for one thing—it has no roof! I rappelled 120 feet into Rigdon Pit Cave on Flint Ridge many years ago and landed softly halfway up to my knees in a long-dead deer carcass. Rigdon Pit is my nomination for the Stinkiest Cave. It was suggested that I be awarded a certificate suitable for framing as the Stinkiest Caver.

No, the Shortest Big Cave is not in New Jersey, home of short caves. The Shortest Big Cave is Ergor's Mauna Loa Cave on the Island of Hawai'i. Mauno Loa is an active volcano currently in a quiet period since it last erupted in 1984. It has erupted thirty-three times since 1843. Its caldera, or peak cone, is floored by a basalt plug. Around the flanks of the volcano are presently inactive lava tube caves. The caves are crusted over pahoehoe lava rivers. A few of these lava tube caves are thousands of feet long and terminate in breakdown, a skylight, or a solidified lava plug. One of the conventions used by the Hawaiian Speleological Society regards lava tube caves that were originally long. If its roof collapses and then terminates in a skylight, the resulting cave is considered a *separate cave* from its original, non-truncated cave length. Ergor's Mauna Loa Cave in the east flank of Mauna Loa is only two hundred feet long but 13,176 feet tall! This dimension makes it the shortest big cave in the world.

I discovered it on an expedition fielded in 1999 to explore the inactive lava tubes in Hawaii. A pineapple business sponsored my expedition during a particularly cold winter on the mainland.

My caving companions included Bill Halliday, a lava tube cognoscenti; Don Coons, co-discoverer of underground Logdson River in Mammoth Cave, Kentucky; and Carolina Shrewsbury, Speleoartist Extraordinaire. We deplaned at the airport and were met with an aloha welcome by traditionally garbed Indigenous Hawaiians who hung leis around our necks. We had provisions for seven days, including Spam, artichokes, and fresh pineapple. (It is *not* true that pineapple tops cannot be told from artichokes when cooked.) We drove by Land Rover to the east flank of the volcano and set off across the scrub toward the peak, which that day was shrouded in clouds.

We made camp at the terminal end of a twelve-hundred-foot-long lava tube that yawned to the sky in a fifty-foot diameter sinkhole. We carried all our water with us as there were no drinking fountains on the basalt flank. The next morning, I checked a clump of scrub bushes beyond the cave end and was amazed to find a two-foot-diameter hole downward. We entered with all our equipment and found ourselves in a twelve-foot-diameter, inactive lava tube with little breakdown on the floor. Lava stalactites adorned the ceiling here and there and were less than three feet long (they were six inches long, but saying less than three feet is also correct).

Imagine my surprise when, after four stations, we were in the middle of a big room 27.5 feet in diameter and higher than our lamp's beams could reach! Our laser rangefinder could not reach the top of the the top of the room. We knew that the summit of Mauna Loa is 13,681 feet above sea level, and the basalt plug in the bottom of its caldera was below that. The problem for us was, how high was the ceiling in the big room? Did it extend higher than thirteen thousand feet (since we had started around two hundred feet above sea level)? We knew that the tall room was directly beneath the caldera, so it must be the main pipe of the volcano, presently inactive, but would be filled to the brim with white-hot magma when the next eruption occurred. Such elevated temperature would surely cook our Spam in the cans and might even make cooked pineapple tops okay to eat. Our immediate problem was to accurately measure the height of the lava cave room. Estimates would not do.

After discussion of alternative methods, we retreated from Ergor's Mauna Loa Lava Cave, hiked back to our Land Rover,

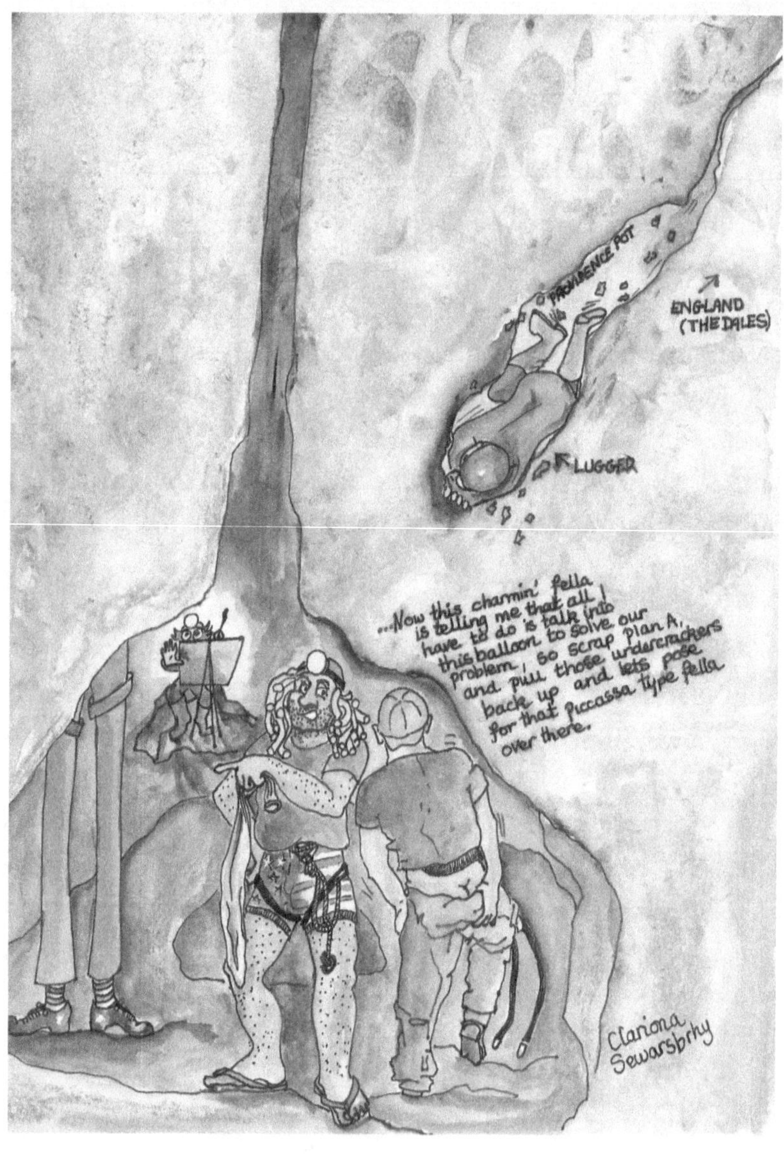
PROVIDENCE POT
ENGLAND
(THE DALES)
F. LUGGER
...Now this charmin' fella is telling me that all I have to do is talk into this balloon to solve our problem, so scrap plan A, and pull those undercrackers back up and lets pose for that Piccassa type fella over there.
Clariona
Sewarsbrhy

and drove to the US Weather Service Observatory atop Mauna Loa. There we "borrowed" a weather balloon and radiosonde to measure the height of the cave room electronically. We loosed the inflated balloon inside the room and watched it float majestically upward. Twenty minutes later we heard a whoosh as the limp balloon fell to the floor of the cave. We speculated that the balloon had been punctured on the rough lava pipe walls or ceiling as it ascended. The radiosonde had ceased its electronic recording at 13,376 feet at its apogee (highest point) when the balloon burst.

Since we had run out of pineapple and had to pay for the weather balloon repair, we were forced to discontinue the expedition. Later, at home, I visited the computer lab at a local university. We knew that Mauna Loa is 13,681 feet high. We calculated the entrance elevation of Ergor's Mauna Loa Cave at two hundred feet above sea level. The radiosonde had quit recording at 13,376 feet. By this measure, the basalt plug atop the volcano was about 105 feet thick, and its underside formed the cave ceiling at 13,176 feet—the pipe ceiling—below the caldera surface. That is how we discovered the *World's Shortest Big Cave*, Ergor's Mauna Loa Cave. And don't you forget it.

FINDING FOSSILS IN CAVE DEPOSITS

Index fossils provide telltale clues to the age of the rock units they are found in. For example, *Platycrinites penicillis*, a crinoid, is an index fossil to the Ste. Genevieve Limestone, a Mississippian-Period formation found in the lower part of Mammoth Cave. It resembles a cross section of a Ticonderoga #2 pencil but without the yellow exterior skin. It is the age-proof fossil for the formation.

My acquaintance with cave fossils is limited but extraordinary. In the abandoned bed of the ancient Root Canal near Sassafras, Wisconsin, I found a 1.7 lb. piece of mystery metal, later identified as amalgam. I believe it was an early filling of a mastodon molar from the Pleistocene epoch and a precursor of veterinary dentistry. Unfortunately, the molar was missing—not at all unusual since amalgam fillings are far more durable than the enamel and dentine themselves. Since it was not a cave deposit per se, I failed to report it to the Wisconsin Molar Society.

In a Nullarbor cave in Australia, I identified a one-meter fossil femur of an emir, thus making an enemy of the expedition leader who claimed it was an emu leg bone. He went so far as to suggest that I knew nothing about paleontology, the study of fossil lifeforms. He was so angry that he omitted my name from the expedition roster, which is why some speleologists still say I never caved in Australia. Believe me, politics is alive and well in some parts of speleology today!

I once found a fossil Model T Ford axle in a cave in the Highland Rim of Tennessee. The carbon steel molecules had been replaced by calcium carbonate molecules thus preserving the original grain structure of the metal part with crystalline limestone. Radiocarbon dating set its origin at 1923 ±6 years. I offered it to the Henry Ford Museum in Dearborn, Michigan, but alas, they explained they had a plethora of fossil Model T parts.

Ferns are related to Hosta plants, and some fern fossils are preserved in rock layers of the Pennsylvanian Subperiod (Carboniferous). I discovered a beautiful, fully formed fossil Hosta leaf on one of my many trips to Mexico. The mouth of the cave in which it occurred overlooked a shining cenote, so I suggested my discovery be named *Hosta la vista*. Sorry to say, the name was already taken.

Everyone knows fossil poop is called (or are called) *coprolites*. Salts Cave in Mammoth Cave National Park has many poop deposits—not fossilized—from which archaeologists recovered and reconstructed the dietary record of the prehistoric Indigenous people who lived in the area. Preserved in their poop are fragments of digested cultigens and undigested detritus. This suite of seeds and fibers shows exactly what was hunted and gathered and what was grown or bought at Indian supermarkets. Most recent studies have revealed that the poop has male origins—female poop has not been found! One conclusion is that the cave was used for male coming-of-age rituals such as is practiced in Indigenous tribes today. "Here, eat this magic white powder . . . ha ha ha . . . it will make a man out of you. Now, pull my finger. . . ." I can see it now.

A recent medical discovery is that fresh poop contains exotic biota and flora that can beneficially ward off diseases and restore a person to healthy immunity. As a result, pharmacologists are now selling donor poop pills from healthy donors at unbelievably high prices to patients who have been prescribed such remedies. My interest is this is as follows.

Since nobody has examined the fossil flora and microfauna of cave coprolites, I have applied for a multimillion-dollar grant to study cave coprolites scientifically for a medical breakthrough. Think of the many benefits for mankind that I may uncover! People nowadays live seventy or eighty years. With ancient, donated fossil poop, life spans of two or three times the present could become routine. I would not only become famous—like Salk, Pasteur, Heimlich, and Lister—but unbelievably rich. Think of all the good I could accomplish with the Ergor Rubreck Poop Prize and Fossil Fecal Scholarship Grant Program.

I guess the first task is crowdfunding an electron microscope, and then second, finding a cave containing lots of coprolites. I'd probably conduct a round-the-world lecture tour to describe the anticipated health benefits. (I will skip Australia because I was underappreciated there.)

There is no reason on Earth why the world's greatest and most wonderful cave explorer could not also be the world's greatest and most wonderful medical researcher of all time . . . is there?

IS THIS THE EVEREST OF CAVES?

National Geographic Magazine publishes cave articles a few times a year. By now, each story has become predictable. It is usually written by a non-caver who just happens to be a submarine parachutist or a skyscraper diver between assignments. Generally, the cave described is equidistant from everywhere on Earth, has never been entered or exited, and everything that ought to be known about that cave is unknown! Could it be the world's longest, biggest, deepest, voluminous? Will it contain diamonds, unobtanium, or unknown species of giant arachnids devouring Homo Sapiens? Huh? Huh? There will be cavers with unpronounceable names from unpronounceable places.

One such story showed photos of speleothems in Mammoth Cave. The photo printed there showed stalactites growing out of the floor. I wrote a letter to the editor pointing out that upside down goof and got an answer back saying, "Everybody knows that."

The March 2017 issue covers an international expedition to a Uzbekistan cave called Dark Star. The cave is eleven miles long and extends three thousand feet from the entrance to the deepest section found so far. "Is This the Everest of Caves?" the caption screams. In a 3D diagram, a note observes that the cave is only 1.1 miles from connecting to another cave! "Will That Be the Next Stupendous Discovery?" If it weren't for the fact that only

National Geographic photographers have cameras with wide angle 7mm lenses, their photos could not hold a carbide light to many that appear in the *NSS News* every month.

Outside Magazine runs breathless cave stories in their adventure magazine. Their stories highlight the dangers inherent in caving and often have one or more cavers die, as happens often on Grotto cave trips. In movies, supernatural creatures devour screaming cave ladies who more often than not become lost in the stygian depths. Of course, those movies claim to be fiction with no resemblance to people living or dead. (Real cavers know that happens all the time on Grotto cave trips.) My mama warned me about caving hazards.

Instead of bitching, I am crowdfunding a magazine that will have well-known cavers authoring stories about subjects they know nothing about (but everybody has access to Wikipedia, right?) Sure, it's a turnabout approach, but writing demands novelty above accuracy. I have chosen *National Geo Logic* for my magazine's title. You can believe it if Ergor Rubreck edits it.

I have already lined up five prominent cavers to write for my slick coffee-table magazine. Here are the story assignments in the works for upcoming issues:

- Wm Shrewsbury: "Flashy Dancers in Gaudy Casinos in Southern France and Northern Siberia"
- Dave Bunnell: "Deep Thermal Vents Under Iceland and Italy"
- Bill Steele: "Bobsled Parachuting Beyond Mali's Farthest Zip Lines"
- Derek Bristol: "Gobi Desert Silk Route Adventures and Double-Yellow-Line Roads"
- Bonny Armstrong: "Great Male Explorers of the Sargasso Sea"

My choices are based on the fact that no mistakes need to be acknowledged or claims retracted if sourpuss expert readers pick at any trivial mistakes. I can just reply, "Everybody knows that."

Of course, how can I, the most honest and wonderful cave explorer the world has ever known, countenance publishing articles that may have one or two mistakes? "True If Interesting." is my credo. Presidents and editors no longer need to apologize for occasional misspeaks; belief beats truth. Here are some of the wild, fantastic, exclusive stories I've lined up for future issues:

- Huautla No Longer Deepest Cave in Mexico
- Treaty of Hidalgo Ceded District to Guatemala in 1907
- Ohio Caverns Could be the World's Longest
- Farmer in Next County Says, "Nobody Knows How Big It Is"
- Grand Canyon Cave Sees Daylight
- Ice Sheet Grinds Roof Away Two Millennia Ago
- I Survived Sand Cave by Floyd Collins, Haddam, Kansas

I'm accepting advanced subscriptions for *National Geo Logic*, at a special price. You can become a charter reader, for $535.00 (four issues). Those wishing to experience a bargain may receive the electronic magazine at the reduced price of $435.00. We pass on the production savings to you. If I get a thousand subscribers, I may just skip publishing and disappear into the caves of Patagonia. Send cash, check, or credit card number and signature.

In the event we do not publish four issues, we may allow you to choose to complete your alternative subscription for your choice of *Child Life*, *House Nifty,* or *Better Homes and Gardenias.*

SPELEOLIDAR QUADCOPTER

Sometimes the best inventions are combinations of various kinds. Like parachutes and ejected aviators. Peanut butter, jelly, sliced bread, and kitchen floors. My latest invention combines the best of several inventions to make cave exploring more scientific. All cavers would like to spend more time exploring the cave than surveying it and drawing cave maps. So, I have combined the best of distance measuring, bearing- and vertical-angle-measurement, photography, real-time telemetry, and cartographic plotting. Furthermore, it requires no hands-on, sump diving, vertical dropping, or ascending. In fact, there's really no reason to go into a cave anymore if you have a bottle of fine merlot.

My SpeleoLiDAR Quadcopter combines a small quad-rotor drone with a lithium-ion battery, a miniaturized LiDAR imager, and a low-frequency transmitter. Sensors originally developed for self-driving cars guide the SpeleoLiDAR Quadcopter along passages large and small, up domes and down pits, without smashing delicate crystals, gypsum walls, or stalactites and stalagmites. It contains a 64TB memory card to record everything in case the rock interval between the SpeleoLiDAR Quadcopter and surface antenna attenuates the radio signal.

How does it work? you may ask. You switch it on at the entrance of your target cave. It will take off your hand (which is why I recommend wearing gloves), launch itself into the stygian dark, and radio all visible and invisible passage information through the rocks to your one-meter receiver on the surface. There, the multiplex signal is computer-processed and fed to a plotter with red and green pens for rendering a 3-D photo-realistic map of the cave, its wall autographs, graffiti, survey stations, and visiting cavers. An available facial recognition module, at extra cost, will tell you the names of the visiting cavers. And through special arrangements with Equifax, also their Social Security numbers, credit score, bank balance, PIN, and underwear size.

Derek Bristol, gadfly caver, tested the prototype at Carlsbad Caverns. "I launched it in the Big Room, and it headed for a tiny hole in the ceiling. When it returned after an hour, I checked the plotter in the basement of the visitor center and immediately saw where I could make a terrific discovery up in Cloudland." He did.

Doesn't it require calibration? (There's always a catch!) No, it is self-calibrating, a technique I picked up from cavers who claim their Disto-X never needs calibrating. It is called Calibration by Assertion. With each order, we send you a calibration certificate suitable for framing attesting to its permanent calibration accuracy and full absolution of the inventor. What could be better than that?

Skeptics have poo-pooed the SpeleoLiDAR Quadcopter's ability to transmit data underground. What they do not know is that low-frequency radio penetrates rock and overburden. The US Navy uses very low-frequency radio, two furlongs per fortnight—to communicate to nuclear submarines deep underwater on the far side of the earth. It is admittedly slow but sure. The message "S h o r e   l e a v e   f o r   a l l   s a i l o r s   t o n i g h t" takes thirty-six hours to transmit, causing unbelievable confusion in Asia Pacific ports.

Alas, full-color LiDAR is not here yet, but I anticipate that will be an available accessory (at extra cost) very soon now. NASA has contacted me about the possibility of using the SpeleoLiDAR Quadcopter on Mars one of these days. We will have to solve the problem of basing the radio receiver, computer, and plotter on the surface, which I assume can be smoothly accomplished so long as money is no object.

Right now the beta test model is flying through Mammoth Cave. I set it to map all the passages and vertical shafts of this 426-mile labyrinth. It has been gone for thirty-four days as I write this, and, unfortunately, there seems to be a glitch in the low-frequency radio. We have not received any data since it entered the Historic Entrance. I am hoping I programmed it to search and image the farthest reaches of the cave first, and that the signal may arrive any day now. I sincerely hope that is the case, because I made so many modifications to the circuitry without recording them that I may not be able to duplicate this remarkable prototype's performance in production versions.

Just to be on the safe side, I am sending an email to cavers in Australia, Italy, Vancouver, Madagascar, Chad, Ukraine, and Bhutan to BOLO for my SpeleoLiDAR Quadcopter. Be on the lookout, cavers everywhere! The email message contains a certificate (suitable for framing) allowing a 20 percent discount on the Mark I SpeleoLiDAR Quadcopter.

The price is yet to be determined, but €247,000 will hold your place for the first units off the assembly line. Proceeds, beyond expenditures, will be donated to the Cave Research Foundation. First adopters will be the envy of their caving clubs and have first claim to bragging rights, wagering rights, and right-as-rain rights. If you order promptly, I'll include a case of fine merlot and two straws.

STYGIAN MUSIC

Cave sounds have always fascinated me, but I had no idea how varied and astounding such sounds could be. I had heard the drip of water from high vertical shafts. They *plunk-plunk* into pools at the bottom with an echo worthy of a large tile bathroom. Two or more can resemble voices heard indistinctly from afar in a cave.

But my first real introduction to underground music was in Steamboat Cave, located in the limestone cliff on the east bank of the river just north of Natchez, Mississippi. I squeezed my way through the breakdown and discovered a two-mile extension of the cave. It paralleled the river. I heard an earsplitting steamboat whistle, intensely loud and long in duration. A distress signal? Probably not—distress is ten frantic blasts. After five minutes, the deafening blast subsided, leaving my ears ringing. Upon investigation around a bend in the passage, I spied two openings—one large, one small. I felt the breeze pick up and accelerate to a strong wind, and the whistle blast assailed my ears again.

The next day, I returned with my iPad oaded with an Acusti-Tek app. The whistle was exactly the same note—a low G—of the famous Robert E. Lee steamboat that blew up and sank in 1897 in the Mississippi River with the loss of eleven crew members. Those two holes leading to daylight formed a natural whistle that, when exposed to a wind of eight mph, created the G blast.

I decided to investigate cave sounds further. I bought a lithium-battery-powered, miniature amplifier and speaker. I visited Great Onyx Cave in Kentucky. Dozens of cave crickets crawled upside down on the ceiling of the entrance building. Imagine my surprise when I cranked up the amplifier to forty dB and heard . . . tap dancing! The crickets were doing an intricate time step in a call-and-response pattern, first the left batch, then the answering right batch. They stopped abruptly and began an unmistakable clogging beat in 4/4 time. I have heard of synchronous fireflies, but these were the Rockettes of the underground world! I considered taking them with me and winning the Dancing with the Stars contest hands down—or feet down. However, Great Onyx Cave is in Mammoth Cave National Park. If I removed the crickets, I could face thirty years in Sing Sing.

Luray Caverns has a Stalactite Electric Organ. The management has rigged solenoids to strike various notes that naturally emanate from the variously sized stalactites. It's entertaining to the tourists. A keyboard "plays" the notes when a skilled organist is seated at the console. Granted, the pedal action is nil, but it is such an unusual instrument that it has been cited by Ripley's Believe It or Not. As the most famous and qualified caver in the world, I negotiated to spend the night in Luray Caverns to learn if electrical leakage from condensers might generate random notes. They might be so faint as to be inaudible, but my amplifier would enable a truly scientific investigation. I set up my equipment in the silent cavern and prepared to spend the night, fully expecting to be disappointed. But hey, lack of music can be proved scientifically, no?

Around midnight, I heard the amplifier buzz and a few faint notes, now amplified, issue from the speaker. Nobody was at the keyboard. The console was empty! The pregnant silence was punctuated by several bars of a song I recognized as "Lady of Spain." How could that be?

I climbed the scientific stepladder I had requested for the scientific test and peered at the lowest-hanging stalactite. Its solenoid was in the retracted position. Suddenly, at the exact instant a note was required, I saw a tiny orange appendage with black spots lash out and strike the stalactite, yielding the required note. It retracted until that specific note was again called for, at which point the appendage again lashed out, hitting the note expertly.

To get to the bottom of this incredible performance, I moved the stepladder to several other stalactites that were wired through solenoids to the cave organ. Peeking with beady black eyes around each stalactite was a cave salamander. They ran through "Lady of Spain" several times, each salamander whacking his or her stalactite in perfect time. Since everybody knows salamanders cannot read music, I concluded that the phenomenon was due to Pavlov's principle—a purely animalistic response to a stimulus. The salamanders had spent their lives in the cave and simply reacted when they heard the stimulus—the previous note. About the only sound the salamanders had heard was the daily playing of the stalactite organ by one of the guide staff. There was nothing of the virtuoso about it, just a perfectly natural and accidental "learning" by animals with no musical ability.

My last musical adventure took place just before I set the "Most Diagonal Cave" record in Huautla, a Mexican cave. In a five-day expedition, I found my way up inside the mountain to a Toltec garbage dump and from there traversed diagonally down inside the mountain to Sump #13, apparently the terminal sump. Near the terminal sump is a tall room with twelve pools of varying sizes. As I neared it on a 532.4-meter rappel, I distinctly heard what I thought were voices. Closer yet, I heard the opening notes of Beethoven's Fifth Symphony. When I popped into the pool room, I saw that the twelve pools formed an octave and a half of musical drip notes. I heard nothing recognizable after that lucky sequence of drips into just the right pools. Coincidences can convince the uninformed of the validity of the supernatural. Unless, of course, you are a highly qualified cave scientist like me.

CLOSE CALLS, NEAR MISSES, AND NARROW ESCAPES

In my lifetime of cave exploring, I have survived risky situations, accidents, and just plain bad luck. For instance, I fell off a forty-foot steel ladder in a cave and lived. I was trapped in a deep pit with my rope to safety short ten feet above me. I was buried alive when an ice cave collapsed. Modest caver that I am, I feel it is time to reveal some scary situations so other cavers may live and learn.

First, part of the art of survival is how you tell the story. For instance, take the time I fell off the forty-foot steel cave ladder. I did not mention that I was on the second step, so I was not hurt. But it makes a better story the way I told it first. "True If interesting" is well worth remembering when you retell your caving experiences.

<hr>

Back in the early days of caving, we had manila rope and Goldline twisted nylon rope. Manila rope was cheap, scratchy, and prone to mold and to fail catastrophically when old. Goldline rope was durable, soft to the skin, and much stronger than manila rope. But Goldline rope was stretchy. It might elongate 10 percent, which was useful if you were climbing a big wall outdoors and fell on a wall anchor or belay. You would bounce like a yo-yo instead of pulling out the anchors one at a time as you free-fall.

I had rappelled into a surface pit on my new hundred-foot Goldline nylon rope, using a hot-seat rappel (a risky maneuver if I ever heard of one). I jumped off the rope at the bottom and was shocked to see the end of the rope spring upward ten feet and dance merrily in the dim light. There was no way to reach it, nothing to stand on. And no more rope to lower to my rescue. I explained my predicament to the cavers on top. "I am trapped—trapped for life! Send away for some more Goldline rope."

"It will take at least two weeks to arrive if we order the rope today. Why don't you turn around and use the horizontal entrance behind the big rock?" I was surprised when a breeze hit the back of my neck. I turned and, sure enough, there was a horizontal entrance to a path leading up the slope to the top of the plateau where I joined the others.

||||||||||||||||||||||||||||||||||||||||||||||||||||

Talus Ice Cave stayed cool way into late July or early August. I explored it on July 4th one year. Unfortunately, I lingered too long taking photographs with my new camera. The heat from my carbide lamp melted some of the ice. I was astonished by a clinking noise above me when all of a sudden, the ice cave totally collapsed with a roar! I was buried under the ice.

I was lucky. The cave ceiling and walls were made of ice cubes that had been frozen together instead of giant blocks of ice. The heat from my carbide lamp had melted the interface between cubes. The roof and wall support gave way. I resembled a can of pop jutting out of an iced picnic cooler.

||||||||||||||||||||||||||||||||||||||||||||||||||||

Not all caving accidents occur in a cave. One year, I joined a Mexican caving expedition. It was a long march to the cave, so we stored our supplies in a house and rented a drover with burros to carry the equipment to the cave mouth eight km away. Onc of our cave packs contained four cases of dynamite to breach a large breakdown. About halfway to the cave, we rested the burros and ate lunch. When we finished our siesta, we discovered the burro with the dynamite pack had nuzzled open the flap and had chewed up and eaten one-and-a-half cases of dynamite!

Farther along the rough trail, the narrow path led beside a limestone cliff. The burro that had eaten the dynamite lurched against the cliff. There was an earsplitting explosion, billowing fumes, and smoke. We were terrified. Our ears rang! In shock, we crept in on the site of the accident. From then on, believe me, we had a mighty sick burro on our hands.

It seldom rains in parts of Texas, so little so that you wonder how there can be any caves in that dry climate. But I was with the Longhorn Kaving Klub when a thick black cloud formed over the entrance to Drygulch Cave. There was a clap of thunder and a bolt of lightning to announce a rain of Niagara proportions that poured for twenty minutes. It was so wet that we had to put our noses under our armpits to breathe. The deluge halted abruptly, and we entered the formerly dusty cave. Rain pouring in had transformed the cave dust into thick Texas mud like no mud ever seen before. It was pure goo—sticky, thick, clingy on boots and trousers.

I was leading a party when we rounded a corner and there on a rock was the biggest diamondback rattlesnake I had ever seen. His rattling was nearly as loud as a machine gun. It lunged at my right leg and sank its fangs deep in my leg. The force knocked me back into the party. Others, wearing gloves, wrenched the rattler off my leg. The second caver in line examined me, fearing they would have to summon the sheriff and coroner. They discovered the snake had 2.1-inch fangs that had sunk into the 3.4-inch mud layer caked on my pants. Another close call!

ER
THE
ICE
CREAM
GUY
ICE
CR
AAHH!

In 1996 I led an expedition to Great Index Cave (so named because it had formations A to Z). It was a rather dodgy cave, a too loose trek for comfort. As we rested in a round room, a 1,324-pound rock let loose from the ceiling and plunged downward. I have read that one's life flashes before one at such moments, but my illustrious life was too freighted with vivid memories of exciting discoveries to just fill a flash. No, the boulder missed all of us by 32.5 inches.

If you are going to relate your narrow cave escapes to other cavers, be sure to use exact figures, not round numbers, to authenticate the closeness of your call, the narrowness of your escapes, and the nearness of your misses.

STRANGE CAVES

The late Rane Curl famously calculated the number of caves with no entrances. He did this by extrapolating the number of caves with five entrances, four entrances, three, two, and one, to yield caves with zero entrances. As I recall, the number was ten thousand more or less.

Now it is my turn. I have calculated the number of entrances with *no caves*. Entrances with no caves are called natural bridges. Since they are all exposed outdoors for all to see, a census of natural bridges would yield the exact number of names with no caves, so my calculation is subject to revision up or down at any time. (That gets me off the guesswork hook.)

The calculated number is 21,150 entrances with no caves. Here is how I figured it: There are an average of 423 natural bridges per state times fifty states = 21,150. You can readily see the absolute power of mathematics. Nobody can dispute that 423 x 50 = 21,150! Now that I have your attention and credibility, I will edify you by telling of strange caves worldwide that most of you did not know about.

The first is Boomerang Cave, a particularly ugly cave located fourteen km east of Newcastle, Australia. No cave map of Boomerang Cave would ever win a cartographic salon. In fact, any map of Boomerang Cave would, when crumpled up and thrown in the wastebasket, rebound and land on the floor. At first, this phenomenon was attributed to a gravitational anomaly (since Australia is in the Southern Hemisphere), but further research revealed that the crumpled map assumes an airfoil shape. The disposal flight lifts the waste map away from its intended target and appears as the map being rejected.

Hockey Stick Cave underlies Montreal, Quebec. The name derives from the cave's survey plot, a straight 0.4 km passage with a 17.5-degree bend of 62m at the end. The so-called hockey-stick curve was similarly named for its resemblance to a hockey stick as used in the national sport of Canada (and you thought it was curling). The hockey stick curve describes global warming temperature recordings, which, according to official executive proclamation, are a hoax). Hockey Stick Cave may also be a hoax if official pronouncements are to be believed.

Off the east coast of Madagascar and the west coast of Africa, some underwater volcanoes have been discovered. They are spewing out lava as you read this. Also, they are creating underwater lava caves. These are the southernmost underwater lava caves, which will require a new category in the official list of record caves.

A paper-mâché cave was discovered in a dumpster behind Central High School (Chattanooga, Tennessee) after the 2022 Science Fair. Apparently, it formerly belonged to Mildred Pond, third place winner. Mildred was a sophomore that year and has since enrolled in TenTech (Tennessee Technical University) where she is majoring in earth science. Her mother, Mrs. Duque Pond, was quoted in the *Chattanooga Call* newspaper as saying, "Millie was not allowed to keep her cave exhibit in her room because it blocked access to her fish tank. Damned if I wanted dead fish stinking up our place."

The winning giant pumpkin in the Circleville, Ohio, Pumpkin Festival of 1939 was a 4,356-pound pumpkin measuring 16 feet, 3 7/8 inches in diameter. Raised by Omar Ponar, he scooped out the seeds and carved a street-level entrance to his Pumpkin Cave. Its convoluted crawlway passages totaled 32 feet. He charged twenty-five cents for admission for six days. He was forced to close Pumpkin Cave due to bad odor on day seven.

Toledo, Spain, was the site of Luz Cave whose walls, ceiling, and floor were covered with a naturally luminous fungus. No artificial lights were ever needed to display the cave for tourists. Unfortunately, the cave grew dimmer in time because tourists grasped souvenir samples of the fungus as a memento of their trip. Lax cave guide standards were blamed on the eventual ruination of Luz Cave. The last faint patch of luminous fungus was extinguished when French cave explorer E.-A. Martel visited the cave in 1897 wearing his "ceiling burner" carbide lamp. Some good came from that event when carbide lamps were subsequently banned in the later-discovered Neanderthal caves of southern France. Ultimately, the premier prehistoric cave with animal paintings was duplicated in concrete to prevent other inadvertent damage in the actual cave due to human visitation. Martel was later called "the father of cave conservation" by the National Speleological Society Cave Conservation Committee Chair in 2013.

Near Athens, Greece, Paradox Cave was advertised as being of "infinite length" by its discoverer and developer, Ajax Zeno. He claimed that the underground passages "could not be measured" because, he said, "Each survey shot ends precisely over the halfway point of the remaining distance of the passage, meaning that the remaining half—no matter how tiny—is *not* the end of the cave." After Zeno's death in 231 BCE, the cave's name was changed to Zeno's Paradox Cave.

Lego Cave may not qualify technically as a cave because it is manmade. Phi Delta Kappa University fraternity students constructed it on a dare from rival fraternity Eata Bita Pi in 2017 during the consumption of fourteen barrels of beer. There is no question that Lego Cave is strange, but its failure as a natural cave definitely disqualifies it from official consideration.

If you wish to nominate a Strange Cave, the nomination fee is €25, payable to Ergor Rubreck, PO Box 1313, Old York, NY 00133.

MY TALK AT THE EXPLORERS CLUB

I was asked to speak next year at the Explorers Club in New York City. Their annual banquet draws members from around the world, including *National Geographic* luminaries such as Jane Goodall, Thor Heyerdahl, and Jacques Cousteau. Naturally, I was highly honored to be invited to such a prestigious event. I understand that one year they served mammoth steaks from an Icelandic woolly mammoth frozen 19,462 years ago in a crevasse. One of the guests at that banquet was overheard saying, "I'd trade for a fried baloney." Now that I have accepted, and I suppose the engraver is hard at work on the invitations, I'd better choose my topic carefully. Where to start?

My exciting rescue of the Vienna Boys Choir and Orchestra from the Hölloch Hölle entrance flood in Switzerland might enliven the evening. Seldom has one man saved so many people with such unselfish courage and at so great a risk to life and limb.

My discovery of the deepest cave in the world, Noböttom Pechera in Ukraine, was not only a world record, but the air was so dense it caused nosebleeds among two of my caver companions. Fortunately, I applied a tourniquet and saved both. Had I had a second bootlace, I could have applied them individually and saved awkwardness.

Or perhaps I might select a true instance of heroic proportions from my many adventures far away, where reporters are not allowed. Modesty has forbidden me from describing many of those bloodcurdling, near-death occurrences.

Since the Explorers Club members have experienced so many unique and astonishing circumstances and examples of bravery, I thought carefully about whether to reveal my story of experiencing two of the most severe instances of pain known to mankind. Some delicacy would be apropos, of course, but I turned that story over in my mind. Dare I tell it?

I was invited many years ago to accompany an expedition to Ultima Thule, Greenland, to explore and map Ursa Major Ice Cavern. It was winter, and the temperature was measured in degrees Kelvin (K). Ten degrees K, not far above zero degrees K, was the outside temperature (had it been windy, the wind chill would have reached absolute zero). The ice cave had been the domain of the giant polar bear of the Pleistocene epoch, extinct for 23,500 years, but whose bones were discovered in 1938 by Nanook del Norte. I knew that no ancient polar bears still lived, but contemporary polar bears might be a menace.

So, one morning I climbed out of my triple eiderdown sleeping bag, pulled on my mukluks, and strapped my Enfield 45 rifle on my back. I staggered to the edge of the yawning cavern. My wrist thermometer read -275° Celsius. I was alarmed by a guttural growl—a bear? I ducked low behind a large ice rill, fearing for my safety. Just then I felt the urgent and irresistible call of nature. Bad timing! What to do?

Slowly I undid my many layers of trousers, a difficult maneuver with heavy mittens. I squatted down as low as I could. *Clank*! Exquisite pain pierced my being, the worst pain I have ever felt! A large white polar bear trap had exploded, clanging shut on my manhood! I knew I would die.

The second worst pain I have experienced in my life was when I ran out of chain!

Perhaps that true account would spoil the dessert course at the banquet (it spoiled mine). Could I relate another one of my adventures that was only half so dramatic?

One year, I participated in a British expedition to the Mulu Cave in Sarawak, New Guinea, based on my proposal to ascend to the ceiling of the Big Room (Gigundo Chambre), some three km in diameter. In correspondence with the sponsors, Michelin Tires and Guinness Stout, I proposed to bring along my aerostat. This hydrogen-fueled dirigible-like mobile balloon would gently lift me in my harness from the rocky floor to the lofty roosts of the Watermelon Bat where I might take DNA samples. *National Geographic* was keen to print my story on Designer Bats when written and splendidly photographed.

We managed to avoid Mulu Foot, a treacherous, physical rot condition, by drying our feet carefully after every day's march through the jungle. Some previous expeditions had been sidelined by this ailment and never set foot—so to speak—in Mulu Cave.

In the center of the Big Room, it was darker than night. My Zebra light illuminated my aerostat kit, which I had assembled with some difficulty because the directions were annotated in roman numerals, and I had forgotten what L stood for. I screwed the hydrogen generator to the gasbag, and it inflated over a period of ten minutes. Thank goodness I did not use my carbide lamp!

It was eerie to see the pools of light on the floor become pin-pricks of light as I rose higher and higher. Suddenly I felt a bump. The ceiling? Then a *whoosh!* as hydrogen exhausted from the bag, jetting me sideways to one side of the room and the other. A stalactite, unnoticed in the gloom, must have pierced the bag, which was rapidly depleted of gas. I fell to the floor two km away from my takeoff. Alas, I had to return home with no DNA samples.

National Geographic was good about it. They said they would put my project at the end of the queue. "We'll let you know when we'll fund you. Don't call us. . . ."

I could hardly talk to the Explorers Club about a failed expedition, could I? Maybe I'll clean up the polar bear story a bit.

RECORD-BUSTING CAVES

Worldwide and statewide record caves are being announced almost daily. There is the longest salt cave in Israel, the probably longest underwater cave in Yucatan, and the largest cave in China (or is it Cambodia or Thailand?), and the largest room cave in Sarawak. The caver that keeps the record of the longest and deepest caves must be suffering from writer's cramp.

Maybe it is time to add to world speleological knowledge some other record caves. For example, the Longest Cheese Cave has been found recently in Wisconsin's Door Peninsula. It is formed in Swiss cheese. An aggressive fermentation process made continuous holes in a large commercial vat of Swiss cheese, discovered on April 1st. The cheese cave does not technically extend into darkness (a requisite for official recognition), but it is located in a cave where the commodity is stored and technically is in the dark all the time.

Officially a cave must be large enough to hold a human being. The new Swiss cheese cave is thirty inches long, so I suppose a newborn baby twenty-one inches long would make it qualify. To be fair, Wisconsin has other cheese caves, but they are limestone caves in which cheese is stored, so they are not in the same category as caves *in* Swiss cheese.

The longest Wisconsin cave is in the country of Switzerland, next to Hölloch Höhle. It is called Wiscönsin Höhle, and it is plugged with ice eleven months of the year and underwater one month. Because of this, it has not yet been mapped by the Society de Spéléologique, but the president of that organization testified, "It's pretty big."

The Shallowest Cave title is held by Scotty's Grotto in Death Valley, Nevada. The surface of Death Valley lies at -282.2 feet MSL and the cave is 42 feet below that. This establishes the Shallowest Cave at -240 feet MSL. At the bottom of this shallow cave is a saltwater sump in which the blind cave pupfish has been seen. They were last seen in 1963, just before the annual banquet of the NYC Explorers Club where the pupfish appetizer was served as the first course of the Woolly Mammoth banquet. (Nothing to do with Mammoth Cave or Wool-Over-Eyes, DC.)

The world's Thinnest Cave is fifty-three miles northwest of Milan, Italy. The cave was used for spaghetti storage for more than eighty-four years (1903–1987). The failure of the spaghetti harvest in 1987 doomed the cave's usefulness. Pasta Italiano Cave is 6.2km long and 0.91m wide by 3.7m high. There is a macaroni cave in Italy that claims the title of the Crookedest Macaroni Cave, but that title belongs to Mafioso Cave in Sicily. Since helictites were accidentally stripped from the cave during the last macaroni inventory, Mafioso Cave has been downgraded to 3.1 on a scale of 100 on the international Cave Desirability Scale.

Sally Hemings Cave, Monticello, Virginia, is the Longest Slave Cave in the Commonwealth of Virginia. The cave housed rutabagas, turnips, and parsnips during the time Thomas Jefferson lived at Monticello. When Jefferson and Sally Hemings moved to Paris, France, (he was appointed ambassador by George Washington), the vegetables were shipped to the Le Cordon Bleu École de Gastronomique where their fragrance established the French preference for odoriferous foodstuffs for the next hundred years. France was famously an ally of the fledgling United States during the Revolutionary War. Sally's Cave was thirty-five feet long by six feet high, and with a semicircular cross section and red brick floor.

Oh sorry, I just wanted to show you my cave Roger.
WORLD'S SMALLEST CAVE
oy! where's my bloody rope?
Clariona Sewkersblary

The term *man cave* comes from Outaluck Cave, the first and longest cave discovered on the Isle of Man. This island is located in the sea between Ireland and Great Britain and is famous for a motorcycle race, castle ruins featuring a multitude of steps, and said cave. Lord Parkbench is said to have retreated to Outaluck Cave after his wife, Lady Parkbench, forbade him from wearing his knickers in bed. He and his King Charles Spaniel, Miffy, lived on and off in the cave for four years. The cave was renamed Man Cave after the Board of Tourism took over its commercial operation in 2006. Its fate in the Brexit controversy is in doubt.

The longest echo cave is Longswallet Cave in Mendip County, England. The cave contains an underground river some thirteen km long with tributaries of various cross sections, all naturally tuned (approximately) to a musical scale. It is said that when the "Hallelujah Chorus" of the Brahms *Requiem* is sung in the cavern, the echo persists through nine stanzas of repeated "Hallelujah," with tributary reverberations added at various pitches. When the sixty-member Mendip Choir attempted to sing the work, it was discovered that the only available staging area was the beach. It was at the only access point, and unfortunately, it was so small that only four members of the choir could stand and sing. A workaround was found after the initial live attempt in 2008 wherein a thirty-two-inch loudspeaker with a subwoofer was mounted in the staging area and connected via Bluetooth to a thousand-watt amplifier of the recording. The pipe organ of the Mendip Cathedral was featured as well as the choir.

What is the Roughest Cave? "Velcro Crack" in the USA's Great X Cave scars up every caver for life and scrapes off most tattoos. However, the Roughest Cave title belongs to Behr-Manning Garnet # 4 Cave in the Bob Marshall Wilderness. Instead of calcite, the BMG cave has orthogonal crystals of pure garnet on walls, floors, and ceilings. Moreover, it varies from seven to nine inches wide by seventy-three inches high for its entire 2.6-mile length. Knowledgeable cavers experimented and learned that only one-direction travel was possible due to roughness. They took explosives on their one-and-only trip and blasted a second entrance (exit) at the end of the expedition. "They resembled eighty/twenty hamburger meat at the end of that trip," said Sheriff Bighat.

Cave of the Winds, located behind Niagara Falls, is the breeziest cave. Visitors and guides wear yellow slickers, and the thundering noise is so loud nobody can hear the guide. International visitors get as much information from the experience of being totally submerged as from being on that cave trip.

Mammoth Cave at nearly 450 miles in length is the world's longest, *but also* it is the Most Surveyed Cave. CRF teams have surveyed it twelve times because they can't seem to get it right. The total surveyed length so far is approximately 4,945 miles. Mammoth Cave "grows" by five or ten miles each year through CRF expedition surveys. That's why its miles cited in this book will never be "correct."

AI EXPLAINS HOW CAVES CHANGE

The cave you see on one cave trip is *not* the cave you see on the next cave trip to the "same" cave. In other words, caves change, and generally, cavers are unaware of this interesting phenomenon. Many cavers believe the cave is eternal, enduring age after age. But the breakdown you see today is *not* the same breakdown you see tomorrow or next year. Artificial Intelligence (AI) explains how this is the surprising reality.

Here is my subjective and objective evidence.

1. Caves I have visited several times over a span of years seem different to me. Have I forgotten what I saw in the past, or has the cave really changed? The cave has really changed, and my memory is as good as the next caver's.

2. A few times I have been stopped by a breakdown. Try as I may, I have not found my way through the rocks. Then, some other caver at a later time finds a way through the breakdown and finds a wonderful passage continuing onward. Was it just that I was not a thorough enough caver the first time I explored the breakdown? No, the breakdown had changed! So much for the subjective evidence. Here is my subjective and objective evidence.

3. Cave Research Foundation teams have resurveyed many passages in Mammoth Cave. They tell you they resurvey "to improve

accuracy." But the fact is no resurveys have identical lengths of the original surveys! This is because the cave changes.

It was not until I became a proficient AI expert that I understood exactly what was happening. I read the Wikipedia article on AI several times until I fully understood how artificial intelligence works on caves and how this new and powerful process unlocks the cave-change problem.

AI has been described as machine learning. It has been a boon for understanding the intricacy of the behavior of neural networks. Neural networks are organic, but caves are inorganic. Nevertheless, caves have patterns. Neuron interactions involve amino acids, which are proteins that can fold and refold in billions of ways and combinations. The equivalent for rocks is they are made up of grains, particles, fibers, granules, and curlicues that combine, and since caves are formed in rocks, AI is appropriate to understand exactly how caves change. For example, in Mammoth Cave, one finds junctions, canyons, tubes, shafts, breakdowns, fills, speleothems, and speleogens, to name a few of the many configuration variables.

The 426-mile length of Mammoth Cave is 2,249,280 feet, and since the average survey shot in Mammoth Cave is 31.51 feet (calculated from 71,383 survey shots in the total survey database), it follows that the combinatorial matrix of variables approaches infinity. In the deep learning mode, the propagation function produces a feedforward recurrent network. Applying a Markov chain analysis, we may calculate the adaptive learning rate creating a stochastic cerebellar model that may be weighted since all of the cave is underground. The vanishing gradient problem is subsumed by the generative adversarial network. Unfortunately, that network lacks robustness, so we apply the Jacobi method to account for the multi-timelines.

In other words, breakdowns change on a shorter timeline than passage cross sections or junctions. But it all changes. I have developed the Rubreck coefficient to calculate from the Jacobi triple product to duplicate the exact differential measurements from observed cave features. The mean square validity of my time-differential method lets us create a table of change values for the entire cave matrix.

You may say, "Ergor, of what practical use is this Rubreck Speleo-AI process?"

If you think deeply about it, it will serve you well on every cave trip! For instance, if you tell some young caver that the crawlway is an interminable belly crawl and she replies, "Well, it surveys to be a hundred thirty-two point six feet long," you have an immediate scientific explanation.

"It used to be far longer than that. After all, caves change through time," you reply.

This is not only true, but also it is factual that cavers change through time. I once wrote in a book that a vertical shaft in a specific cave measured 240 feet from top to bottom. Years later, some cavers tried to embarrass me in a large meeting by saying that I failed to account for the fifty feet below the drain. At the time, I felt contradicted, belittled, and humiliated. Knowing what I know now, I can say authoritatively, "Yes, that's right, I measured to the drain before it was open to the last fifty feet."

Lechuguilla Cave in New Mexico has chandelier crystals some two feet long. I described these to a caver who said, "I've been to Lech, and those crystals are three to five feet long." I was able to say that I was talking about their size ten thousand years ago, and of course, they are much longer now.

A few days ago, some new cavers asked me to show them the way to Indian Cave. We drove to the site, donned our gear, and trudged down the path. Indian Cave as I remembered it was about 325 feet long. But after two hours, it was certain that the cave was almost a mile in length! I naturally explained to the youngsters that caves do change over time.

They immediately suggested that we change the name to Native American Cave. It would be more politically correct. But renaming that cave changed the subject away from my faulty recollection to my cultural insensitivity.

When I got home, I looked at the topographic map and discovered that Indian Cave was located in the next valley over.

BREATHLESS STORIES!

I have seen numerous breathtaking stories on Facebook. They all promise sensational information but deliver far less. No cave stories have appeared. They are not far behind. As a former advertising agency owner, I pay attention to clever ads.

Floyd Collins Alive!

Floyd Collins was trapped in Sand Cave, Kentucky, and pronounced dead on February 16, 1925. He was subsequently buried five times, once near the Crystal Cave ticket office, once in the Grand Canyon of Crystal Cave, reburied in Crystal Cave after his body was stolen, and finally in a church cemetery on Flint Ridge. But Floyd Collins is actually alive and the oldest cave explorer. He's hiding today in the White House. You'll never believe what's next! **Advertisement** _______________

Ergor's Cave Helmet Polish, Million-Dollar Miracle!

Ever wonder how some cavers win the World Speleological Association Brightest Helmet Award, with its $10,000 prize, three years running? Hard-hat detailer Shynee Dome reveals his secret, "I use Ergor's Marvelous Silicone Ceramic Helmet Dressing." You, too, can claim valuable prize money by using this high-tech formula after long cave trips. Scratches disappear! Looks better than new!

3oz. bottle $89.95 plus $19.25 S&H. Ergor Chem Co., PO Box 1492 Columbus, OH 41537.

Mammoth Cave Only 14 Miles Long!

After pretending that Mammoth Cave is 426 miles long, the truth is out! Mammoth Cave is only fourteen miles long according to a deathbed confession of Austin Washington, former superintendent of Mammoth Cave National Park. "We superintendents were paid $425,000 per year to fudge the numbers. The park service will deny it, but I have the check stubs to prove it."
Advertisement _________

Hear Across the Football Stadium!

A miracle new hearing aid, the Frozen Niagara™, is sweeping Hollywood by storm! The technology is brand new but was first hinted at in an inscription smoked on the ceiling of Gothic Avenue in Carlsbad Caverns in 1936. You can hear a bat pee on a washcloth in the Big Room with the Niagara Model 230 Skidoo, with Lithium Lifetime batteries. It's offered in a limited edition. First come, first served. $7,296 plus S&H, Ikinhear LLC, PO Box 3, Rome, GA 30149.

Lottery Decides King of England

A new monarch was crowned king of England in a surprise coronation ceremony on April 30, 2023. Alice Markowitz of Liverpool held the winning number in the King for Life Lottery, sponsored by the Belfast Hospital Association. "I just bought two tickets on a lark, so now I'll have to sell my Cooper," Alice said. She said she always wanted to be king but felt unqualified. You cannot imagine what her genealogy revealed!
Advertisement _________

Pickle Juice Kills Toe Fungus,
Apple Cider Cures Cancer!

Discovered by the potholing family Markowitz, whose roots go back to William the Conqueror, this all-vegetable formula with special secret ingredients kills all diseases when blended with ice cubes. Say goodbye to COVID-19 and chicken pox forever. And you may lose some weight. PIK-CIDR, 4oz. £35.

Canadian Cave Connects
to England

Cross-Channel Tunnel is eclipsed by a new cave discovery—a limestone cave extending from British Columbia in Canada to Wales in the UK. The cave passage is just wide enough for a passenger car but too small for a lorry. The mud floor in the cave is one meter deep, so driving is not advised. The discoverer is Hugh St. Lawrence, a British caver on holiday in Canada. He and his chaps made the discovery "behind a rock." They have yet to name the cave but will soon. Suddenly, the strangest event took place, which surprised everybody!

Advertisement ________

Smart Watch Displays
13 Functions

Apple has developed a new smartwatch that will simultaneously display twelve bodily functions: resting heart rate, blood pressure, temperature, active pulse, humor condition, battery level, inoculations, height, weight, shirt size, snot volume, ear wax level, and age. Better get two. $389.95 each, $350.00 for two. APP WATCH, RR Station, Salt City, UT 84103

Intermittent Foul Air Cave
Kills Visitors

Deadly CO (carbon monoxide) vapor from fumaroles inside Chance Caverns, Arizona, periodically issues forth in an invisible cloud and overcomes visitors. There were six victims in 2022 and four victims in 2023. "We are on top of the situation," said Owen Bucks, owner. "The bad gas gets the two -hundred-thirty-seventh person, so we keep count. When we hit two-thirty, we close the cave." Everyone has a chance. A lawsuit for $256 billion has been filed, with sensational lawyers on both sides.
Advertisement _______

Natural Balance Supplement
Restores Life

Fruits and Vegies are in short supply in diets of Americans. Those near the end of life especially need these capsules. They'll restore vigor and vim, pep-up lassitude, and reinvigorate lifelessness. Mildred A. was on her last legs with the coroner standing by and the undertaker just outside her door. She took three capsules of each supplement. She jumped up from bed and danced several steps of the Charleston.

John W. was about to have his casket lid closed when he opened his eyes and begged for Fruits and Vegies. Try it and get 35-percent off as an introductory user if you use the code word LIVE. Mail $435 for a month-long supply of Fruits and Vegies, to P.O. Box 69, Dayton, OH 45432.

CHATGPT CAVE REPORTS

ChatGPT is an AI tool that can write answers to questions, short stories, and school papers, and, according to some, can put everybody out of work. There is a version you can install for free on your computer. A full-featured version sells for $20 per month. I asked ChatGPT to describe my most recent cave trip. Here is the output:

Rubreck Explores Obsidian Abyss

Having accomplished what mere mortals can only dream of, I, Ergor Rubreck, now grace you with the tale of my most recent subterranean conquest. My unmatched expertise in the art of spelunking saw me deep in the heart of the dreaded Obsidian Abyss, a pitch-black chasm that has claimed the sanity of lesser explorers.

As I ventured into the abyss, my footsteps echoed off the jagged obsidian walls—my own daring soundtrack. I could feel the collective shivers of those who had dared and those who had failed to explore this depth. But fear is a stranger to me.

Each twist and turn within the bowels of the abyss was a new chapter of courage. With no light to guide me but the trusty glow of my lantern, I navigated treacherous passageways and avoided the hidden threats of the abyss with an ease that would make a mountain goat weep with envy.

I descended to where no other dared—the belly of the beast—where countless generations of explorers' tales and whispers warned of monstrous, unseen dangers. In the frigid, inky darkness, I could hear the low growl of subterranean beasts—or was it just the abyss echoing my own audacity?

Against the odds, I emerged victorious, unscathed, and, dare I say, slightly bored by the ease of my conquest. No monstrous horrors were waiting—just the thrill of uncharted depths now stamped with the mark of Ergor Rubreck.

Oh, how mundane must the life of an ordinary person be, never knowing the exuberant thrill of conquering the earth's belly, the pure ecstasy of being the very first to cast light into the eternal darkness? Alas, my heart weeps for you, dear reader, but take solace in this thrilling account, a meager glimpse into the extraordinary life of the world's greatest cave explorer ever—me, Ergor Rubreck.

||||||||||||||||||||||||||||||||||||||||||||||||||

Now that I am a master of GPT and AI, I am about to sell my newly invented CaveReportGPT-8 tool. It will generate any number of cave trip reports and please cave newsletter editors who always complain about not having enough cave trip reports to publish.

I created a cloud database of 2.3 billion pieces of searchable cave information, together with Grammarly spellcheck and an app to handle questions.

Here's my secret: I created all the required categories and populated them with variables. CaveReportGPT-8 tool has eleven categories—Cave names 87 variables, Landowners 365 variables, Participating cavers 423 variables, Weather 8 variables, Equipment 44 variables, Entrance configuration 18 variables, Means of entrance 9 variables, Going forward 15 variables, Footing composition 36 variables, Crux of conflict 72 variables, Conclusion 7 variables.

Through the magic of stochastic and Monte Carlo technology, my CaveReportGPT-8 tool generated the following trip report:

Barnyard Cave Gives and Takes

By CaveReportGPT-8

The cave is on the farm of Barnby Yardly, and three of us, me (Ergor Rubreck), M.T.Pockets, and Esmeralda Stromboli set out on a snowy day last Saturday. We carried 120 feet of rope, a Disto-X, two sections of deer stand ladder, and lunch. We rappelled thirty-five feet into the sinkhole entrance and started a survey.

A dusty crawl led 1,231.4 feet to a stream that terminated in 842 feet at a 154-foot diameter, forty-foot-high speleothem room with a spectacular proliferation of six-foot stalactites, forty-foot columns, basketball-size cave pearls, and gypsum flowers.

On the return trip, Ms. Stromboli fell into a hole in the bed of the stream. She could not swim, so drowned. Efforts to resuscitate her failed. We notified the landowner and the sheriff. I suggest PFDs for the next trip.

CAVE RADIOS

Cave radios were developed in France by Maurice Codé, an assistant to Édouard-Alfred Martel, the father of speleology, in 1872. The first message sent from the Grotte de Mayonnaise was, "*Apportez plus de vin*" (Bring more wine). Other cave radio pioneers were Frank Reid of Indiana, Alan Hill of (then) Michigan, Brian Pease of New England, and Stan Sides of Missouri. All of these found that low-frequency radio waves penetrated the rocks in which caves form (that attenuated or stopped higher-frequency radio transmission). This is why only in movies do cave explorers use short-wave walkie-talkies.

And, this is why navy headquarters communicate with sub-merged submarines with extremely low-frequency transmissions using antennae miles long. The first submarine radio message in World War I was from the British submarine *Insipid*, 215 km from Gibraltar. The message was, "Send more rum."

My first radio experiment in a cave took place in 1961 when I carried a "portable" (eight D-cells) receiver through the Austin Entrance of Crystal Cave in Kentucky trailing a thirty-foot antenna. I could pick up a 650 kHz station in Horse Cave all the way through from the Austin Entrance, Pohl Avenue, up Brucker Breakdown, and 150 feet south in Turner Avenue. The cave walls were wet up to that point whereas in Turner Avenue the cave passage was beneath the sandstone and caprock, and water could not penetrate. Wet walls may conduct radio waves, or the radio waves may enter where the water enters. Another time, I was on a trip into Morrison Cave in which Geary Schindel carried a forty-five-pound loop antenna for Jim Quinlan's radio-locating efforts for the Doyel Valley entrance to Mammoth Cave. Thus, my cave radio experience is ephemeral if not full of expertise.

Several months ago, cave radio pioneer Stan Sides brought his newest cave radios to Hamilton Valley in Kentucky. He had a low-power rig and a high-power rig. He took me to test his low-power radio. I carried the loop antenna and transmitter into the cave. The antenna was on an eighteen-inch-square of plywood, and the radio transmitter was fitted into a small Kleenex-sized box. He said, "This radio is foolproof, which is why I selected you, Ergor. All you do is crawl to the end of the cave, level the antenna, and turn on the transmitter with this switch. It will beep regularly so you will know it is working. Then come out, and I will show you the exact location of the cave radio." I did as ordered and pushed the antenna into the farthest end of a tiny crawlway and turned on the transmitter.

When I joined him on the surface, he was thrashing to and fro through the briar patch. I'm traversing," he said, "trying to find the null." I learned he was unable to pick up the signal, let alone where the quenched signal nulled out. He never did.

Some people near the road junction miles away claimed they heard one of his earlier signals. It would not surprise me to learn he had transmitted the submarine launch codes unleashing a salvo of Poseidon missiles toward Moscow.

Several months later, Stan greeted me with the news that he had unsoldered all the rare parts in his radio and found that the framis was disconnected from the darber-go and that reconnecting them should fix everything. He showed up today saying he had three radios now. I did not ask him if any of them worked. "Of course, they all work . . . I'm leaving a high-power cave radio and a low-power radio in Kentucky for regular use."

The bottom line is that some cave radios actually work. Brian Pease brought his cave-locating rig to a cave where the owners wanted to construct a back entrance. Several cavers carried in the loop antenna and transmitter and turned it on. The surface locating team picked up the in-cave signal immediately. The "right spot" for the entrance was directly beneath a sixty-degree slope that was too steep for an entrance of any kind. Other cavers have located the right spot for monitoring wells and entrances, saving thousands of dollars over precision surveys. But my luck has not been so hot—beyond picking up Horse Cave and hearing about cemetery cleanup weekends and country music.

Some cave radio aficionados claim their rigs will do two-way voice transmission up to hundreds of feet deep. *I do know about that!* Fuhgeddaboudit!

Back in 1954, the NSS ran the C-3 expedition in a big cave in Kentucky. They ran telephone lines from the surface deep into the cave and installed hand-crank telephones. The cavers in Camp One were able to order oatmeal, Spanish rice, raisins, and Ry-Krisp and exchange weather information. Later on, some Cave Research Foundation hot-shot cavers found a way to lay lightweight phone wire as fast as a caver could travel and use sound-powered phones that didn't need batteries. This advanced high-tech phone system enabled such edifying conversations as: "It's beginning to rain up here on the surface. What's the weather like down there?" "The weather down here is . . . *dark*! . . . har har har." Cave phone systems were abandoned shortly after that. For good reason.

Yet, technology marches on. I am sure the low-frequency cell phone is not far off, and you know what that means: "Welcome to Mammoth Cave National Park, home of the five-hundred-mile cave. Please switch off your cell phones so as not to disturb our superb underground wilderness experience. Also, we ask you to turn off your Go-Pro X-Ray cameras because that will spoil the wonder of what's around the next bend. Those of you with porta-ble LiDAR survey instruments should extinguish them at this time as these will interfere with those of you listening to downloaded music with your earbuds and 6G Wi-Fi.

"For those of you with low-light visual acuity, you may wish to view the 3D narrated Historic Tour AV Smellovision presentation in the visitor center. For those of you who may be hungry, we have closed the Snowball Dining Room, but I am authorized to issue complementary eight-course dinner pills and a package of dehydrated water to drink. Do not litter but instead use the recycle stations clearly marked in the cave.

"I am terribly sorry, but the period of time allotted for our tour has been used up by these public service announcements. Please follow me out of the cave, and it has been our pleasure to serve you."

I BUY THE SMALLEST CAVE IN KENTUCKY

The longest cave and deepest cave statistics have always intrigued me. So much so that I subscribed to a service to read advance, smuggled page proofs of the forthcoming *Guinness Book of Records*. Then the late Bob Gulden published a far more comprehensive yearly listing of the longest caves, deepest caves, longest ice caves, longest underwater caves, deepest caves in granite, and so on.

I wished with all my heart to contribute to this list, if only for a year or two. I knew that as sure as I discovered a record-breaking cave, some spelunker with a flashlight would go another ten feet in it to set a new world record.

Try as I might, I could not find a list of the shortest caves or smallest caves. Nobody brags about finding a short cave. In fact, the remedy is to call your small cave *Stupendous Caverns.* Throw in an additional *Crystal* or *Onyx* and your dinky find may attract tourists with money. I felt that my destiny was to find a record cave.

A couple of years later, while attending a flea market in Somerset, Kentucky, my opportunity arrived! I purchased the smallest cave in Kentucky.

I brought the cave back to Ohio to add to my collection of unusual speleogens. The cave is 9.7 feet long (2.96 m) and it allows me to penetrate exactly one body length into it. As you know, an official cave must extend into total darkness. While crawling into the cave, I struck my head a resounding blow and immediately blacked out completely. According to the Somerset EMT Squad, I was unconscious for seventeen minutes.

The lesson is I should have worn my hard hat on my head. It would not fit, so I removed it (the hat). Yes, this sounds incredible, so I have taken a photo of my truck and the limestone rock containing the smallest cave in Kentucky. You can see the entrance at the end of the rock. Now it is the smallest cave in Ohio.

I may haul it around to the forty-eight contiguous states to establish the Guinness Record for the smallest cave in forty-eight states. I am willing to give the profits from my tour to a charity as a token of my generosity. Can I find local cavers to volunteer to help me unload it?

I offered to place it in the front yard of the Thomas A. Edison home in Milan, Ohio where it would probably qualify as the largest cave in Ohio as well as the smallest. The caretaker respectfully declined, saying his city's zoning ordinance prohibited large rocks with small caves in the front yard. I think he had bought a new lawnmower and was afraid the rock would cast a shadow that would destroy his grass. Edison's loss is somebody else's gain.

A longtime caver friend suggested I prop up the rock vertically so I could also claim the World's Shallowest Cave. If I repositioned the rock so a hydraulic dumping cylinder could alternately position the cave horizontally then vertically, I could charge for viewing both phenomena. Could I qualify it as the first *shortest diagonal* cave? That record might last for a month or two at best.

In desperation, I called the Ripley's Believe It or Not Museum in Florida. They seemed interested in my offer to let them exhibit the World's Shortest Cave. We discussed payment terms. They would give me thirty-five cents for every ticket sold, and they would charge me $12 per day to park my truck. I could break even monetarily on volume if I could convince 34.3 of my friends and relatives to visit the museum daily. I did the math. That's 12,520 visitors per year for me to break even. I figured my chances of profit were somewhere near Power Ball lottery odds.

Somebody will want the shortest cave. I contacted the president of the Cave Research Foundation. He said he would love to install the cave on the front lawn of the CRF Headquarters in Hart County, Kentucky, but unfortunately, Hart County has a zoning ordinance that prohibits small caves. The fine for violation of that law is $12 per day and thirty days in the electric chair.

I wonder if they have any show caves in the Grand Duchy of Lichtenstein.

REPORT ON THIN CAVERS

In 1953, I was taken into Floyd Collins's Crystal Cave by Bill Austin, a famous caver long before I became the most famous and wonderful caver. After many hours of crawling, canyon straddling, walking, and creeping we came to a crack in the floor. "You must squeeze down through this crack to get to Floyd's Kitchen and a good meal," said Bill. I lowered my legs and wiggled my butt to fit. It was so tight I thought I was stuck, but when I moved sideways, I sank deeper into the tight squeeze. My breastbone hung up on the lip, but a diagonal move and twist allowed me to inch my chest into the crack. Again, I thought I could not move from the vise-like grip of rock. After resting a few seconds, I wiggled deeper and felt my feet swing free in the room below. With one mighty heave that scraped skin painfully off my chest, I popped out below in a walking passage. Bill was smiling—he had gone around the crack in the floor through a generously sized passage—a bypass.

I learned two things: I could just fit through a seven-and-a-half-inch crack, and if you hunted hard enough, you could find a larger bypass. Still, I realized that in caving, thinner is better. Small, thin people in reality and fiction have always been great cave explorer candidates. General Tom Thumb, a real little person, was born Charles Sherwood Stratton in 1838, and he stopped growing by the age of six months when he was just twenty-five inches tall. He stood three feet 3.6 inches tall and weighed seventy pounds at age eighteen. P.T. Barnum found him and trained him to become a circus performer. He married a fellow little person, Lavinia Warren, in 1863. After a successful life, he died in 1883 at age forty-five. We don't know how small a crack he might have squeezed through, but I'll bet it was three or four inches!

In fiction, the Brothers Grimm wrote a fairy tale that in 1937 was made into an animated movie, *Snow White and the Seven Dwarfs.* The Seven Dwarfs were miners, not cavers, but one look would show you they could easily squeeze through something three inches wide. Author William Haponski wrote a kids' novel, *The Cave of Healing: Adventures in the Worlds of In and Out,* about a race of cave-dwelling people who for millions of years lived in the cave world of "In." These one-inch-tall people could "form" and "unform" from their diminutive size to human size at will. While anything is possible in fiction, there's no argument that small size is a big asset in caving.

Will the Zika virus change the size equation for cavers? One catastrophic result of Zika is infants born with microcephalic defects—abnormally small heads. Generally speaking, human head size is not the cave-limiting factor. It is chest cavity size and pelvic bone size. Flesh compresses; bones don't.

But not all cavers are thin. Some are thick! The thickest cavers sought ways to eliminate the too-small squeezes. Dynamite could clear the way, but cave conservationists objected. So, a clever caver invented "microshaving." Plastic soda straws are filled with black gunpowder with a Nichrome wire inserted. When voltage from a battery is applied, the wire heats up to red hot and explodes the gunpowder. Explosive straws are packed into small holes drilled in rock, electrical wire stretched away, and the charges detonated to blast off the obstructing rock. "Shaved caves" have enabled too-thick cavers to make many discoveries. I myself developed rock-dissolving aerosol spray. Its only limitation was its great expense. I am thinking of my next invention—a spray that will transform solid rock into elastic rock. Alas, its expense is proving to be a too-formidable obstacle.

Isn't enlarging tight spots in caves morally reprehensible? Absolutely not in the case of rescuing a stuck victim trapped in the pinch of unyielding stone. Smart cave rescuers have used auto crankcase oil to lubricate trapped victims. Clothing is peeled off insofar as possible, and cooking oil or other slippery substance is poured around the visible body parts of the desperate caver. Some have popped out like a cork in champagne and were forever indebted to their rescuers. There can be a downside, however. In 1986, Willow D. Wisp, twenty-two, became stuck fast in a Tennessee cave. Her boyfriend squirted a bottle of what he thought was salad oil around her. It was really Elmer's glue. Willow set a state record for days underground, exceeded only by those resting in cemeteries across the state.

One of the strangest of and most extreme of all stories of tight places in caves occurred in Mulu Cave in Sarawak. Those caves are best known for giant rooms as big as football stadiums—not tight squeezes. The beautiful Vava La Voom, a French movie star, now caver, seemed to be stuck after squeezing painfully through a tiny crack in the back of the cave. Another member of the French expedition, Aver duPoise, who accompanied Vava, saw her plight and waited silently to see how she would extricate herself.

She removed her helmet and carbide lamp and shoved them both through the crack. She then removed her wig and passed that through the small opening. A glass eye and false teeth came next. She passed through her bra (falsies evident), and then a bustier and bustle. After passing through her artificial left leg Vava looked up, startled, at Aver silently watching her.

"Well!" she said, "What do you want?"

Aver replied in French, "You know damn well what I want. Unscrew it and pass it up here."

COLORFUL CAVE WRITING

Once I read a caving account that was so boring and so drawn-out that reading it was like watching paint dry. I knew a caver many years ago who was so boring his dog left him. Don't you just hate dull cave stories? Every caving adventure I have experienced was exciting, Earth-shaking, stupendous, erotic, exotic, or surprising. I have advice for those who aspire to write more vividly. First: read stories in *Outside Magazine*. Those writers use every action word and breathlessly suspenseful literary construction known to man or beast. Some writing is so excruciatingly alive that the reader is forced to visit the bathroom before continuing.

Since I believe truthfulness is golden and facts are silver, I try to respect my own standards of sober reality and impeccable reason in everything I write. "True If Interesting," I always say. Leave leaden prose to spelunkers.

Why don't I use the word *spelunker*? It is a pejorative word used in cross-word puzzles. Cavers rescue spelunkers, No self-respecting caver *ever* calls himself a spelunker.

Less than

One of the best phrases to pep up your cave writing is *less than*. For example, if you have measured a cave to be 245 feet long, describe it thus: "Baddass Cave is *less than* a mile in length!" (Note the added emphasis of the exclamation point.) Drops are best described as, "*less than* 2,547 feet." If you can add a decimal at the end, it sounds even better.

Stygian

If you can insert the word *stygian* here and there, it will let the reader know you have read a great deal of cave literature, and that you know the word *stygian* means darker than a black cat on a moonless night in Level Five in Mammoth Cave. That is really black! Consider this example: "I tossed a rock into the pit." vs. "I wrenched a rock from its mud matrix with a great sucking noise and heaved it into the *stygian* blackness of Suicide Pit!" Doesn't the word *stygian* in there just make you want to count the seconds until a faint *splat*?

Ominous

If you are going to describe rocks in a cave, always prefix *ominous* to those rocks. There may be friendly rocks in a cave, but who cares? "Bone-tired, the cavers dragged their muddy frames into a room with *ominous* rocks looming overhead."

Rhetorical questions?

Enliven your cave writing by adding frequent rhetorical questions. "The cavers stepped across the canyon." is a pedestrian description. Consider this improvement: "At the edge of a wet-slick canyon, the cavers asked, 'Will I slip and plunge into the void? How far is it to the bottom, hidden in stygian darkness? Will sharp rocks impale my body? Will my blood rain down?'"

Abyss

No, this is not the chief operating officer of a nunnery. If you refer to drops—no matter how small—as an *abyss*, readers will be reminded that they are in a cave rather than on some prairie in Kansas. Remember, most *abysses yawn*. "Naked fear jumped in my gut as I peered down the *yawning abyss*." Now, isn't that better than, "I looked down the deep pit."?

Meanwhile

If you want readers to stay up all night reading your stories, place the main characters at the point of greatest peril, and start the next paragraph with *Meanwhile . . .* A Mexican cave trip serves as an example of the effectiveness of the term:

> *Jim crawled to the bottom of the 135-foot sheer entrance drop. The team below had been starving for two days without food, and Jim was determined to bring succor. Just then he heard a voice at the top, "Hey, Manuel, I have found this new rope. Hand me the machete!" The last figure-eight on the end of the rope rose above Jim's highest reach.*
>
> *Meanwhile, back at the camp, the cooks were arguing about whose turn it was . . .*

Endurance barrier

Joe Lawrence Jr. and Roger W. Brucker wrote a book about an expedition. They did not describe the end of the cave. Rather, the explorers reached the *endurance barrier*. In other words, they pooped out, but the cave did not poop out. So, any time you decide to leave a cave, mention you are returning after encountering the *endurance barrier*. Maintain self-respect and your richly deserved reputation.

> *Less than a thousand miles up the Amazon River, I, Ergor Rubreck, famous cave explorer, entered the stygian blackness of Shrunken Cabeza Cave. Stalactites with*

razor-sharp points dangled ominously over my tender body. Would I dislodge one and pierce my spine, leaving me a hopeless paraplegic? I willed myself to shrink small as I crept through ammonia-oozing bat guano to the fragile edge of a yawning abyss. I could shine my $2,112, million-candlepower Scurry-On spotlight down from a jutting ledge. So, I slithered outward and aimed the beam downward. Suddenly, behind me, I heard a loud crack!

Meanwhile, at Camp Number Nine, scuba diver Spike Bubbles gasped, "I've reached the rebreather endurance barrier at sump twenty-three. Afraid I can't set a world record this trip."

MOVIE TECH ADVISER

I was contacted by 21st Century Fox Vice-President Havens Tbetsi. Was I interested in being the technical advisor on a film now green-lighted for production in a few months? "It's a cave movie, Ergor, and your name came up when we Googled on 'foremost cavers.' You were also listed among 'wonderful cavers,' so I think we've got the right guy," said Havens.

"What's the movie about?" I asked. I would not serve as tech adviser on just a run-of-the-mill B movie—the awful ones where women cavers scream, and the wise guy gets tangled in the ropes and hangs himself. Havens Tbetsi told me the budget called for A-List stars, male and female, and $259 million had already been underwritten. "Can you give me a rundown of the plot?" I asked.

Tbetsi said it was "E.-A. Martel meets Stephen Bishop, Anna Bandana, Darryl Ripplesix, and Billy Eyelash, and they find gold in Mammoth Cave. It's based on a true story—it'll be big, short-listed for an Oscar for sure." He said they really wanted a cave expert because Tbetsi, also the producer–director, wants it to be 110 percent authentic. When I heard the tech adviser budget was $485,350, I said I would do a good job for them. I was on the next plane to Hollywood.

At the first production conference, Havens Tbetsi introduced the scriptwriter, W. Summersault Moron, who gave a quick summary of the plot. "Édouard-Alfred Martel arrives from France and hears from Jesse James and Floyd Collins about the hoard of federal gold secreted in Mammoth Cave. They decide to find it. Meanwhile, Jim White and his two girlfriends, who run a bordello in Carlsbad, New Mexico, also decide to search for the same hoard of federal gold stashed inside Mammoth Cave. The stage is set for the epic confrontation. . . ."

I spoke up, which is what I thought I was being paid for: "When did this take place?"

"About 1813, more or less, back in the old days."

I introduced the facts: "In the interest of truth, E.-A. Martel went to Mammoth Cave in 1812. So, we're okay so far. Jesse James was born in 1847 and died in 1888, so I don't see how he could tell E.-A. Martel anything in 1813. Floyd Collins was born in 1887 and died in 1925 so that part is also not okay. Jim White, who discovered Carlsbad Caverns in 1901, was born in 1882 and died in 1946, so not okay. The only gold hoard known in Kentucky was the Fort Knox Gold Bullion Depository, a vault-like building constructed in 1936 and first used for gold bar storage in 1937. So, the gold hoard is out," I concluded. I tried not to smile.

"Well, Ergor, for your information, Jesse James is a cameo in the background. Floyd Collins and E.-A. Martel, *father of modern speleology*, carry the scene. As for the gold hoard, this is *not* the US gold—this is Frank James's gold. Jesse's brother Frank hid it in James Cave and later moved it to Mammoth Cave." W. Summersault Moron either had a kangaroo-jump style of history or knew more than I did.

We stopped for a liquid lunch and resumed the meeting at two o'clock. I continued the conversation: "Cavers have scoured James Cave for the gold hoard of the James brothers for five decades. There's no gold hoard."

Summersault replied, "I just said it was *moved* to Mammoth Cave, probably in 1910, by Frank James, who was fifty-seven at the time. A little liberty taken here. But to tell the rest of the story, E.-A. Martel and Floyd Collins descend a thousand feet into Mammoth Cave on an electric winch that Martel has brought from

France. Meanwhile, Jim White, played by Daryll Ripplesix, piano player in the bordello with two of his team, Anna Bandana and Billy Eyelash, have entered the cave underwater, found the gold, and are setting an ambush for Martel and Collins." Summersault enthralled everybody.

I said, "A couple of little problems here. You can't descend a thousand feet into Mammoth Cave unless you start fourteen hundred feet in the air. You might get four hundred feet starting from the surface. Also, the electric winch for cave entry was invented about 1950 in France. French caver Marcel Loubens was killed in Gouffre de la Pierre Saint-Martin in France when he fell off an electric winch in 1952. And another thing, the first underwater entry to Mammoth Cave was a swim by two Louisville, Kentucky, cave scuba divers in 1974. The amateurs could not have made the half-mile swim underwater or above."

W. Summersault Moron was hot: "I suppose you are going to claim there was no bordello in Carlsbad, New Mexico, in 1813!" Summersault turned in fierce anger to producer–director Havens Tbetsi and shook his finger at him, "Either you fire Ergor Rubreck, or I quit!"

"Let's see, Ergor, I am paying you $485,350 as tech adviser, and I'm paying scenario writer W. Summersault Moron $4,850,000, and our budget is $259,000,000. Given the circumstances, Ergor, I'm going to have to let you go. But we'll keep your name on file."

That was a bitter pill to swallow. I was sure that with good technical advice, the film would be a great success—maybe win Tbetsi an Oscar. But I could not have foreseen the writer's thin skin and the investment already committed to him. On the other hand, there were a few hints already that the writer and I might tangle in earnest as the project progressed.

However, I'm an optimist. Havens said he'd keep my name on file, so I knew that when the next big cave movie came up, I'd get my shot if I were a good sport about this setback. I submitted my expenses for round-trip airfare and two nights in Motel 6, plus incidentals. The bill came to $2,200. Havens opened his wallet at the same time W. Summersault Moron took out his billfold. Both of them peeled out a thousand-dollar bill and two hundreds. Havens Tbetsi gave me another hundred-dollar bill, and said, "Nice to know you, Ergor, and good luck to you."

Days later I remembered that Stephen Bishop (1810–1857) couldn't be in an 1813 film as a three-year-old. Then, last week I learned the film had been retitled "Cave of Godzilla" and that "Based on a True Story" had been replaced by "Authentic Horror! You'll scream!" I can hardly wait to receive Havens's phone call. And see the electric winch explode.

VOIDS UNDER GREAT MONUMENTS

When I was a very young boy, I used to listen to the radio. In conjunction with offers of an Ovaltine decoder pin, I heard the phrase, "Void where prohibited." I asked my mama what it meant. She said, "Look it up." I did. A void is a space, and it also means to urinate. In other words, "void where prohibited" means *pee where illegal to pee*. Like many other facts we discover, this fact has no useful purpose, except maybe to impress friends with trivia. But void can also be a noun referring to a cave or mine. In my lifetime of cave exploring, I have discovered many useless facts that could help readers impress friends and confuse enemies.

As a young man, I reported on the caves of Put-in-Bay (South Bass Island in Lake Erie). The Perry Victory and International Peace Memorial is a 352-foot Doric column of limestone commemorating victory in the Battle of Lake Erie. Since it is managed by the National Park Service, I asked the park superintendent if there was a cave beneath the monument. He withdrew a large key and opened a side door in the rotunda. Beneath the monument was a hollow basement, full of echoes, dripping water, and *white stalactites*! The rainwater had leached through the terrace paving cracks, dissolving carbonate mortar and pavers and depositing the minerals in the basement void. It looked like a cave!

The stainless-steel Gateway Arch memorial in St. Louis is a 630-foot-tall parabolic arch designed by Ero Saarinen and completed in 1965. Unknown to all except a handful is the fact that to prove the concept of an electric railcar to carry visitors to the top, the engineers first dug a parabolic tunnel beneath the site. They installed a prototype railcar that descended 630 feet and proved the principle. Only a few people who knew about the prototype have ridden this underground railcar, but you might ask for a ride next time you visit the arch. If the officials feign ignorance, remember, Ergor Rubreck spilled the beans.

Bunker Hill Monument is a 121-foot granite spire erected on Breed's Hill in Charleston, MA to commemorate the US victory in the Revolutionary War against the British. It was completed in 1843. Shortly after learning about the Gateway Arch subterranean railcar, I visited the Bunker Hill memorial. I asked the park super-intendent if there was a void beneath the column. He looked at me as if I had discovered he'd paid no income tax for ten years. "How do you know about that?" He looked hot. I told him he could trust me to keep my guess confidential for ten years if he would show it to me. Otherwise, his secret was out! He met me after hours and opened a manhole. The secret small room beneath the monu-ment contained three casks of tea from the Boston Tea Party, Paul Revere's lantern from the Old North Church, and an original pot of Boston baked beans. You are now wiser, but no richer.

In the District of Columbia is the Washington Monument. This 555.625-foot-tall white obelisk took thirty-six years to build, interrupted by the Civil War. It is constructed of marble, granite, and bluestone gneiss. It is estimated to weigh ninety-one thousand tons and was completed in 1884. A tiny elevator takes visitors to a small viewing area near the top, where they can see many miles in four directions. The National Park Service operates the Wash-ington Monument.

I asked the ranger-in-charge if I could see the cave below the monument. "What cave?" she asked. "In my six-year tenure, I have never heard of a cave beneath the Washington Monument."

I pointed out my discoveries of voids beneath other great monuments and my conclusion that all truly great monuments harbored voids beneath. "We could make history if we find the cave . . . it should take only a few minutes to look for it," I said. I disclosed that if successful, I intended to search beneath the Eifel Tower in Paris, inside the Presidents' Monuments in the Black Hills, and below the Sphinx in Egypt. The findings would serve trivia buffs for centuries. She said, "I suppose it wouldn't hurt to look."

We crawled down through a hole behind a slop sink in the mop closet, Cobwebs parted as we beamed our flashlights into the gloom. The tight squeeze made this a painful discovery at best. We dropped into a tiny room, barely as big as an ancient telephone booth. On a shelf were the following: five desiccated cherry pits, a rusty hand axe, and an upper dental plate. There was no documentation or identification as to what these items may have been.

My final monument to investigate was the Statue of Liberty in New York Harbor. In 1886 the statue was erected on a special crowdfunded pedestal. Its shell, made of copper two pennies in thickness and reinforced with an inner steel framework, is estimated to weigh the equivalent of thirty million pennies. She has a shoe size of 879 (although she wears a sandal).

Lady Liberty herself is 151 feet tall and stands on a 154-foot pedestal (305 feet total height). She was a gift from France. The site of the statue was an old military star fort, Fort Wood, part of the defense of New York for the War of 1812. The pedestal rests on this old star fort. I reasoned that Fort Wood must have had a powder magazine that was still there beneath the Statue of Liberty. If so, what could be found within it? Gold? Silver?

The National Park Service processed my paperwork for a research permit after three years of negotiations. I would have one week to complete my research. Inside, the underground powder magazine was vivid green flowstone! At first, I thought maybe it was a trick of Irish St. Patrick's Day partisans. But chemical analysis revealed that the green flowstone was mineral dissolved from cracks in the fort and pedestal, redeposited, and the green color was verdigris from the weathering of Lady Liberty's copper surface!

Whether a void beneath a major monument is a cave, a basement, or a mine tunnel makes little difference. It has no value. But armed with my revelations, you can stupefy your friends, confuse your enemies, and maybe win a beer. Above all, do not void where prohibited.

EXCLUSIVE LIGHT-LINE CAVING CLASS

A field course for cavers to teach "light-line" cave climbing techniques will be offered May 18 through June 22 at the Museum of Natural History in Little Rock, Arkansas. I, Ergor Rubreck, famous caver and big wall climber, will organize and personally teach the class on the latest techniques in "minimally invasive cave climbing." The fee for the course is $437 in small, unmarked bills.

All cavers are familiar with five-eighth-inch static climbing rope, considered by some to be the standard for rappelling and ascending. Anyone who has worked with these ropes knows they are overkill. They are too heavy to carry, difficult to coil neatly, and entirely too strong by a factor of nine. I will teach students how to use lighter lines and hardware that will conserve the cave *and* the caver.

Light-line caving uses multiple strands of military surplus parachute cord instead of heavy, bulky static ropes. These cords have a test strength of five hundred pounds, so two of them can replace a six-thousand-pound static kernmantle rope at less cost. How often do you drop a Volkswagen on your caving rope? I claim the lighter lines are entirely safe when used in multiples.

For anchors, I use rubber-like suction cups instead of bolts or large rocks. The suction cups are made of a transparent elastomer that is waterproof and equipped with a ring for clipping on the light line. I use shower curtain rings instead of expensive carabiners to clip into the anchors. I dismiss criticisms about poor safety with the fact that I use multiple suction cups and multiple shower curtain rings to anchor the multiple light lines. We teach high redundancy techniques, so the climber *never* depends on just one cord or one suction cup. Also, we teach each student to lick the suction cup before applying it to the wall for better adhesion. Where the walls are already wet, it's a no-brainer.

Nobody has ever been killed using my novel light-line techniques. I do admit that nobody has taken my class before, since this is its first class-offering of the new techniques. Technology in caving is moving toward the use of smaller, lighter equipment. Cavers used to use bulky and dangerous carbide lamps, but now they use tiny LED lamps. We must conserve materials as well as money, so my new techniques are essentially green and environmentally friendly.

What about future developments in light-line caving techniques? I am experimenting with wearing shower clogs on my feet instead of heavy mud-clinging Vibram-soled boots. I am planning tests of novel headgear with a shower cap instead of a bulky hard hat. It should save weight and reduce caver fatigue. I have not thought about how to mount a light on the shower cap as it may be too flimsy. Maybe some LEDs attached to the hair or scalp would make the shower cap glow overall, a sort of diffused, shadowless light. A pink shower cap would shed a very flattering light on any cavers accompanying your explorations.

The idea of lighter helmet alternatives came to me when I considered dipping my head in rubber cement to create a more form-fitting, blow-resistant headgear. However, that proved to be too tough to comb out, and I decided it was probably impractical unless I shaved my head in advance of each trip.

Surely the wave of the future is lightweight caving equipment, and there can be no argument about that. Recently I have experimented with using air packing materials as knee and elbow pads. Sealed air packing materials are often included in Amazon shipping containers. The trouble with using them in a cave is they tend to go "pop" when you get too close to a wall, ceiling, or floor. Their abrasion resistance is nil, but their cost is attractive.

Bubble wrap holds promise if you can stand the "pop, pop, pop" as you crawl along the passage. Bubble wrap clothing could provide allover protection unless you approach too close to carbide lights. Those who savor the sound of popcorn popping could actually enjoy that audio experience.

The choice of beverages for cavers can facilitate weight reduction. If you drink light beer instead of dark beer from your canteen, you may save a few ounces. A light snack could consist of Cheez-Its or popcorn instead of Snickers or Vienna sausages.

I have saved the plastic bags from grocery stores and used them in place of my heavy cave bag on a few trips. Alas, they developed holes after a few feet of travel. Perhaps the trail of spilled equipment could be useful for showing rescuers where you went in the cave if you did not return. By lining the plastic bags with orange mesh onion bags, I discovered I could extend their undamaged range to tens of feet. More research and development are clearly needed.

My course in light-line caving is not just to introduce you to Ergor's fabulous breakthroughs in caving techniques and equipment, but to also stimulate your thoughts about lightening the explorer's load. Your innovations may well surpass mine for better safety, endurance, and freshness. (If you develop usable ideas, email them to me and we can split the profits.)

A brochure and course enrollment form can be downloaded from www.scamRus.com. Must be seventeen to apply. No scholarships are available.

MAGNIFICENT CARBIDE LAMP COLLECTION

Many years ago, I attended a National Speleological Society convention and saw a large collection of carbide cave lamps. There were most of the familiar brands: Autolite, Justrite, and Guy's Dropper. There were exotic European ceiling burner lamps with names that read like an eye chart. I saw a carbide lamp about six feet tall for outdoor night construction. The smallest was about the size of a thimble and may have been an earring. Common to all of these lamps was the use of calcium carbide fuel. When water is dripped on lumps of carbide, it fizzes and gives off acetylene gas. Ignited, the burning gas produces a warm white flame.

My own carbide lamp collection contains some of the rarest carbide lamps on Earth, worth untold millions of dollars. Most are one of a kind. The rarest belonged to the Egyptian Pharaoh Tootwhistle II. Famed as the inventor of the upside-down pyramid, his was the first of several unsuccessful pyramids. He reigned until his death in 1333 BC from falling blocks of stone. When I was in Egypt as a guest of the government to inspect the cave tombs of Aswan, a shabby beggar beckoned me into a dark alley and offered to sell me an intricately worked, solid stone carbide lamp that was thirty-three hundred years old. "Very rare," he said, "There is none like it."

I said, "In 1892 Thomas Willson perfected the electric arc furnace method of making calcium carbide, Two years later the carbide lamp was invented by E. Harrogate Gearing, who received a patent. There weren't any carbide lamps three thousand years ago!"

"Yes, sahib, that is what makes it so rare." His asking price of one thousand pounds seemed a bit high, despite it belonging to Tootwhistle II, so I offered him 120. "Sold!" he said. A man in a police uniform appeared several shops away, "Beware of that man," said the frowning beggar. "He has been known to steal valuable antiques from unsuspecting tourists." With that, he drew his cloak up shielding his face and slinked away. I regretted not knowing the full story of my rarest carbide lamp, dating some eleven hundred years before the manufacture of calcium carbide.

My next purchase was my winning bid at an odd lot auction at Ellis Island in New York Harbor. I had purchased — sight unseen — antiques sealed in an abandoned storage shed. I used bolt cutters to sever the hasp of an ancient padlock and swung wide the door to see what fate had allowed me to purchase. There was a large green carbide lamp, apparently copper. It stood sixteen feet tall and resembled a flame. With the help of three friends, I turned it over and saw the inscription on the bottom: Liberty Lamp 1880. I pored through archives of the New York Public Library and found that it was the original Statue of Liberty torch lamp, part of the beaten copper fabrications assembled in Brooklyn as a gift of the French to the United States in 1886. Thomas A. Edison's invention of the electric light made the intended carbide lamp obsolete before it was ever installed in the statue being erected on Liberty Island.

One July 4th, we hauled the Liberty carbide lamp into the Grand Canyon of Floyd Collins's Crystal Cave and loaded it with three large drums of carbide and seven gallons of water. When I combined the water and carbide, there was a tremendous hissing and fuming. Most of the cavers ran out of the cave before I lit the match. There was a terrific *Booomm*! and a brilliant flash of light.

It took four hours before the ringing in my ears subsided. All the light bulbs in that vast cave room were shattered. Several days later, when the smoke settled, we found the pristine white walls of Crystal Cave were now a toasty tan color, like meringue on a coconut cream pie. The Liberty Lamp lay battered and crumpled like a metal roof after a tornado. I decided against an expensive restoration of the Liberty Lamp, no matter how patriotic. Some fool might try to fire it up again, and that just wouldn't be safe.

My collection includes several carbide caving lamps from Bulgaria. Probably the most notable has a five-liter carbide chamber with a water reservoir secured to a stout leather belt. A rubber garden hose leads upward to a felt cap (before hard hats) containing an array of ceramic burners closely resembling a garden rake with some eleven tines. (I have seen modern LED cave lamps with multiple sources of illumination that are no doubt based on this carbide lamp.) I used the eleven-burner carbide lamp on several cave trips. It was okay in borehole passages, even though its wide wings introduced some tippy balance issues. However, in lower walking passages, it created eleven soot trails on the passage ceiling, so I had to avoid using it in passages without sufficient headroom.

One day I took several members of the Bach Choral Society on a cave trip. Unknown to me, my eleven-burner lamp had a clogged center burner. As we strolled through a five-foot-high passage, my lamp traced ten lines on the ceiling with a space in the middle where the defective burner was located. The musicians following me noted the resemblance to a musical staff. They noted that irregularities in the ceiling produced large soot smudges that they said resembled musical notes. Soon they were singing the notes as the lamp-generated staff and notes led onward down the passage. Echoes from their singing filled the passage with splendid four-part choral music. We reached the end of the low passage where the ceiling went up and the lines stopped. The singers refused to go on and insisted on singing their way back through the low passage, with some developing intricate counterpoints and fascinating rhythm changes. We made seven transits of that eight-hundred-foot passage. I insisted that we end the trip, as the ceiling was now utterly defaced with crisscrossing staff lines and soot smudges.

Each year Choral Society singers call and ask me to take them caving again. I haven't invited them since I myself prefer cool jazz.

Now that LED cave lamps have totally replaced carbide lamps—except among a few cranky diehards—I suppose my collection will slowly increase in value. Maybe one day some aficionado of carbide lamps will offer me $2,500 for my collection.

That should be enough to buy that new, totally cool Mega-Lumen 27-LED Seven-Way Sahara Sun Brilliant Cave Lamp with lithium batteries, 120 VAC/12 VDC charger, waterproof carry case, elk skin leather belt with LED studs, and automatic power wine bottle opener.

FEET ON THE CEILING

The images of splayed handprints and hand stencils outlined by dark pigment on cave walls are the ubiquitous icons of prehistoric cavemen and Indigenous people of North America. Such hands are not limited to North American Indigenous artists. European Neanderthal and Cro-Magnon peoples created similar artwork that survives to this day on cave walls, ceilings, and occasional canyon walls. French caves contain whole menageries of now-extinct, local animals as well, but the hands seem mysterious to modern observers.

It's been suggested these images are the result of placing the artist's hand with fingers spread on the wall and blowing or spraying dark pigment over the hand. The reverse image of the hand glows in the tan ocher of the bedrock. Occasionally, probably as a joke, the artist would place a leaf beneath one finger or joint, apply pigment, and then flick the leaf to the floor of the cave. The shocking sight of a "mutilated" hand would frighten the observer until he or she began to see the obvious joke played by the artist. One can imagine a cave filled with hysterical laughter as the understanding of how the missing digits were done. "Ha, ha, ha, Swift Antelope, good one! You had us going for a time there. Busted finger . . . ha, ha. ha!"

It is against this heritage of handprints that I made the most amazing scientific discovery since fire, water, or firewater.

In Copper Mountain Cave in the Andes Mountains of Chile, I found footprints on the ceiling. Not handprints—footprints! They appeared to have been made by the same techniques as the handprints—blowing or spraying pigment on a physical foot. The puzzle was, why were the footprints located on the ceiling? A human being could not place his feet so high up unless hoisted by fellow humans or resting on a scaffold.

The more I examined these footprints, the more I realized from their large number (436 right, 412 left) that the real mystery was far greater than how the subjects had been lifted into position for the artist to enshrine them.

Suddenly, in a flash of genius, I had the answer. *Deformation*! From time immemorial, catastrophic geological deformation, uplifts, downdrops, eruptions, and shifts have taken place. Today we have the irregular drift of magnetic north. We have come to recognize continental drift due to plate tectonics. We know about orogeny— mountain-building processes that have formed mountain ranges such as the Andes, Alps, Himalayas, and Rockies.

The most spectacular we have seen are recumbent folds in which rock formations were overturned so much that the younger rocks are on the bottom lying almost horizontally on top of older rocks due to folding and faulting in some landscapes. Yes! The rock formations containing Copper Mountain Cave in the Chilean Andes were overturned after the cave had formed, and the natives walked on what was the floor but is now the ceiling. So, of course, they depicted footprints by spraying pigment on the ancient feet as they trod what was then the floor of the cave!

I am sure of this conclusion since what I interpret as a reminder still exists in North America. The name by which the Indigenous people who are now called the Blackfoot Nation knows itself is Niitsitapii (The People). The Niitsitapii have an oral tradition of at least ten thousand years in the Rocky Mountains of what is now Montana and Canada. However, the Niitsitapii Nation is today called the Blackfoot Nation because of the name given to them by the Crow Nation: Siksika, which refers to the people's black moccasin soles, whose color was caused either by paint or by walking through prairie grasses burned in a fire. Extrapolating to South America, it is easy to conclude that high on the ceiling of Copper Mountain Cave are footprints (127 right, 103 left) of those ancient Indigenous peoples of Chile.

Scrapings from the Andean cave revealed that some of the models for the footprints showed fossilized traces of athlete's foot fungus in the footprint! I'm indebted to Dr. Pie Scholl, MD, Dean of the America del Sol Escuela de Pies for identifying this sample. "Sr. Ergor, you have established the origin of athlete's foot as originating in Chile, since nobody else has claimed this resource," said Dr. Scholl. (It's nice to be first in something.) But I digress.

Further examination of Copper Mountain Cave took me to a niche in the back wall. An amorphously shaped green rock lay there. I found it surprisingly heavy. So, I scraped it with my knife. Beneath the verdigris color was the gleam of copper metal. Since this was copper country, I realized this was a nugget of pure copper. I rubbed off more of the green oxide, and as I rubbed, the cave passage began to slowly invert! It clicked into place upside down—the way it must have been when the footprint icons were added to the "floor." I tumbled against the wall, then down the wall as the tilt became pronounced. I landed on the new floor (old ceiling). Could it be I had discovered the magical copper inversion nugget?

Outside the cave, I stood under a tree and rubbed the nugget. As the tree bent down to the ground, its roots came out showering dirt on me, and it finally stood inverted, green leaves and branches on the ground, roots high in the air! A little later, I rubbed the copper nugget inside my Land Rover. In a few seconds, my Land Rover rested upside down on its top, tires up, with me suspended from my seat belt.

Sitting there upside down, I considered my options. I could turn apartment buildings upside down, causing bathwater and bathers to crash against the inverted ceiling. Or, get paid for *not* inverting buildings. I could invert the Pyramid of Cheops, the Statue of Liberty, or the Empire State Building. I could make history. There is no law against inverting things.

But I thought of the downside. Misery and shame, hardship, ill will. I could become richer than Midas but probably extremely unhappy in the end. I decided to put the nugget back in its niche after re-inverting my Land Rover, the tree, and the cave. Maybe one day the truth would be revealed—how I saved the world from an inversion worse than death. Perhaps I would win a prize, or even a certificate suitable for framing. On my tomb would be an epitaph: "Here lies a nice caver who saved the world from inversion."

I haven't given the coordinates of the cave. No sense in tempting unscrupulous people.

MARS CAVE VIDEO

I had been reading about the several Mars Explorers sent by NASA to scope out the red planet. Some astronomers examining orbiter photos of the planet surface said they saw cave entrances. If there are caves on Mars, they speculated, those might offer shelter from the sizzling heat and near absolute zero temperatures, not to mention protection from deadly cosmic ray bombardment. Caves could guard the astronauts' privacy from the prying gaze of remote astronomers, too.

Since I am the foremost expert on caves in the world, I dashed off a white paper to the authorities at NASA with my idea. I could make a virtual video of a trip through a Mars cave as a training aid for future astronauts. I thought I knew enough to make a realistic simulation—a true, if interesting—twenty-minute production of what space cavers might encounter as they enter the Martian caverns.

To my great pleasure, I received an urgent RFP (request for proposal) from NASA. They wanted me to submit a formal contract proposal for producing the Mars caving simulation video. Furthermore, since I was the most technical expert on caves in the universe, I was asked to apply on a sole source basis. In other words, no competitors would bid against me. Naturally, I should spare no expense to make the video authentic.

You may think that my technical problem was not knowing *if* there are caves on Mars, and how they might look if indeed they do exist. I could allow for that by submitting a high dollar amount. If funded, I'd spend the money learning from astronomy experts who reported the possibility of caves in the first place. So I drew up a seventeen-page contract for $69,432,824.16 for my twenty-minute training film. I figured there was enough money in the contract to design a lot of specialized caving equipment, such as lights, asbestos rope, breathing gear, and thermal candy bar holders. But a friend urged me not to throw in all that stuff but to make a proposal for it separately later. "Don't leave any money on the table," he urged.

In a week the authorization from NASA arrived to go ahead. My first concern was over public reaction to my large contract. I hired a PR (public relations) firm, the one used by the gas and oil fracking companies in New York State. They would make several infomercials putting the best spin on my project; maybe a beautiful woman would stroll around extolling the value and benefits of a Martian cave video simulation. They'd create fancy charts and cutaway models.

I realized that without my cave lights, the video simulation would be black. I had not included artificial lighting in my contract. So I made a video of twenty minutes of pitch black. After all, this is exactly what future astronaut cavers would see in a Mars cave, unless I invented a $7,936,467.16 artificial light. Oh well, there would be time to worry about that when I landed the NASA lighting contract.

In Washington, DC, I took my simulated video to NASA headquarters for the grand presentation. I made a few extemporaneous remarks that my PR firm had scripted for me and mounted on the Teleprompter. They had even composed background music for my twenty-minute video. I regarded their contribution well worth the $1,603,657.13 their PR services had cost me up to that point.

The NASA procurement team had assembled all the astronomers, Mars mission astronauts, former Space Station crews, Russian cosmonauts, and three monkeys left over from the Aerobee days. Theater Number 27 was packed. On the platform, I said that the

CAVES
of
MARS
ARMSTRONG
ALGOR NO
BURT'S
BOG
SEATS
TAX MONEY
WEDGLEWOOD
SECONDS
Clariona
Bussuiherry

video simulation they were about to see was as accurate as science and engineering could make it. They would see in breathtaking realism exactly what an astronaut cave explorer would see during a twenty-minute exploration into a cave on Mars. The projectionist rolled the video. The main titles and thrilling musical title overture rolled. Then came twenty minutes of pitch blackness. I thought it was extremely effective when the PR guy said, "This video would make Mars cave exploration safe, fuel-efficient, and wonderful!"

Frankly, I was unprepared for the reaction after the screening. I had anticipated shock and awe. Instead, the NASA director said, "That's it?" Audience members looked befuddled, whispering among themselves. There was an air of unease.

I quickly explained: "When astronauts enter the caves of Mars, they will see exactly what you have just witnessed . . . total darkness. They cannot see their hands or space gloves two inches from their eyes. It is a universe of abject silence and a realm of unrelenting blackness. All astronomical authorities agree that without light there is no seeing anything in a Mars cave. Absolute darkness reigns! It is *not* like movies you may have seen, where mysterious off-stage lights cast menacing shadows. To bring light to Mars caves will require a follow-on contract—preferably sole source—to develop a cave light that is safe, fuel-efficient, and wonderful."

Two months later I received sad news. My $69,432,824.16 contract had been officially sequestered and terminated. Therefore, I would not be paid, even though I had delivered the final product. It seems the government had to choose between buying 6,943 ten-thousand-dollar toilet seats, the spare left wing of an F-35, or my NASA Mars cave simulation training video.

I surely hope the admirals and generals enjoy their plush seats.

MARVELOUS CAVE LIGHT

Back in the 1950s, the carbide lamp was standard issue for cave explorers. Those unfamiliar with this piece of equipment should envision a shiny brass, two-part, cap lamp with a round reflector on the front and a yellow-white flame burning from a ceramic tip. The lower part of the lamp is a base that unscrews and allows the caver to pour in several tablespoons of calcium carbide lumps resembling gray gravel. The bottom chamber is screwed onto the top chamber containing water. A lever atop the water tank adjusts the rate of drip of the water into the bottom. Water activates the carbide to produce a jet of stinky acetylene gas, which is ignited by rubbing the heel of one's hand over a wheel on the reflector to generate a spark. The carbide lamp was once popular in mining until a number of mines blew up, hundreds of miners were horribly burned to a crisp, and canaries were denuded of all feathers. No wonder electric lamps replaced carbide lamps in mining and then caving.

Early electric cap lamps used either eight D-cell batteries or heavy lead-acid batteries. The latter burned for eight and a half hours per shift and weighed thirty-two pounds, and the former burned seventeen and a half minutes before winking out due to wire breakage, battery corrosion, battery-case failure, bulb burn-out, or any one of twenty-six other ailments. The revolution came in the form of the Wheat Lamp, an incandescent bulb attached to an army surplus guided missile battery.

Since then, Petzel developed smaller cap lamps using AA and AAA dry cells, in which LEDs gradually replaced incandescent bulbs. Then came the stun light costing $300 and most recently the Scurry-On costing $4,000. You must empty your bank account to go caving with one of these babies, but you will be able to see fossils three hundred feet up the walls in TAG caves, and one kilometer across the rooms of Chinese caves. Darkness in caves is a thing of the past; good riddance, some say.

These marvelous lights today, combined with helmet cams, allow you to make color videos of cave trips. Cave divers use variations of these compact lights to make underwater videos. Next, I expect to see lights so powerful as to see under mud and through solid rock walls.

A whole different class of cave lighting is under development, and I will reveal the details of some of these inventions for the first time. First is Ergor Rubreck's Emergency Batteryless Lamp; second, a remarkable fuel cell light that uses only organic heat conversion; and finally a Chemlight that uses cloned fireflies to do away with the need for scarce resources.

I got the idea from hand-cranked emergency flashlights that give you light so long as you squeeze the handle vigorously. My prototype uses an electric generator driven by a bicycle wheel that is raised on a spring-loaded boom to track along the ceiling, much like a streetcar boom. It is mounted on a cave helmet. Spring tension keeps the wheel on the ceiling of the cave as you go along the passage. What about domes? My bike wheel is rigged to a heavy flywheel that spins on ball bearings. When the ceiling contact is lost, the flywheel keeps rotating for four and a half minutes. I am perfecting a hinge that will allow repositioning the boom toward either cave wall if the ceiling is too high. Also, I am thinking of replacing the twenty-pound flywheel with a thirty-five-pound wheel to increase the spin time to seven and a half minutes. The difficult part of my development program is recruiting test subjects who are strong enough to support my wonderful emergency light. They quit and complain of fatigue. Why can't these whiners appreciate true science?

The next development is not mine. Dr. Alan Mountain calls his novel fuel cell lamp the Analite®. It uses no batteries but instead adapts the space-age technology of the fuel cell. The lamp has a three-foot cord that one inserts in one's rectal cavity where it converts 98.6° F heat into electrical current. Its drawback could be its unreliability during hypothermic episodes, not to mention discomfort. When I asked Dr. Mountain how reliable his Analite® will be, he replied, "You can bet your ass."

A few cavers have used Cyalume chemical light sticks for emergency lights in caves. In its present form, the stick is a glass tube covered in tough plastic. When broken, the glass shatters, allowing the two liquids contained within to mix and give off a weird greenish glow. Recent improvements have widened the color spectrum, so the sticks give off a bluish, pinkish, or purplish glow. The problem is that after fifteen minutes or so, the glow fades, and the caver is forced to crack another Cyalume stick—if available.

My improvement on the Cyalume stick is an environmentally friendly solution. The whole world will benefit. Each year hundreds of thousands of fluorescent tubes are disposed of when they burn out. My plan is to use old four-foot-long fluorescent tubes, fill them with fireflies, and dip the tubes in rubber cement. If you crack one of those, you will have almost the illumination of the Scurry-On, but easier on the eyes than the Scurry-On's blinding beam. A caver could carry a golf bag of these natural chemical lights and find their way out of Mammoth Cave. It took me all summer to catch enough fireflies to build my prototype, but when I sealed them into the fluorescent tube and coated it with rubber cement, the fireflies died due to lack of air. I have yet to pull off a practical test.

I am reading scientific papers on cloning fireflies to see if I can build an environmental generator within the tube and use cloned insects to reduce lethality and increase longevity. When I asked

Dr. Alan Mountain for his advice on sustainable cave lighting, he said, "Bug off."

At first, I was insulted, but then realized he had inadvertently given me a catchy name for my new and marvelous cave lighting invention—Bug-On™* light.

---

* Patent pending. All rights reserved. Violators will be shot. Mama would be impressed.

DARK MATTER SECRET OF THE UNIVERSE

Dark matter is mysterious, invisible, subject to vociferous argument, and illusive. Some scientists endlessly write about it. Is it the key to understanding the universe? Or, is it fake news? Many scientists believe that dark matter makes up about 27 percent of the universe. If you think that is bad, dark matter makes up about 85 percent of the mass of the universe! Unlike regular matter, such as airplanes that can be detected by radar, dark matter cannot be detected by any waveform in the electromagnetic spectrum. That spectrum runs from DC to daylight and beyond.

I, Ergor Rubreck, have discovered that almost all caves are filled with dark matter. The very definition of a cave states that it only begins past the daylight at the entrance. Think of it—dark matter is present in a cave until you switch on your light. Of course, you cannot see or hear dark matter. I do not know why scientists think they have to look at galaxies to find dark matter when the caves are full of it! (I have been similarly accused by ignorant cavers!) All seriousness aside, dark matter is just around the bend in the next cave you visit.

Every caver knows that handheld radios do not work in caves. Only movie directors think they do, especially when the explorer drops his radio clicking and clacking down the walls of the Bottomless Pit. "We're cut off!" the hero yells to his companions just before a mighty rockfall seals off the only passage to the outside. Could it be that one of the reasons walkie-talkie radios don't work in caves is that their high-frequency reception is blocked by dark matter? Think about it: without a landline telephone, you cannot talk to people on the surface when you are deep in a cave. Could dark matter be blocking your audio signal? An AM/FM radio does you no good, either. Nor could you rely on that famous French caver Maurice Codé to get your message through. No, you are trapped in stygian darkness!

Commercial cave exhibitors try to get around dark matter by stringing electric lights through the cave, but the cave reverts to its dark energy state when the lights are extinguished. Dark matter rushes in at the speed of . . . dark energy. Breathing dark matter continuously is not recommended. In the historic section of Mammoth Cave, many of the tuberculosis patients became sicker and died when exposed to dark matter. A face mask is no protection.

In the interest of science, I sought to gather and examine dark matter, but I knew better than to bring a glass collection bottle into the cave. I brought in a lead-sealed zinc box. However, when I reached the deepest, darkest part of the cave, I could not open the box—I'd failed to install hinges and a door. I exited the cave and reworked the box by adding a door baffled by light traps so the dark matter could not escape. Back in the deepest part of the cave, where cosmic rays could not penetrate, I snapped open the box, counted to three, and snapped the lid shut. My box of dark matter stayed secure all the way back to my lavishly equipped laboratory.

I turned off all the lights and opened the box. Alas, the dim glow of instrument panels and LED lights on switches corrupted the dark matter I had so carefully sequestered.

Weeks later I returned with a new sample. I had placed film detectors around the lab to ensure all lights were indeed off. Their transparency in the developer attested to totally absent light. I admit it was difficult to administer the spectrophotometer tests to break down the elemental constituents. I spilled a cup of hot coffee on my pants and did the Macarena in the dark. (In excruciating pain, I thought of the song "Dancing in the Dark.") The spectrophotometer buzzed and hummed and finally shut off. The mystery of dark matter would be revealed for the first time by my printed results.

NONEXISTIUM	0.4 %
UNOBTANIUM	0.2%
NOSEEUM	0.3%
INVISIUM	0.5%
ETHER	0.6%
UNIDENTIFIED	0.01%
INERT INGREDIENTS	97.99%
	100%

Now that we know the composition, what do we know? There was a trace of zinc and lead that I threw out, reasoning that it was a residue from the sample box, and I rounded the printout figures for clarity.

Alas, my mentor, Bob Lodge, pointed out that my spectrophotometer works by burning the sample in a concealed arc of dazzling light, which probably contaminated my sample, making the analysis worthless. However, it stands as the only *attempted* analysis of dark matter in the history of science.

But, I know where to collect a plethora of additional samples of dark matter!

PSYCHIC PHENOMENA AT MAMMOTH CAVE

On an obscure TV channel, I saw an episode of *Expedition X* in which psychic investigators searched for signs of extraordinary psychic activity in Mammoth Cave. They encountered "probable" signs of a "presence," feelings of "something ominous," and a warm image on a thermal screen. Near the end of the program, they had to rush to an entrance before an instantaneous flood was about to drown them like the Egyptian chariot army in the Red Sea. Fortunately, they also escaped the giant ceiling slabs of rocks that were poised to flatten them like pancakes. I resolved to see for myself, so I armed myself with suitable instruments and personnel for a thorough scientific investigation.

First, a tambourine. Then a three-foot length of chain. I borrowed a thermal screen from a nearby university lab. My own Apple iPad would serve to receive any messages from the other side. A friendly spiritual adviser and investigator from Madagascar agreed to accompany me. Her name, Krystal Bawl, suggested competence in psychic matters. She had been part of the staff on numerous TV psychic investigations.

We entered Mammoth Cave at 6:00 p.m. on June 6 (666) and headed for the "Haunted Chambers." I had purchased two All-Day tour tickets, and I figured that twenty-four hours would give us enough time to conduct a thorough investigation.

I turned on the thermal screen; it glowed a beautiful golf-green hue. I pointed it at the ceiling. There were flashes and slashes of orange indicating life! Sure enough, solitary bats were clinging to the ceiling. Then I discovered an amazing psychic phenomenon—an orange streak every time my finger passed near the screen. What an astounding coincidence, a spirit passing simultaneously with my finger! Krystal Bawl pronounced it as solid proof that the room was occupied by supernatural beings.

My iPad chimed. I opened it and found the word PICARD. There have been French explorers by that name, but who was here? iPad signals cannot penetrate the hundreds of feet of limestone over our heads. We searched the shadows for entities. Back in the center of the room, the iPad chimed again. The image: 5S. It must have stood for something, but what? Now I could understand. The ghostly magician present had wanted us to pick a card. And it knew the card would be the five of spades. Unfortunately, we had not brought a deck of cards. But still, how could the mysterious entity know the card selected would be the five of spades? Incredible—a one-in-fifty-two chance that ruled out coincidence. More proof of supernatural activity!

Krystal said she felt a shiver, a light breeze on her face. I was about to explain that air currents often spring up in Mammoth Cave. But she pointed to a dark corner. "There!" she screamed. (I had forgotten we were on TV.) I balled up the chain and hurled it into the darkness she pointed to. It clanked and clanked far longer than any chain I had thrown in a cave. "There is the ghost of a slave here, and he is clanking the chain, protesting his captivity and the injustice that kept him here." Those of you who have thrown a chain in a cave before should be alert for such clues the next time you throw a chain.

We decided to conduct a séance. We sat cross-legged in the center of the room with the tambourine between us. We switched off our lights and concentrated our hearing on the inert instrument. After many minutes of pitch-dark silence, Krystal began to chant a Madagascan dirge. It was not long before the tambourine began to jingle in time with the exotic chant. The chant varied in tempo from slow to extremely fast. Finally, the chant ended and so did the tambourine's jingle. When we switched on our lights the tambourine was in exactly the same location between us. I picked it up and turned it carefully in my hands looking for a thread or stick that could have actuated it. Nothing! I felt a weird feeling rippling through me. Had we been visited by a spirit? If so, why a Madagascan spirit? Could Mammoth Cave connect with Madagascar?

According to the spiritual authority, an Indian woman on the *Expedition X* team, hundreds of people had died in Mammoth Cave. That sounded like bad news. I knew Lost John, a prehistoric mummy, had died in the cave excavating gypsum under a twenty-ton rock, but now hundreds of deaths? Only that Indian lady knew.

About this time, the room seemed to sway. Then it seemed to shake. We decided it was time to move. As we backed away from our séance site, a massive limestone boulder, perhaps weighing a thousand tons, peeled off the ceiling and landed with an eerie *boom*! on the tambourine. If you don't believe me, you can bring in jacks to raise the rock slab and see the crushed tambourine for yourself. "We'd better get out of here before the cave floods," said Krystal. "The spirits don't like our being here. Mammoth Cave is a sacred place."

My iPhone rang. Who could call me here? "Hello, who is this?"

"The last elevator has left," said a sepulchral voice. I asked who was calling. But there was no further answer! Krystal Bawl asked if we were being left to die down here. I replied that the elevator was in another part of the cave. We would be safe. Just then I caught a fleeting glimpse of a blind white crocodile flashing by my face and a shark darting after it. I asked Krystal if she had seen animals. She had not seen any, so we were spared a TV scream.

There were thuds . . . *boom*! . . . *boom*! . . . *boom*! behind us as we hurried out the way we had come in. I was sure that slab after slab of the ceiling was crashing down behind us. We escaped just in time.

At the top of the stairway at the entrance of Mammoth Cave, I saw a crackle of lightning, and the clouds burst with a drenching Niagara Falls of rain. The downpour overwhelmed the stairway and began to fill the cave with angry, swirling water. Blind fish swirled by. I am still a skeptic concerning psychic phenomena at Mammoth Cave. I don't know about Krystal Bawl. She was talking animatedly to the TV cameraman . . . and screaming.

MY CAVING AWARDS

Lew Bicking was a hard-charging, go-go-go caver, full of energy and always ready to tackle the toughest caves. To honor his memory, the National Speleological Society (NSS) created the Lew Bicking Award for the caver who that year exemplified the energetic spirit exhibited by Mr. Bicking. Some of the world's leading cave explorers have been nominated and a few selected for this singular honor. Alas, I have not, perhaps because the speleo world is waiting until my demise to establish the Ergor Rubreck Award for supercharged caving and indefatigable spirit. To tell the truth, the only award I have been given was the Gold Bricking Award by my fellow soldiers. They never explained it to my satisfaction, so I assume it was for valor, efficiency, conservation of energy, and scouting missions out of sight of confirmatory testimony.

Awards, like icebergs, have a lot going on below the surface: The visible symbol only hints at the bravery and heroic performances of the recipient. I know that modesty prohibits me from describing my most wonderful accomplishments and examples of self-sacrificing heroism. For example, I once saved twenty-one Ukrainian cavers from freezing to death. I had to leave their party early and locked the cave gate behind me on my departure. I was awakened from a sound sleep to rush to rescue them when they failed to return at the appointed time for their emergence. It turned out they had returned to the gate, and, finding it locked, saw their life slipping away—abandoned to the freezing drafts whistling through the gate. When I arrived at the gate, I found a pitiable lot of blue Ukrainian cavers reaching their hands through the gate in desperation.

"Silly cavers," I said, "the gate key is under that rock on the left side of the gate below the bottom hinge where I placed it." (It was a struggle fitting together the Ukrainian words to advise them, but eventually, they put together my utterings and pointing and found the hidden gate key.)

Surely my rescue should have earned me an award of some kind, such as the Carnegie Medal, but they probably had no such award in that country. Instead, they awarded me a one-way ticket on the next train.

Tommy Brucker won the Lew Bicking Award one year. I had taught him everything he knows about caves and caving. But I didn't tell him everything I know. His friends affectionately call him "Tommy Death," but I know that is an exaggeration. He is still alive! Part of his reputation is deserved, part not so much. He once climbed by stemming (mountain climbing lingo for chimneying) a wide slippery canyon to the amazement of his caving companions. Nobody could follow him. His reach and his daring were no match for the others. "How do I get down?" he shouted.

His companions immediately recognized this as only a rhetorical question, calculated to force his fellow cavers to analyze the problem. Natural teachers use this technique to inspire learning by engaging students at a "teachable moment." Instead, the two-inch-thick ledge he had just crawled across emitted a loud crack and plunged sixteen feet to the floor, barely missing the onlookers. Not one of the lesser-experienced cavers could give now-stranded Tommy a feasible alternative for his impending gravity descent.

Tommy yelled, "Give up? You don't get down from a canyon, you get down from a goose!" This truly educational response was punctuated by the obvious peril that seemed to await Tommy. Calmly, Tommy asked the cavers below to use their carbide lamps to smoke a ladder rung on the wall. The carbon buildup soon made

WATER
Clariona
Sewwursbhg

a step, allowing one of the cavers to mount the rung and smoke another rung on the wall. Within four hours they had smoked a carbon soot ladder up to Tommy, allowing him to descend smoothly and safely to the floor.

The not-so-remarkable contribution to his reputation was to always arrive back in camp several hours *after* his sign-in time expectation. The missing Tommy created a heightened air of expectation back at camp. Would he come back alive this time? Would his fellow cavers escape the flooding waters? Would they be forced to mount a rescue? A recovery?

Upon his late return, he would shrug and roll his eyes, never explaining the risky escapes and sudden rock falls that probably beset his party. His companions, white with fatigue and fear, would give only faint accounts of the feats they had witnessed. I think he delayed their exit from the cave by telling stories, knowing full well the powerful effect of a last-minute arrival of a missing cave party.

The award I propose is the Flatrock Award. Everybody who has caved for a couple of years has experienced the odd caver on his party who was so inept as to be an enigma. How could anyone be so stupid, so clumsy, so unsafe, so boring, so obnoxious? The party leader who is eligible for the Flatrock Award is the one who brings down a flat rock with stunning force on the head of the odd caver and has sworn his party members to silence as to the real circumstances.

I am quite sure there will be many winners of the Ergor Rubreck Flatrock Award.

AFTERWORD

I hope you have enjoyed reading *Mama says, DON'T CAVE.* Please give this book to all your many friends and relatives as presents. Your enemies, too.

Hats off to John Weldon "J.J." Cale whose song lyrics reminded me of how my mama feared caving. Thanks to The National Corvette Museum provided the photo used in "My (SECRET) Corvette Adventure."

Big reveal: Ergor Rubreck is a pseudonym invented by Richard A. Watson in 1976. It is the anagram pen name of Roger W. Brucker, NSS #1999RLF, PH, HM, FE, CM, CM, AL. Red Watson selected Roger to illustrate the 1976 version of *MAWS Cave* Books by Erd Noswat (Cave Books, 1976). Roger has illustrated other books, including *Scary Stories of Mammoth Cave* by Colleen O. Olson and Charles Hanion (Cave Books, 2009). Roger is the author or coauthor of several cave books: *The Caves Beyond* by Joe Lawrence Jr. and Roger W. Brucker (Cave Books, 1975); *The Longest Cave* by Roger W. Brucker and Richard A. Watson (Southern Illinois University Press, 1987); *Trapped! The Story of Floyd Collins* by Robert K. Murray and Roger W. Brucker (University Press of Kentucky, 1982); *Beyond Mammoth Cave: A Tale of Obsession in the World's Longest Cave* by James Borden and Roger W. Brucker (Southern Illinois University Press, 2000); and *Grand, Gloomy, and Peculiar; Stephen Bishop at Mammoth Cave* by Roger W. Brucker (Cave Books, 2009)

Clariona Sewursbhry is the anagram pseudonym of Carolina Shrewsbury (NSS #46182F), who is the masterful and creative illustrator of many of these stories. She held two positions with the NSS: the first chair of the Arts and Letters Section and chair of the Fine Arts Salon. She was part owner of On Rope, a caving equipment outfitter.

ACKNOWLEDGMENTS

Mama Says, Don't Cave would not have been possible without the contribution of the following individuals: I thank them profusely and gratefully acknowledge their hard work and encouragement. My wife Lynn Brucker provided tolerance and editorial suggestions, as well as essential computer help. Cory BlackEagle copy edited Ergor's stories one-by-one over many years. Danny Brass faithfully dared to publish many of these stories over a ten-year period. My son Tom Brucker suggested stories and boosted my morale throughout several decades. My daughter Ellen B. Marshal pulled alongside and offered editorial help, graphic assistance, and design ideas. Brooke Warner, President of Warner Coaching, Inc., wrangled the thousand and one details of book publishing. Jennifer Caven copy edited the book in its entirety a second time and discovered the CMOS (Chicago Manual of Style) Alternative Rule 9.3 regarding numbers. Tabitha Lahr designed the book cover using my illustration from *The Longest Cave*. She also designed the rest of the book. All these creative professionals have my abundant thanks and profound gratitude for a good job, They will receive certificates suitable for framing.

— ER and RWB